THE MIND OF CLASSICAL JUDAISM
Volume II

SOUTH FLORIDA STUDIES IN THE HISTORY OF JUDAISM

Edited by
Jacob Neusner
Bruce D. Chilton, Darrell J. Fasching, William Scott Green,
Sara Mandell, James F. Strange

Number 150
THE MIND OF CLASSICAL JUDAISM
Volume II
From Philosophy to Religion

by
Jacob Neusner

The Mind of Classical Judaism
Volume II
From Philosophy to Religion

by

Jacob Neusner

Scholars Press
Atlanta, Georgia

THE MIND OF CLASSICAL JUDAISM
Volume II
From Philosophy to Religion

by
Jacob Neusner

©1997
University of South Florida

Publication of this book was made possible by a grant from the Tisch Family Foundation, New York City. The University of South Florida acknowledges with thanks this important support for its scholarly projects.

Library of Congress Cataloging in Publication Data
Neusner, Jacob, 1932-
    The mind of classical Judaism / by Jacob Neusner.
      p.   cm. — (South Florida studies in the history of Judaism ; no. 148-151)
    Includes bibliographical references.
    ISBN 0-7885-0351-0 (v. 1 : pbk. : alk. paper). — ISBN 0-7885-0352-9 (v. 2 : pbk. : alk. paper). — ISBN 0-7885-0353-7 (v. 3 : pbk. : alk. paper). — ISBN 0-7885-0350-2 (v. 4 : pbk. : alk. paper)
    1. Judaism—History—Talmudic period, 10-425. 2. Rabbinical literature—History and criticism. 3. Jews in rabbinical literature. I. Title. II. Series.
BM179.N4775 1997
296'.09'015—dc21   97-3014
                                      CIP

Printed in the United States of America
on acid-free paper

Table of Contents

Preface vii

Introduction 1
    i.   From Philosophy to Religion 1
    ii.   Counterpart Categories 10
    iii. Comparison and Classification of Systems 17
    iv. Methodological Considerations: Comparing Systems of the Same Religion 25

I.   Learning and the Category, "Torah" 31

II.   The Transvaluation of Value 63

III. Empowerment and the Category, "The People Israel" 93

IV. The New Learning: The Gnostic Torah 119

V.   The New Order: The Political Economy of *Zekhut* 143

VI. Enchanted Judaism and *The City of God* 171

Preface

"The mind of Judaism" refers to those processes of thought that taught people to see things in one way and not in some other and to say things in this way, not in that way. An ongoing social entity inculcates in age succeeding age modes of thought that, shared by all, impart self-evidence and enduring sense to transient propositions. Minds may change on this and that. But mind does not, mind meaning modes of patterned thought on ephemera. Accordingly, while the social entity undergoes change, rules of deliberation dictate the range of permissible deed, and the realm of choice honors limits set by sense deemed common. *How* people think dictates the frontiers of possibility. The mind of Judaism, that is to say, process, is what will define Judaism in age succeeding age, so long as a Judaic system endures.

This is a trilogy about a very particular Judaism, that represented by Rabbinic culture or what I call the "mind" – the intellectual life that animates the writings of the textual community responsible for the classical canon of classical, normative, or Rabbinic Judaism in its formative age. These writings are comprised by authoritative documents of exposition and exegesis of the Mishnah, ca. 200 C.E., by the Talmud of the Land of Israel, ca. 400 C.E., through the Talmud of Babylonia, ca. 600 C.E., along with the Midrash-compilations of that same age devoted to the recapitulation of Scripture. By "textual community" I mean, people who wrote the books, valued and preserved them, and defined their social world by reference to them. By "mind" or thought, I mean, specifically, two things, first, how people connect one thing to something else, one fact to another, in literary terms, one sentence to another; and, second, the ways they form connections into large-scale conclusions, encompassing statements, that is to say, how the result of connection generates large-scale composition of ideas.

These two stages – the perception of connection, the discernment of (self-evidently valid) conclusions based on the connection – characterize the public thought, the mind, of those who stand behind the authoritative documents, those educated to value and adhere to them, and the generations raised in the enduring culture embodied in those writings. The intellectual protocol represented by thinking in one way, rather than some other, then governs the formation of thought – "mind" in a broader sense still – as to both modes of thought and the consequent messages. In this trilogy, having worked out the matter of making connections and drawing conclusions, we turn to the examination of modes of thought, philosophical versus religious and theology, and the message of fundamental importance: the definition of "Israel."

The character of these writings further allows us to explore the potentialities and also the limitations of intellect, what people are likely to see or to miss. The way in which people use language places on display the modes of thought that yield the connections and conclusions they propose. That is why throughout I appeal to the syntax and grammar of writings of the Judaism of the Dual Torah in expounding the modes of thought presented in that syntax and grammar. What we say indicates how we think: I know no other data of a concrete order, available for analysis, than the workings of language in literature. In examining the modes of thought of canonical writings, therefore, I show the range of choices.

But in referring to the textual community of classical Judaism, I signal that I do not speak of what is private and personal. Like all religions, this Judaism is public, forming a statement of culture, not only conviction – what is shared, not only what is, or may be, merely idiosyncratic. By "the mind of classical Judaism," I therefore mean the public, social rules of thought that defined the framework of the world-view, the way of life, and the definition of the social entity ("Israel") that all together formed the Judaic religious system of the social order put forth by "our sages of blessed memory" in the Rabbinic literature. These rules of thought affected how, in general, people defined rationality – what made sense, what did not, what belonged in one category, what in some other. In that way the rules of thought defined the world view of that theory of the social order. For when people knew how to make self-evidently valid connections, they also could draw the necessary conclusions therefrom. An encompassing culture defined by principles of self-evidence, rules of rationality, then came before and defined the structure and system of classical Judaism: the details of its way of life, world view, and theory of the social entity ("Israel") – chapters, dimensions, sectors, details of that encompassing culture.

That is because it was in the rules of rationality that that Judaism's account of the principal components of a well-constructed religious system took shape. The system cohered, each of the principal components working out the details of a cogent and integrated whole.

Preface

What the system said about one component it said about all others, but each contributed an essential element to the whole statement. A single mode of thought governed, so that conclusions were reached in one and the same way concerning a broad range of topics. In this trilogy, I recapitulate for a broad audience some of the main results of systematic monographs, noted in a moment, concerning the modes of thought and analysis characteristic of classical or Rabbinic Judaism.

The Mind of Classical Judaism: I. Modes of Thought: Making Connections and Drawing Conclusions: in the first of the three statements, we review the modes of thought characteristic of Rabbinic literature. My fundamental argument is that the paramount documents of classical Judaism not only preserved, but also inculcated, a particular way of forming propositions, of making connections and drawing conclusions. Specifically, I refer to as putting two *and* two together to *equal* four – the italicized words forming the hinge on which all else turns – and also a particular mode of joining these propositions together into sizable compositions of thought. Thus I mean the modes of thought characteristic of the normative statements of a particular Judaism.

The Mind of Classical Judaism: II. From Philosophy to Theology: in the second of the three statements, I deal with the transformation of the cultural patterns of that same Judaism in the shift from one mode of thought to another. That shift took place when the essentially philosophical modes of thought characteristic of the Mishnah gave way to the religious and theological modes of thought dominant in the Talmud of the Land of Israel and the Talmud of Babylonia, that is, a movement from ca. 200 to ca. 400 to ca. 600. Three sets of writings attest to each of the stages, respectively. These point, specifically, as follows: the Mishnah and Tosefta and associated Midrash-compilations, Sifra, Sifré to Numbers, and Sifré to Deuteronomy, to a Judaic system that was philosophical; the Talmud of the Land of Israel and its companion-Midrash-compilations, Genesis-Rabbah and Leviticus Rabbah, to a Judaic system, in writing continuous with the foregoing, in morphology quite different, that was religious; and the Talmud of Babylonia and its related Midrash-compilations, Lamentations Rabbah, Ruth Rabbah, Esther Rabbah I, and Song of Songs Rabbah, that was theological. What do these terms, philosophical, religious, and theological, denote?

A philosophical system forms its learning inductively and syllogistically by appeal to the neutral evidence of the rules shown by the observation of the order of universally accessible nature and society. A religious system frames its propositions deductively and exegetically by appeal to the privileged evidence of a corpus of writing deemed revealed by God. A theological system imposes upon a religious one systematic modes of thought of philosophy, so in its message regularizing and ordering in a cogent and intellectually rigorous way the materials received from a religious system. The movement from the religious to the theological will involve the systematization and harmonization of the religious categories, their re-formation into a single tight and cogent statement, one that leaves no doubt on what is right and what is wrong, what we are supposed to think and to do, and how all that we are to think and to do coheres. It is an initiative as radical, in its way, as the passage from the philosophical to religious formation is in its way. For the modes of thought, media of expression, and, as a matter of fact, categorical structure and system are reworked in the enterprise of turning a merely imputed order, imputed within the single heart of the faith, into a wholly-public order, subject to sustained and cogent representation and expression, each component in its place and proper sequence, beginning, middle, and end. Religious conviction differs from theological proposition as do bricks and mortar from a building.

Religious and the theological systems of course work over the same issues in ways that are common to themselves and that also distinguish them jointly from philosophical ones. But the rigorous task of forming from religious attitudes and convictions a cogent composition, a system and not merely a structure of beliefs, imposes on systems of the theological sort disciplines of mind and perception, modes of thought and media of expression, quite different from those that characterize the work of making a religious system. The connection is of course intimate, for a theological system succeeding and reshaping a religious one appeals to the same sources of truth in setting forth (often identical) answers to (ordinarily) the same urgent questions. But the theological type of system is different from the religious type in fundamental ways as well, for while there can be a religious system without theological order, there can be no theological system without a religious core.

The Mind of Classical Judaism: III. *What is "Israel"? Social Thought in the Formative Age:* in the third of the three statements, I turn to a concrete example of the modes of thought and the shift in their character that are described in the first two parts. My example is the thought of classical Judaism about "Israel," that is, the kingdom of priests and the holy people, on the one side, the supernatural family, children of Abraham, Isaac, and Jacob, on the other. There is illustrate in specific ways the movement of modes of thought from philosophy to religion (and theology) that Parts I and II set forth in theoretical terms. In Part III of the work I show how people bring to concrete and vivid expression their thought about the social entity that in their minds they imagine that they, with their families and others of like opinion and life-pattern, constitute. That thought in practical ways illustrates the modes of thought characteristic of the several successive ages in the formation of classical or Rabbinic Judaism. When in the Mishnah and related writings they speak of "Israel," to what sort of social group do they refer, and how do they think about that group? And, in the later documents, thinking in different ways altogether, how do they deal with the same issue? At stake in the answer is insight into the solution of a much larger problem, the way in which systems take shape, the relationship, in the formation of systems, between circumstance and context, contents and convictions – above all, modes of thought in general and the specific results of thinking about particular questions. What we address, therefore, in this study is a striking example of how people explain to themselves who they are as a social entity. For religion as a powerful force in human society and culture is realized in society, not only or mainly theology; religion works through the social entity that embodies that religion. Religions form churches or peoples or nations or communities or other entities that, in the concrete, constitute the "us," as against "the nations" or merely "them." And religions carefully explain, in deeds and in words, who that "us" is – and they do it every day. If we wish to know how that "we" or "us" attains concrete definition within the larger religious world-view and way of life of a particular religious system, we do well therefore to invoke the case of Judaic systems or Judaisms, because in nearly all known Judaisms the "us" of "Israel" forms an indicative and critical element.

The Philosophy and Political Economy of Formative Judaism. The Mishnah's System of the Social Order: Initially, the modes of thought and consequent world view took shape along conventional, philosophical lines; the way of life incorporated an economics and a politics worked out within the framework of a single system of category-formation. That entire structure is to be set forth in its own terms. The work on philosophy and political economy in a single volume presents the theory of the social order put forth by the philosophical Judaism of the Mishnah. There I condense and abbreviate the results of three other monographs, *Judaism as Philosophy. The Method and Message of the Mishnah.* Columbia, 1991: University of South Carolina Press; *The Economics of the Mishnah.* Chicago, 1989: The University of Chicago Press; and *Rabbinic Political Theory: Religion and Politics in the Mishnah.* Chicago, 1991: The University of Chicago Press. I treat the philosophical phase by itself, because, while the Rabbinic system is constructed upon that basis and is set forth, in important statements, as a mere exegetical continuation of it, in fact the philosophical formulation has its own shape and structure. More to the point, the ultimate social vision of Rabbinic Judaism, building upon the Mishnah, sets asymmetrically to the Mishnah's system of the social order, going over details of the Mishnah's picture without attempting to replicate the main point, the system as a whole. Attaching its ideas to the

Mishnah's statements in the form of commentaries to phrases and sentences, the Rabbinic statement absorbed the Mishnah's system but also recast it within a quite different structure from the one put forth by the Mishnah. Consequently, the Mishnah's deeply philosophical system found itself obscured and distorted in the prism of the Rabbinic re-presentation of the whole, and, not examined in its own terms. As a result, the Mishnah's account, delivered through masses of details, of how its framers conceived that Israel should live together, rarely has enjoyed its hearing, even while those very details would find their way into another system altogether.

In *The Philosophy and Political Economy of Formative Judaism* I have secured for it its own statement, and in the present trilogy, I proceed to rehearse the main lines of thought and expression of the world view and way of life that followed, in the manner that I have now explained. The books that are condensed in this series are as follows:

I. MAKING CONNECTIONS AND DRAWING CONCLUSIONS: MODES OF THOUGHT IN CLASSICAL JUDAISM

The Making of the Mind of Judaism. Atlanta, 1987: Scholars Press for Brown Judaic Studies.

The Formation of the Jewish Intellect. Making Connections and Drawing Conclusions in the Traditional System of Judaism. Atlanta, 1988: Scholars Press for Brown Judaic Studies.

II. FROM PHILOSOPHY TO THEOLOGY

The Transformation of Judaism. From Philosophy to Religion. Champaign, 1992: University of Illinois Press.

III. WHO AND WHAT IS "ISRAEL"? THE SOCIAL THOUGHT OF CLASSICAL JUDAISM

Judaism and its Social Metaphors. Israel in the History of Jewish Thought. N.Y., 1988: Cambridge University Press.

This book is part of a long-term project of mine, to make accessible to a broader audience the main results of my research into the history of Judaism. Specifically, in teaching a graduate seminar at the University of South Florida in fall, 1996, on the Formation of Judaism, I realized that my presentation of matters is spread over a number of books, too many, and too long, for students to read in a single semester. That is why, as is clear, I determined to condense and then join together in *The Philosophy and Political Economy of Formative Judaism: The Mishnah's System of the Social Order* three free-standing monographs. That provides the first step in the work. Then I determined to condense three other works into a matched trilogy, covering problems of philosophy, religion, and the history of religion. This companion trilogy goes over counterpart issues in the formation of Rabbinic Judaism once the Mishnah attained closure, that is, how the Mishnaic system was transformed and amplified in the next phase in the history of that Judaism. My hope is that by issuing condensing a number of monographs and simplifying the presentation, putting the whole out in a less expensive format, students will gain greater access to how Judaism took shape in its formative period.

No work of mine can omit reference to the exceptionally favorable circumstances in which I conduct my research. I wrote this book at the University of South Florida, which has afforded me an ideal situation in which to conduct a scholarly life. I express my thanks for not only the advantage of a Distinguished Research Professorship, which must be the best job in the world for a scholar, but also of a substantial research expense fund, ample research time, and some stimulating and cordial colleagues. In the prior chapters of my career, I never knew a university that prized professors' scholarship and publication and treated with respect those professors who actively and methodically pursue research. The University of South Florida, and all ten universities that comprise the Florida State University System as a whole, exemplify the high standards of professionalism that prevail in publicly-sponsored higher education in the USA and provide the model that privately-sponsored universities would do well to emulate. Here there are rules, achievement counts, and presidents, provosts, and deans honor and respect the University's principal mission: scholarship, scholarship alone – both in the classroom and in publication. Here at last I find integrity, governing in the lives of people true to their vocation and their mission.

For support for my research in a professorship that I greatly value, my thanks go also to the President of Bard College, Leon Botstein, and Dean of the Faculty, Stuart Levine, as well as to my colleague, the chairman of the Department of Religion and co-worker in many projects, Bruce D. Chilton. Their encouragement and practical support of my research work mean a great deal to me. The opportunity to teach such varied but equally worthwhile types of students as I find at USF and at Bard particularly stimulates a fresh view of scholarship for me.

JACOB NEUSNER
Distinguished Research Professor of Religious Studies
UNIVERSITY OF SOUTH FLORIDA, TAMPA
AND
Professor of Religion
BARD COLLEGE
ANNANDALE-ON-HUDSON, NEW YORK

Introduction

I. From Philosophy to Religion

The system of Judaism put forth by the first set of canonical writings of Rabbinic Judaism – the Mishnah and associated writings – is best classified as a philosophical one, the system portrayed in the next set of writings – those built on the Mishnah as exegetical statements – as a religious one. These continuator-documents therefore transformed the character and structure of the system that was fully set forth in its initial document..[1] By comparing one set of writings with another, we are able to contrast one system of a religion with another system within that same religion. The second system is represented as a gloss upon the first; the connections therefore are formal and literary.

The foundation-document is the Mishnah, a philosophical law code brought to closure at about ca. A.D. 200 and presents a theory of the social order that comprises a world-view or philosophy, way of life or economics, and an account of the social entity or politics. Why do I call the theory a philosophical one? By philosophy I mean very simply, a system of thought that, in the context of the same time and place, people generally deemed philosophers will have recognized as philosophical, with the proviso that there be no error as to the facts of the matter. The Mishnah, the first canonical writing of Judaism after the Hebrew Scriptures of ancient Israel ("the Old Testament") in important ways is to be read as philosophy in accord with the generally accepted

---

[1] The traits of mind of two sets of documents – the Mishnah, ca. A.D. 200, with its associated Midrash-compilations, Sifra, Sifré to Numbers, and Sifré to Deuteronomy, and the Talmud of the Land of Israel (a.k.a the Yerushalmi), a commentary to the Mishnah and associated Midrash-collections, Genesis Rabbah, Leviticus Rabbah, and Pesiqta deRab Kahana, ca. A.D. 400-450 – permit us to undertake this exercise in the comparative study of category-formation. A continuous literary tradition – the Yerushalmi is represented as a (mere) continuation of, and commentary to, the Mishnah, and the several distinct groups of Midrash-compilations are presented as (mere) commentary to Scripture – in fact attests to two distinct religious systems.

understanding of philosophy in the time, ca. A.D. 200, and place, the Greek-speaking Near East. By philosophy both in that study and here, therefore, I mean specifically the philosophical tradition of the Greco-Roman world of the Second Sophistic, in particular the method of Aristotle and the proposition important to Middle Platonism. But philosophy in a generic sense demands its place, and by philosophy in general I mean disciplined, rigorous thought, in accord with rules subject to application without limit as to topic, that intelligibly produces generalizations demonstrated on the basis of correct principles of thought concerning this-worldly facts to govern or explain a variety of circumstances. A philosophy forms cogent system of rational thought that treats diverse cases by appeal to a limited set of internally coherent generalizations. Such a system, as to method, abstract and intelligible, subject to reasoned explanation, as to topic, concerning a variety of concrete cases or problems, defines what I mean by (a) philosophy and, consequently, philosophical.[2]

Among the philosophers of the Greco-Roman philosophical tradition, the Mishnah's Judaic system can have been perceived as philosophical not merely in method but also in message. The Mishnah's method of hierarchical classification in important ways is like that of the natural history of Aristotle, and the central component of its message, congruent to that of neo-Platonism. Specifically, the Mishnah's Judaic system sets forth in stupefying detail a version of one critical proposition of neo-Platonism, demonstrated through a standard Aristotelian method.[3] The repeated proof through the Aristotelian method of hierarchical classification demonstrates in detail that many things – done enough times, *all* things – really form a single thing, many species, a single genus, many genera, an encompassing and well-crafted, cogent whole. Every time we speciate, – and the Mishnah is a mass of speciated lists – we affirm that position; each successful labor of forming relationships among species, for example, making them into a genus, or

---

[2] I have further worked out in great detail an account of those passages in the entire Mishnah that are to be classified as philosophical, within the stated criterion, in my *The Philosophical Mishnah*. Volume I. *The Initial Probe.*; Volume II. *The Tractates' Agenda. From Abodah Zarah to Moed Qatan*; Volume III. *The Tractates' Agenda. From Nazir to Zebahim;* and Volume IV. *The Repertoire.* Atlanta, 1989: Scholars Press for Brown Judaic Studies.

[3] And I need hardly add that the very eclecticism of the philosophy of Judaism places it squarely within the philosophical mode of its time. See J. M. Dillon and A. A. Long, eds., *The Question of "Eclecticism." Studies in Later Greek Philosophy* (Berkeley and Los Angeles, 1988: University of California Press). But these are only general observations, not meant to suggest direct connection or even to imply that an explanation drawn from "what was floating in the air" seems to me to pertain; I have no explanation.

Introduction

identifying the hierarchy of the species, proves it again. Not only so, but when we can show that many things are really one, or that one thing yields many (the reverse and confirmation of the former), we say in a fresh way a single immutable truth, the one of this philosophy concerning the unity of all being in an orderly composition of all things within a single taxon. Accordingly, this Judaism's initial system, the Mishnah's, finds its natural place within philosophy because it appeals to the Aristotelian methods and medium of natural philosophy – classification, comparison and contrast, expressed in the forms of *Listenwissenschaft* – to register its position, which is an important one in Middle Platonism and later (close to a century after the closure of the Mishnah) would come to profound expression in Plotinus.

Let us dwell on the philosophical classification of the Mishnah's mode of thought. The Mishnah's method of inquiry is that of natural history, corresponding with that method of natural history characteristic of Aristotle. I do not claim that our sages of blessed memory read, or could have read, Aristotle or any other Greek philosopher. Aristotle's work on natural history, his reflections on scientific method, for example, the *Posterior Analytics*[4] – these works speak in their own language to their own problems, and the Mishnah's authorship has written in a different language about incomparable problems. But when we compare our philosophers' method with that of Aristotle, who also, as a matter of fact, set forth a system that, in part, appealed to the right ordering of things through classification by correct rules[5] the simple fact becomes inescapable. Before us are different people, talking about different things, – but in the same way.

The philosophical Judaism moreover utilized economics – the rational disposition of scarce resources – in order to set forth a systemic statement of fundamental importance. Entirely congruent with the philosophical economics of Aristotle, the Mishnah's economics answered the same questions concerning the definition of wealth, property, production and the means of production, ownership and control of the

---

[4] I consulted Jonathan Barnes, *Aristotle's Posterior Analytics* (Oxford, 1975: Clarendon Press).

[5] And, as to proposition about the hierarchical ordering of all things in a single way, the unity of all being in right order, while we cannot show and surely do not know that the Mishnah's philosophers knew anything about Plato, let alone Plotinus's neo-Platonism (which came to expression only in the century after the closure of the Mishnah!), we can compare our philosophers' proposition with that of neo-Platonism. For that philosophy, as we shall see, did seek to give full and rich expression to the proposition that all things emerge from one thing, and one thing encompasses all things, and that constitutes the single proposition that animates the system as a whole.

means of production, the determination of price and value and the like. And that fact signifies that the Judaic system to which the Mishnah attests is philosophical not only in method and message but in its very systemic composition. The principal components of its theory of the social order, its account of the way of life of its Israel and its picture of the conduct of the public policy of its social entity, – all of these in detail correspond in their basic definitions and indicative traits with the economics and the politics of Greco-Roman philosophy in the Aristotelian tradition. Specifically, the Mishnah's economics, in general in the theory of the rational disposition of scarce resources and of the management and increase thereof, and specifically in its definitions of wealth and ownership, production and consumption, point by point, corresponds to that of Aristotle.

The power of economics as framed by Aristotle, the only economic theorist of antiquity worthy of the name, was to develop the relationship between the economy to society as a whole.[6] And the framers of the Mishnah did the same when they incorporated issues of economics at a profound theoretical level into the system of society as a whole that they proposed to construct . That is why the authorship of the Mishnah will be seen as attacking the problem of man's livelihood within a system of sanctification of a holy people with a radicalism of which no later religious thinkers about utopias were capable. None has ever penetrated deeper into the material organization of man's life under the aspect of God's rule. In effect, they posed, in all its breadth, the question of the critical, indeed definitive place occupied by the economy in society under God's rule. The points in common between Aristotle's and the Mishnah's economics in detail prove no less indicative. Both Aristotle and the Mishnah presented an anachronistic system of economics. The theory of both falls into the same classification of economic theory, that of distributive economics, familiar in the Near and Middle East from Sumerian times down to, but not including, the age of Aristotle (let alone that of the Mishnah five centuries later). But market-economics had been well-established prior to Aristotle's time.[7] Aristotle's economics is

---

[6]Polanyi, "Aristotle Discovers the Economy," in Polanyi, Karl , Conrad M. Arensberg, and Harry W. Pearson, *Trade and Market in the Early Empires. Economies in History and Theory* (Glencoe, 1957: Free Press), p. 79.

[7]Let me briefly explain the difference between the two, which is a fundamental indicator in classifying economics. In market economics merchants transfer goods from place to place in response to the working of the market mechanism, which is expressed in price. In distributive economics, by contrast, traders move goods from point to point in response to political commands. In market economics, merchants make the market work by calculations of profit and loss. In distributive economics, there is no risk of loss on a transaction. In market

distributive for systemic reasons, the Mishnah's replicates the received principles of the economics planned by the Temple priests and set forth in the Priestly Code of the Pentateuch, Leviticus in particular. The result – fabricated or replicated principles – was the same. Both systems – the Mishnah's and Aristotle's – in vast detail expressed the ancient distributive economics, in their theories of fixed value and conception of the distribution of scarce resources by appeal to other than the rationality of the market. The theory of money characteristic of Aristotle (but not of Plato) and of the Mishnah for instance conforms to that required by distributive economics; exchange takes place through barter, not through the abstract price-setting mechanism represented by money. Consequently, the representation of the Mishnah as a philosophical Judaism derives from not only general characteristics but very specific and indicative traits held in common with the principal figure of the Greco-Roman philosophical tradition in economics.

There was a common social foundation for the economic theory of both systems.[8] Both Aristotle and the Mishnah's framers deemed the fundamental unit of production to be the household, and the larger social unit, the village, composed of households, marked the limits of the social entity. The Mishnah's economic tractates, such as the tractates on civil law, invariably refer to the householder, making him the subject of most predicates; where issues other than economics are in play, for example, in the political tractates such as Sanhedrin, the householder scarcely appears as a social actor. Not only so, but both Aristotle and the authorship of the Mishnah formed the conception of "true value," which maintained that something – an object, a piece of land – possessed a value extrinsic to the market and intrinsic to itself, such that, if a transaction varied from that imputed true value by (in the case of the Mishnah) 18%, the exchange was null. Not only so, but the sole definition of wealth for both Aristotle's and the Mishnah's economics was real estate, only land however small. Since land does not contract or expand, of course, the conception of an increase in value through other

---

economics, money forms an arbitrary measure of value, a unit of account. In distributive economics, money gives way to barter and bears only intrinsic value, as do the goods for which it is exchanged. It is something that people accept not for its inherent value in use but because of what it will buy. The idea of money requires the transaction to be complete in the exchange not of goods but of coins. The alternative is the barter transaction, in which, in theory at least, the exchange takes place when goods change hands. In distributive economics money is an instrument of direct exchange between buyers and sellers, not the basic resource in the process of production and distribution that it is in market economics.

[8]Though the politics of the Mishnah was disembedded from its economics, while the politics of Aristotle was embedded, so that the latter presents a political economy, the former does not.

than a steady-state exchange of real value, "true value," between parties to a transaction lay outside of the theory of economics. Therefore all profit, classified as usury, was illegitimate and must be prevented.

The Mishnah's politics – its theory of the legitimate use of violence and the disposition of power in society, – describes matters in a manner that is fundamentally philosophical in the Aristotelian context. Israel forms a political entity, fully empowered in an entirely secular sense, just as Scripture had described matters. To political institutions of the social order, king, priest, and court or civil administration, each in its jurisdiction, is assigned the right legitimately to exercise violence here on earth, corresponding to, and shared with, the same empowerment accorded to institutions of Heaven. These institutions moreover are conceived permanently to ration and rationalize the uses of that power. The picture, of course, is this-worldly, but, not distinguishing crime from sin, it is not secular, since the same system that legitimates king, high priest, and court posits in Heaven a corresponding politics, with God and the court on high exercising jurisdiction for some crimes or sins, the king, priesthood, or court down below for others. Three specific traits, direct our attention toward the philosophical classification for the Mishnah's politics in framing a systemic composition, even though, to be sure, the parallels prove structural and general, rather than detailed and doctrinal as was the case with economics.

First, like the politics of Plato and Aristotle, the Mishnah's politics describes only a utopian politics, a structure and system of a fictive and a fabricated kind: intellectuals' conception of a politics. Serving the larger purpose of system-construction, politics of necessity emerges as invention, for example, by Heaven or in the model of Heaven, not as a secular revision and reform of an existing system. While in the middle second-century Rome incorporated their country, which they called the Land of Israel and the Romans called Palestine, into its imperial system, denying Jews access to their capital, Jerusalem, permanently closing their cult-center, its Temple, the authorship of the Mishnah described a government of a king and a high priest and an administration fully empowered to carry out the law through legitimate violence. So the two politics – the Mishnah's, the Greco-Roman tradition represented by Plato's and Aristotle's – share in common their origins in intellectuals' theoretical and imaginative life and form an instance, within that life, of the concrete realization of a larger theory of matters. In strange and odd forms, the Mishnah's politics falls into the class of the *Staatsroman*, the classification that encompasses, also, Plato's *Republic* and Aristotle's *Politics*. But, admittedly, the same may be said for the strange politics of the Pentateuch.

Introduction

Second and more to the point, the Mishnah's sages stand well within the philosophical mode of political thought that begins with Aristotle, who sees politics as a fundamental component of his system when he says, "political science...legislates as to what we are to do and what we are to abstain from;" and, as to the institutionalization of power, I cannot imagine a more ample definition of the Mishnah's system's utilization of politics than that.[9] While that statement, also, applies to the Pentateuchal politics, the systemic message borne by politics within the Pentateuchal system and that carried by politics in the Mishnah's system do not correspond in any important ways. Aristotle and the philosophers of the Mishnah utilize politics to make systemic statements that correspond to one another, in that both comparison and contrast prove apt and pointed. Both spoke of an empowered social entity; both took for granted that on-going institutions legitimately exercise governance in accord with a rationality discerned by distinguishing among those empowered to inflict sanctions. Both see politics as a medium for accomplishing systemic goals, and the goals derive from the larger purpose of the social order, to which politics is subordinated and merely instrumental.

But, third, the comparison also yields a contrast of importance. Specifically, since political analysis comes only after economic analysis and depends upon the results of that prior inquiry into a social system's disposition of scarce resources and theory of control of means of production, we have no choice but to compare the politics of Aristotle and the politics of the Mishnah, just as we did the economics of each system. For when we know who commands the means of production, we turn to inquire about who tells whom what to do and why: who legitimately coerces others even through violence. And here the Mishnah's system decisively parts company with that of the Pentateuch and also with that of Aristotle. As to the former, the distributive economics of the Pentateuch, in the Priestly stratum at the foundations, assigns both economic and political privilege to the same class of persons, the priesthood, effecting distributive economics and distributive politics. But that is not the way things are in the Mishnah's politics, which distinguishes the one in control of the means of production from the one control of the right legitimately to commit violence. The former, the householder, is not a political entity at all, and, dominant as the subject of most sentences in the economic tractates, he never appears in the political ones at all.

---

[9]Cited by R. G. Mulgan, *Aristotle's Political Theory* (Oxford: Clarendon Press, 1977), p. 3.

The point of difference from Aristotle is to be seen only within the context of the similarity that permits comparison and contrast. While the economics of Aristotle and the economics of Judaism commence with the consideration of the place and power of the person ("class," "caste," economic interest) in control of the means of production, the social metaphors that animate the politics of the two systems part company. Aristotle in his *Politics* is consistent in starting with that very same person ("class") when he considers issues of power, producing a distributive politics to match his distributive economics. But the Mishnah's philosophers build their politics on with an altogether different set of building blocks. The simple fact is that the householder, fundamental to their economics, does not form a subject of political discourse at all and in no way constitutes a political class or caste. When the Mishnah's writers speak of economics, the subject of most active verbs is the householder; when they speak of politics, the householder never takes an active role or even appears as a differentiated political class. In this sense, the economics of the Mishnah is disembedded from its politics, and the politics from its economics. By contrast the economics and politics of Aristotle's system are deeply embedded within a larger and nurturing, wholly cogent theory of political economy.

The successor-system, represented by the Talmud of the Land of Israel and related writings, ca. 400-450, presented a theory of the social order lacking any theory politics, philosophy, and economics of a conventional order. So while, as a matter of hypothesis, we must assume that a system formed in theory to describe the social order by definition attends to the way of life, world view, and definition of the social entity, that that system puts forth, in practice that is not what happened. For by "way of life"– economics – or "world view" – politics – the successor-system did not mean – or even refer to – exactly the same category of data that initial system had adopted for itself. It is that fact that makes urgent for the study of world history the unfolding of the two distinct Judaisms, the one philosophical, the other, religious. For herein we find a case in which establishing connections is complicated by the incongruity of categories.

The claim, "this is what functioned for this system in the way in which, in that system, that accomplished the (same) task," proves simply irrelevant. Such a claim forms an excuse, not a reason, for difference among systems, and, since what is at stake is establishing connections from society to society through systemic comparison, it hardly explains why one system sets forth its way of life by selecting data of one kind, while another one chooses data of a completely different order altogether, for the same purpose. Not only so, but what we seek to describe, analyze, and interpret are systems, on their own and (in the

Introduction

case of systems that prove continuous in their canonical express) also in relationship with one another. So let me restate matters as I think a rigorous definition requires us to see them. A system selects its data to expose its systemic categories; defines its categories in accord with the systemic statement that it wishes to set forth; identifies the urgent question to which the systemic message compellingly responds. To understand a system, we begin with the whole and work our way inward toward the parts; the formation of categories then is governed by the system's requirements: the rationality of the whole dictates the structure of the categorical parts, and the structure of the parts then governs the selection of what fits into those categories.[10]

Now that we have seen the philosophical character of the initial system's world-view, way of life, and theory of the social entity, that is, its philosophy, economics, and politics, we ask how these same categories fared in the successor-system's documentary evidence. As a matter of simple fact, while sharing the goal of presenting a theory of the social order, as to their categorical formations and structures, the initial, philosophical Judaic system and the successor system differ in a fundamental way. Stated very simply, what happened is that the successor-system held up a mirror to the received categories and so redefined matters that everything was reversed. Left became right, down, up, and in a very explicit transvaluation of values, power is turned into weakness, things of real value is transformed into intangibles. This transvaluation, yielding the transformation of the prior system altogether, is articulated and not left implicit; it is a specific judgment made concrete through mythic and symbolic revision by the later authorships themselves.[11] A free-standing document, received with reverence, served to precipitate the transvaluation of all of the values of that document's initial statement.

The categorical transformation that was underway, signaling the movement from philosophy to religion, comes to the surface when we ask a simple question. Precisely what do the authorships of the successor-documents speaking not about the Mishnah but on their own account, mean by economics, politics, and philosophy? That is to say, to what kinds of data do they refer when they speak of scarce resources and legitimate violence, and exactly how – as to the received philosophical

---

[10] None of these points intersects with either relativism or functionalism; the issues are wholly other. At stake in systemic description, analysis, and interpretation, after all, ultimately is the comparative study of rationalities.

[11] I underline that fact, since all that follows on the transvaluation of values through the formation of what I have invented as "counterpart-categories" appeals to explicit statements, not a very general, post facto observation on my part.

method – do they define correct modes of thought and expression, logic and rhetoric, and even the topical program worthy of sustained inquiry? The components of the initial formation of categories were examined thoughtfully and carefully, paraphrased and augmented and clarified. But the received categories were not continued, not expanded, and not renewed. Preserved merely intact, as they had been handed on, the received categories hardly serve to encompass all of the points of emphasis and sustained development that characterize the successor-documents – or, as a matter of fact, any of them. On the contrary, when the framers of the Yerushalmi, for one example, moved out from the exegesis of Mishnah-passages, they also left behind the topics of paramount interest in the Mishnah and developed other categories altogether.[12] Here we find that, in these other categories, the framers of the successor- system defined their own counterparts. These counterpart-categories, moreover, redefined matters, following the main outlines of the structure of the social order manifest in the initial system. The counterpart-categories set forth an account of the social order just as did the ones of the Mishnah's framers. But they defined the social order in very different terms altogether. In that redefinition we discern the transformation of the received system, and the traits of the new one fall into the classification of not philosophy but religion.

II. Counterpart Categories

For what the successor-thinkers did was not continue and expand the categorical repertoire but, rather, set forth a categorically-fresh vision of the social order – a way of life, world view, and definition of the social entity – with appropriate counterpart-categories. And what is decisive is that these served as did the initial categories within the generative categorical structure definitive for all Judaic systems. So there was a category corresponding to the generative component of world-view, but it was not philosophical; another corresponding to the required component setting forth a way of life, but in the conventional and accepted definition of economics it was not an economics; and, finally, a category to define the social entity, "Israel," that any Judaic system must explain, but in the accepted sense of a politics it was not politics.

---

[12]That fact is demonstrated in my *Talmud of the Land of Israel. A Preliminary Translation and Explanation. 35. Introduction. Taxonomy* (Chicago, 1983: The University of Chicago Press). There I show that when Mishnah-exegesis is concluded, a quite separate agendum takes centerstage, the emphases of which find no counterpart in the Mishnah. That seems to me to justify the consideration of counterpart-categories, such as I introduce here.

Exactly how was this categorical reformation accomplished? To state matters first in the most abstract way, it was done by reversing the flow of language, specifically taking the predicate of a sentence and moving it to the position of the subject, that is, commencing not from subject but from predicate. From "[1] economics is [2] the rational disposition of scarce resources," the category of way of life was rephrased into, "[2] the rational disposition of scarce resources is [1] (their, in context, systemic) economics." The reverse reading therefore yields the counterpart category, defined by this sentence: "*a (any) theory of rational action with regard to scarcity...*, then: is (for the system at hand) its economics." The same procedure serves,, too – *mutatis mutandis* – for discerning the later systems' politics and science or learning or philosophy. The result was a quite new system. This transvaluation of values, through not merely the re-formation but the utter transformation of categories, set forth an essentially fresh answer to a fundamentally new urgent question. But here, the answer is the main point of interest. To give a simple instance, when we say, "a (or any) theory of rational action with regard to scarcity *is* (an) economics," we mean, any account of what is deemed scarce and therefore to require rational action as to allocation, increase, and disposition, functions to define the category that is the counterpart, in the philosophical system of the Mishnah, to economics. It answers the same question, but it utterly recasts the terms of the question. True, standard topics such as wealth and money, production and distribution, work and wage, ownership and conduct of economic entities play no role. But the issues of tangible wealth and materials goods do emerge, and, it follows, the system identifies something other than real wealth (real estate, capital, for instance) – but this "wealth in another form" also is claimed to put bread on the table.

That fact raises the question of how to deal with such accounts of the social order that, while answering the questions that pertain, nonetheless lack an economics or a politics or a philosophy in the familiar senses of these categories? To answer that question of method in the analysis of category-formation, I have to discover and define what serves, in such a system, the task of economics in a philosophical system. To do so – as stated in abstract form just now – I propose the notion that, "[2] a (any) theory of rational action with regard to scarcity *is* [1] economics." Matters that hardly fall into the category of economic theory at all may yield points of congruency. As a matter of fact they may also validate those systemic comparisons and contrasts that permit us to trace the history of an on-going system from its philosophical to its religious formulation. We know that we are right when we find that the authorships of the successor-systems recognize and select the principal symbolic expression of a received category and turn it on its head: land becomes Torah-learning, and that is made explicit, for one stunning instance. Then it is not merely my post-facto reading of one system as a reversal of a prior one that has yielded the counterpart-category, but the documents themselves.

When we see that a category for an alien system and its rationality constitutes *its* economics and therefore forms a counterpart to economics as we understand that subject within our rationality, we learn how in a critical component to translate system to system. We may then make the statement, "In that system, within their rationality, that category of activity forms a component of economic theory, while in our system, within our rationality, we do not think of that category of activity as a component of economic theory at all." And this we do without assuming a posture of relativism, for example claiming that their economics, and, with it, their rationality, is pretty much the same, or as at least as valid, as ours. Framing the relativist judgment in that way, we see that it is simply not relevant to what is at stake. That kind of interpretation of matters is not pertinent to my exercise in translation and comparison carried out through the definition and examination of counterpart-categories. We begin with the systemic counterpart to philosophy, then proceed to economics, and conclude with politics. Our first task is to follow the categorical formation of a new world-view generated by the received mode of thought, a world-view that fundamentally differed from the philosophical one at every point.

What the philosophical Judaism kept apart, the religious Judaism portrayed by the Talmud of the Land of Israel and related writings now joined together, and it is just there, at that critical joining, that we identify the key to the system: its reversal of a received point of differentiation, its introduction of new points of differentiation altogether. The source of generative problems for the Mishnah's politics is simply not the same as the source that served the successor-system's politics, and, systemic analysis being what it is, it is the union of what was formerly asunder that identifies for us in quite objective terms the critical point of tension, the sources of problems, the centerpiece of systemic concern throughout. Let me show how this process of reintegration was worked out in the categorical reformation underway in the Yerushalmi and related writings.

We begin with the shift from philosophy to Torah-study, that is from abstract reflection to concrete text-exegesis and digression out of sacred scripture; philosophy yields accurate and rational understanding of things; knowledge of the Torah, by contrast, yields power over this world and the next, capacity to coerce to the sage's will the natural and supernatural worlds alike, on that account. The Torah is thus transformed from a philosophical enterprise of the sifting and classification of the facts of this world into a gnostic process of changing persons through knowledge. It is on that basis that in the Yerushalmi and related writings I find in the Torah the counterpart-category to philosophy in the Mishnah. Now we deal with a new intellectual category: Torah, meaning, religious learning *in place of* philosophical learning. What is the difference between the one and the other? First comes appeal to revealed truth as against perceived facts of nature and their regularities, second, the conception of an other-worldly source of explanation and the development of a propositional program focused upon not nature but Scripture, not the nations in general but Israel in particular, and third, the gnosticization of knowledge in the conception that knowing works salvation.

What was to change, therefore, was not the mode of thought. What was new, rather, was the propositions to be demonstrated philosophically, and what made these propositions new was the focus of interest, on the one side, and data assembled by way of demonstrating them, on the other. From a philosophical proposition within the framework of free-standing philosophy of religion and metaphysics that the Mishnah's system aimed to establish, we move to religious and even theological propositions within the setting of contingent exegesis of Scripture. Then how do we know that what was changing was not merely topical and propositional but *categorical* in character? The answer lies in the symbolic vocabulary that would be commonly used in the late fourth and fifth century writings but not at all, or not in the same way, in the late second century ones. When people select data not formerly taken into account and represent the data by appeal to symbols not formerly found evocative or expressive, or not utilized in the way in which they later on were used, then – so I claim – we are justified in raising questions about category-formation and the development of new categories alongside, or instead, of the received ones. In the case at hand, the character of the transformation we witness is shown by the formation of a symbol serving to represent a category.

To signal what is to come, we shall find the quite bald statement that, in the weighing of the comparative value of capital, which in this time and place meant land or real property, and Torah, Torah was worthwhile, and land was not – a symbolic syllogism that is explicit, concrete, repeated, and utterly fresh for the documents we consider. On the basis of that quite explicit symbolic comparison I speak of transformation – symbolic and therefore *categorical* transformation, not merely thematic shifts in emphasis or even propositional change. And that is why I hold that we witness in the successor-writings the formation of a system connected with, but asymmetrical to, the initial, philosophical one. Then for the world-view of the transformed Judaism, the counterpart-category to philosophy is formulated by appeal to the symbolic medium for the theological message, and it is the category, the Torah, expressed, as a matter of fact, by the symbol of *Torah*.[13]

Philosophy sought the generalizations that cases might yield. So, too, did religion (and, in due course, theology would too). But the range of generalization vastly differed. Philosophy spoke of the nature of things, while theology represented the special nature of Israel in particular. Philosophy then appealed to the traits of things, while theology to the special indicative qualities of Israel. What of the propositional program that the document sets forth? The philosophical proposition of the Mishnah demonstrated from the facts and traits of things the hierarchical order of all being, with the obvious if merely implicit proposition that God stands at the head of the social order. The religious propositions of the successor-documents speak in other words of other things, having simply nothing in common with the propositional program of the Mishnah's philosophy.

The shift in economics is no less striking. Consideration of the transvaluation of value brings us to the successor-system's counterpart category, that is, the one that in context forms the counterpart to the Mishnah's concrete, this-worldly, material and tangible definition of value in conformity with the familiar, philosophical economics. We have now to ask, what, in place of the received definition of value and the economics thereof, did the new system set forth? The transformation of economics involved the redefinition of scarce and valued resources in so radical a manner that the concept of value, while remaining material in consequence and character, nonetheless took on a quite different sense altogether. The counterpart category of the successor-system concerned themselves with the same questions as did the conventional economics, presenting an economics in function and structure, but one that concerned things of value other than those identified by the initial system. So indeed we deal with an economics, an economics of something other than real estate.

But it was an economics just as profoundly embedded in the social order, just as deeply a political economics, just as pervasively a systemic economics, as the economics of the Mishnah and of Aristotle. Why so? Because issues such as the definition of wealth, the means of production and the meaning of control thereof, the disposition of wealth through distributive or other media, theory of money, reward for labor, and the like – all these issues found their answers in the counterpart-category of

---

[13] Much that is said here alludes to the results of my *Torah: From Scroll to Symbol in Formative Judaism* (Philadelphia, 1985: Fortress; second printing: Atlanta, 1989: Scholars Press for Brown Judaic Studies).

Introduction

economics, as much as in the received and conventional philosophical economics. The new "scarce resource" accomplished what the old did, but it was a different resource, a new currency. At stake in the category meant to address the issues of the way of life of the social entity, therefore, were precisely the same considerations as confront economics in its (to us) conventional and commonplace, philosophical sense. But since the definition of wealth changes from land to Torah, much else would be transformed on that account.

Land produced a living; so did Torah. Land formed the foundation of the social entity, so did Torah. The transvaluation of value was such that an economics concerning the rational management and increase of scarce resources worked itself out in such a way as to answer, for quite different things of value from real property or from capital such as we know as value, precisely the same questions that the received economics addressed in connection with wealth of a real character: land and its produce. Systemic transformation comes to the surface in articulated symbolic change. The utter transvaluation of value finds expression in a jarring juxtaposition, an utter shift of rationality, specifically, the substitution of Torah for real estate. We recall how in a successor-document (but in none prior to the fifth century compilations) Tarfon thought wealth took the form of land, while Aqiba explained to him that wealth takes the form of Torah-learning. That the sense is material and concrete is explicit: land for Torah, Torah for land. Thus, to repeat the matter of how Torah serves as an explicit symbol to convey the systemic world-view, let us note the main point of this passage:[14]

Leviticus Rabbah XXXIV:XVI

1. B. R. Tarfon gave to R. Aqiba six silver centenarii, saying to him, "Go, buy us a piece of land, so we can get a living from it and labor in the study of Torah together."
   C. He took the money and handed it over to scribes, Mishnah-teachers, and those who study Torah.
   D. After some time R. Tarfon met him and said to him, "Did you buy the land that I mentioned to you?"
   E. He said to him, "Yes."
   F. He said to him, "Is it any good?"
   G. He said to him, "Yes."
   H. He said to him, "And do you not want to show it to me?"

---

[14]While the attributions are to first century figures, the story appears in a document that reached closure in the fifth century, and I take the story to represent opinion deemed authoritative in the fifth century. For extensive explanation of what is at issue, see my *The Canonical History of Ideas. The Place of the So-called Tannaite Midrashim, Mekhilta Attributed to R. Ishmael, Sifra, Sifré to Numbers, and Sifré to Deuteronomy* (Atlanta, 1990: Scholars Press for South Florida Studies in the History of Judaism).

I. He took him and showed him the scribes, Mishnah teachers, and people who were studying Torah, and the Torah that they had acquired.

J. He said to him, "Is there anyone who works for nothing? Where is the deed covering the field?"

K. He said to him, "It is with King David, concerning whom it is written, 'He has scattered, he has given to the poor, his righteousness endures forever' (Ps. 112:9)."

The successor-system has its own definitions not only for learning, symbolized by the word Torah but also for wealth, expressed in the same symbol. Accordingly, the category-formation for world-view, Torah in place of philosophy, dictates, as a matter of fact, a still more striking category-reformation, in which the entire matter of scarce resources is reconsidered, and a counterpart-category set forth.

Philosophical politics tells who may legitimately do what to whom. When a politics wants to know who ought *not* to be doing what to whom, we find in hand the counterpart-category to the received politics – anti-politics, a theory of the illegitimacy of power, the legitimacy of being victim.[15] The received category set forth politics as the theory of legitimate violence, the counterpart-category, politics as the theory of *illegitimate* violence. The received politics had been one of isolation and interiority, portraying Israel as sui generis and autocephalic in all ways. The portrait in the successor-documents is a politics of integration among the nations; a perspective of exteriority replaces the inner-facing one of the Mishnah, which recognized no government of Israel but God's – and then essentially ab initio. The issues of power had found definition in questions concerning who legitimately inflicts sanctions upon whom within Israel. They now shift to give an account of who illegitimately inflicts sanctions upon ("persecutes") Israel. So the points of systemic differentiation are radically revised, and the politics of the successor-system becomes not a revision of the received category but a formation that in many ways mirrors the received one: once more a counterpart-category. Just as, in the definition of scarce resources, Torah-study has replaced land, so now weakness forms the focus in place of strength, illegitimacy in place of legitimacy. Once more the mirror-image of the received category presents the perspective of the counterpart-category.

Now we find the answers to these questions: to whom is violence illegitimately done, and also, who may not legitimately inflict violence? With the move from the politics of legitimate to that of illegitimate power, the systemic interest now lies in defining not the who

---

[15]That is, of course, as much as, in the contrast of real wealth and true value, that is to say, land and Torah-learning, we identify not a revised economics but a counterpart-category to the familiar economics.

Introduction

legitimately does what, but rather, the to whom, against whom, is power illegitimately exercised. And this movement represents not the revision of the received category, but its inversion. For thought on legitimate violence is turned on its head. A new category of empowerment is worked out alongside the old. The entity that is victim of power is at the center, rather than the entity that legitimately exercises power. That entity is now Israel *en masse*, rather than the institutions and agencies of Israel on earth, Heaven above – a very considerable shift in thought on the systemic social entity. Israel as disempowered, rather than king, high priest, and sage as Israel's media of empowerment, defines the new system's politics. The upshot is that the successor-system has reconsidered not merely the contents of the received structure, but the composition of the structure itself. In place of its philosophy, we have now a new medium for the formulation of a world-view; in place of a way of life formulated as an economics, a new valuation of value, in place of an account of the social entity framed as a politics, a new conception of legitimate violence. So much for the formation of counterpart categories.

III. Comparison and Classification of Systems

What philosophy kept distinct, religion joined together: that defines the transformation of Judaism from philosophy to religion. The reliable rules of sanctification – to invoke theological categories – are joined with the unpredictable event of salvation, and the routine – to call upon the classification of Max Weber – meets the spontaneous. Not to be gainsaid, the social order is made to acknowledge what, if disorderly, also is immediate and therefore necessary. History, that omnipresent but carefully ignored presence in the philosophical Judaism, in the form of not change but crisis, regains its rightful place at the systemic center.

The classification of the new system is religious and not philosophical. Precisely what I mean must be made clear, since the Mishnaic system also was a religious one. But the received system was a religious system of a philosophical character, and the successor-system was not of a philosophical character. What I mean by a religious system of a philosophical character is readily explained: this worldly-data are classified according to rules that apply consistently throughout, so that we may always predict with a fair degree of accuracy what will happen and why. And a philosophical system of religion then systematically demonstrates out of the data of the world order of nature and society the governance of God in nature and supernature: this world's data pointing toward God above and beyond. The God of the philosophical Judaism then sat enthroned at the apex of all things, all being hierarchically classified. Just as philosophy seeks the explanation of things, so a philosophy of religion (in the context at hand) will propose orderly explanations in accord with prevailing and cogent rules. The profoundly philosophical character of the Mishnah has already provided ample evidence of the shape, structure, and character of that philosophical system in the Judaic context. The rule-seeking character of Mishnaic discourse marks it as a philosophical system of religion. But, we shall now see, the successor-system saw the world differently.

It follows that a philosophical system forms its learning inductively and syllogistically, by appeal to the neutral evidence of the rules shown to apply to all things by the observation of the order of universally accessible nature and society. A religious system frames its propositions deductively and exegetically by appeal to the privileged evidence of a corpus of truths deemed revealed by God. The difference pertains not to detail but to the fundamental facts deemed to matter. Some of those facts lie at the very surface, in the nature of the writings that express the system.

As we have now seen, these writings were not free-standing but contingent, and that in two ways. First, they served as commentaries to prior documents, the Mishnah and Scripture, for the Talmud and Midrash-compilations, respectively. Second, and more consequential, the authorships insisted upon citing Scripture-passages or Mishnah-sentences as the centerpiece of proof, on the one side, and program of discourse, on the other. But the differences that prove indicative are not merely formal. More to the point, while the Mishnah's system is steady-state and ahistorical, admitting no movement or change, the successor-system of the Yerushalmi and Midrash-compilations tells tales, speaks of change, accommodates and responds to historical moments. It formulates a theory of continuity within change, of the moral connections between generations, of the way in which one's deeds shape one's destiny – and that of the future as well. If what the framers of the Mishnah want more than anything else is to explain the order and structure of being, then their successors have rejected their generative concern. For what they, for their part, intensely desire to sort out is the currents and streams of time and change, as these flow toward an unknown ocean.

But these large-scale characterizations in well-crafted systems do not provide the only pertinent evidence. Details, too, deliver the message. The indicators for each type of system, as these are attested in their written testimonies, derive from the character of the rhetorical, logical, and propositional-topical traits of those writings. The shift from the philosophical to the religious modes of thought and media of expression – logical and rhetorical indicators, respectively – come to realization in

Introduction

the recasting of the generative categories of the system as well. That is the lesson of Part Two of this book. These categories are transformed, and the transformation proved so thorough-going as to validate the characterization of the change as "counterpart-categories." The result of the formation of such counterpart-categories in the aggregate was to encompass not only the natural but also the supernatural realms of the social order.

That is how philosophical thinking gave way to religious. It sets forth the category-formation that produced in place of an economics based on prime value assigned to real wealth one that now encompassed wealth of an intangible, impalpable, and supernatural order, but valued resource nonetheless. It points toward the replacement of a politics formerly serving to legitimate and hierarchize power and differentiate among sanctions by appeal to fixed principles by one that now introduced the variable of God's valuation of the victim and the antipolitical conception of the illegitimacy of worldly power. This counterpart-politics then formed the opposite of the Mishnah's this-worldly political system altogether. In all three ways the upshot is the same: the social system, in the theory of its framers, now extends its boundaries upward to Heaven, drawing into a whole the formerly distinct, if counterpoised, realms of Israel on earth and the Heavenly court above. So if I had to specify the fundamental difference between the philosophical and the religious versions of the social order, it would fall, quite specifically, – to state with emphasis – *upon the broadening of the systemic boundaries to encompass Heaven*. The formation of counterpart-categories therefore signals not a reformation of the received system but the formation of an essentially new one.

But the critical issue addressed by the new system and the central point of tension and mode of remission thereof, the exegetical focus – these remain to be identified even after we have noted the extension of systemic boundaries. And, as a matter of fact, the counterpart categories in hand themselves do not help to identify the generative problematic that defined the new system and integrated its components. For the issues I have located as the systemic economics and politics – Torah in place of land, the illegitimacy of power and the priority of the absence thereof – while present and indicative in the documentary expression of the system, assuredly do not occupy a principal position within those documents. For the successor-documents' categories are not those of philosophy, on the one side, and a politics disembedded from economics, on the other.

In the nature of systemic analysis, therefore, I have brought the categories of one system to the data of another, those of the initial system to the ones of the successor-system, and the result is to discover only how different are the latter from the former. So concerning the transformed Judaism of the late fourth and fifth century we now know everything but the main thing. True, since we compare the given to the new, I had no choice but to proceed as I have. But what I have done thus far is ask only *my* questions – that is, the systemic questions of philosophy and political economy or philosophical economics and politics. And these questions have been turned upon a literature that dealt with such questions essentially by dismissing them. For the upshot of the formation of counterpart-categories turns out to be the destruction of the received categories, now turned on their heads and emptied of all material and palpable content, refilled then with intangibles of intellect and virtuous attitude alone. Knowing how a system has revalued value and reconstructed the sense of legitimate power by deeming legitimate only the victim and never the actor, does not tell us what the system locates at its center.

To identify the systemic foci, *its* – and not my – sources of the exegetical problematic and its definition of its generative issues, I must propose as the answer not a subjective judgment as to what is dominant and commonplace. I have, rather, to set forth an entirely objective claim as to what is essential and definitive and integrating (which, as a matter of fact, in this context also happens to be commonplace). By objective I mean simply, my results should emerge for anyone else examining the same evidence in accord with the same principles of description and analysis (interpretation is always subjective). Once we concur that a Judaic system by definition responds to the questions deemed compelling with truths regarded as unavoidable and self-evident., then, reading the evidence at hand, anyone should reach the conclusions I present here, if my indicative evidence is correctly identified and accurately described So the task now is to identify those urgent questions and define the self-evident truths that came about by way of response: the way of life, the world view, formed by the Israel that the successor-system defined for itself. And the issue is joined for us when we can identify the point of differentiation of one system and integration of another: surely an objective fact.

Where to begin? It is in the specification of what in fact is integrating. For in general, historians of religion concur, the power of religion lies in its capacity to integrate, to hold together discrete components of the social order and explain how they all fit together. And, in general, it seems to me a simple fact that the power of philosophy lies in its capacity to differentiate, discriminate, make distinctions and clarify the complex by showing its distinct parts. Then a successor-system, connected to but autonomous of its antecedent, will prove philosophical if it continues the labor of differentiation, religious if

Introduction

it undertakes a work of integration. And the Judaism before us addresses the principal, and striking, distinction characteristic of the philosophical system it had inherited, the one between economics and politics, (re)integrating what had been kept apart in a theory of political economy such as the Pentateuch and Aristotle had laid out, but the framers of the Mishnah had not composed at all.

Let me spell out what I conceive to be the principal success of integration, within a supernatural framework that must be deemed religious and only religion, accomplished by our sages of blessed memory in the Yerushalmi and related writings. We recall,[16] the one striking contrast between the social system put forth by Aristotle and that set out by the framers of the Mishnah lay in the superior systematization of politics within the frame of economics accomplished by Aristotle and not achieved at all by the Mishnah's social system. Aristotle's systemic message, delivered through his philosophy, economics, and politics, was carried equally by economics and politics in such a way that the two formed a single statement, one of political economy. To state the matter very simply: the principal economic actor of Aristotle's social system, the householder (in the language of our sources, the landholder or farmer for Aristotle and Xenophon) also constituted the principal political figure, the one who exercised legitimate power, and the joining of the landholder and the civic actor in a single person moreover accounted for Aristotle for the formation of society: the polis or lowest whole and indivisible social unit of society.

But for the framers of the Mishnah, the economic actor, the one who controlled the means of production, was the householder, while the householder never played a political role or formed part of the political classes at all. That fact is shown by the simple distinction of usage, in which the subject of most sentences involving the disposition of scarce resources was the householder, while that same social entity ("class") never made an appearance in any of the political tractates and their discourses, which choose, for the subjects of their sentences, such political figures as the king, high priest, (sages') court, and the like. These usages signal the disembeddedness of economics from politics, a fact further highlighted by the Mishnah's separation between the economic entity, the village or town made up of householders, and the political entities, royal government, temple authority, sages' court; none of these, as a matter of fact, correspond with the village or town, that is, the polis, in the Mishnah's philosophical system.

---

[16] I refer to my *Rabbinic Political Theory: Religion and Politics in the Mishnah* (Chicago, 1991: The University of Chicago Press), briefly summarized in Chapter Three.

What the philosophical Judaism kept apart, the religious Judaism now joined together, and it is just there, at that critical joining, that we identify the key to the system: its reversal of a received point of differentiation,[17] its introduction of new points of differentiation altogether. The source of generative problems for the Mishnah's politics is simply not the same as the source that served the successor-system's politics, and, systemic analysis being what it is, it is the union of what was formerly asunder that identifies for us in quite objective terms the critical point of tension, the sources of problems, the centerpiece of systemic concern throughout. And one fundamental point of reversal, uniting what had been divided, is the joining of economics and politics into a political economy, through the conception of *zekhut,* a term defined presently.

The other point at which, we find, what the one system treated as distinct the next and connected system chose to address as one and whole is less easily discerned, since to do so we have to ask a question the framers of the Mishnah did not raise in the Mishnah at all. That concerns the character and source of virtue, specifically, the affect, upon the individual, of knowledge, specifically, knowledge of the Torah or Torah-study. To frame the question very simply, if we ask ourselves, what happens to me if I study the Torah, the answer, for the Mishnah, predictably is, my standing and status change. Torah-study and its effects form a principal systemic indicator in matters of hierarchical classification, joining the *mamzer-*disciple of sages in a mixture of opposites, for one self-evident example.

But am I changed within? In vain we look in the hundreds of chapters of the Mishnah for an answer to that question. Virtue and learning form distinct categories, a point I shall underline in the pertinent chapter, which follows, and, overall, I am not changed as to my virtue, my character and conscience, by my mastery of the Torah. And still more strikingly, if we ask, does my Torah-study affect my fate in this world and in the life to come, the Mishnah's authorship is strikingly silent about that matter too. Specifically, we find in the pages of that document no claim that studying the Torah either changes me or assures my salvation. But, we shall presently see, the separation of knowledge and the human condition is set aside, and studying the Torah deemed the source of salvation, in the successor-system. The philosophical system, with its interest in *homo hierarchicus,* proved remarkably silent

---

[17]For, after all, the problematic of the Mishnah's politics is the principle of differentiation among legitimate political agencies, first between Heaven's and humanity's, second, among the three political institutions of the Mishnah's "Israel."

Introduction

about the affect of the Torah upon the inner man.[18] The upshot is at the critical points of bonding, the received system proved flawed, in its separation of learning from virtue and legitimate power from valued resources. So to the simple conclusion:

So, it must follow, the comparison between one system and its connected, but distinct successor points to quite objective evidence on the basis of which we may characterize the successor in its own terms. For the categories that present themselves now derive from the system subjected to description, and not from those of the prior system (let alone from my own theory of the components of a theory of the social order). They emerge at that very point – the joining place of differentiation or its opposite, integration – at which systemic description begins, the exegesis of the system's exegesis. Why virtue joins knowledge, politics links to economics, in the religious system but not in the philosophical one is of course obvious. Philosophy differentiates, seeking the rules that join diverse data; religion integrates, proposing to see the whole all together and all at once, thus (for an anthropology, for example) seeing humanity whole: "in our image, after our likeness." Religion by its nature (so it would seem from the case at hand) asks the questions of integration, such as the theory intended to hold together within a single boundary earth and Heaven, this world and the other, should lead us to anticipate. So our observations about the broadening of the frontiers of the social order turn out to signal a deeper characteristic of the analysis at hand.

Why should we have taken the route that has led us to this mode of analysis? The reason is that of special interest in the work of systemic description is not so much theology or doctrine or belief as the interplay of religion and society, that is, the relationship between contents and context, conviction and circumstance, each viewed as distinct and

---

[18]That the system neglected woman altogether, except as a subordinated outcaste, achieving caste-status only through the father at first, and then the husband, served the systemic purpose. By the theory proposed here, however, woman (nearly) as much as man should form a systemic actor, since while for hierarchical purposes, woman can be treated as collective and abnormal, for the work of integration, woman, as much as man, will exhibit the besought unities. We shall note a number of points at which a woman is a principal figure, either counseling the right response to a dilemma, or forming a major actor in a tale. But these are only preliminary observations, and a study of the comparison between the role and representation of woman in the various documents of the unfolding canon will show whether my guess on the systemic difference, and my implicit explanation of that difference, make sense when tested against evidence. In my *The Place of the So-called Tannaitic Midrashim. Methodological Experiments in the Intellectual Situation of Documents, with special reference to Mekhilta Attributed to R. Ishmael, Sifra, Sifré to Numbers, and Sifré to Deuteronomy*, I shall begin part of this inquiry.

autonomous, an independent variable. Religion is a decisive fact of social reality, and not merely a set of beliefs on questions viewed in an abstract and ahistorical setting. Our task is now to identify the system that the successor-documents' authorships formed, and this we do by proposing to define the questions they pursued, the self-evidently-valid answers they set forth, in making a single and coherent statement about their own condition.

The final part of the book then follows an obvious path. The two chapters of systemic description and analysis represent what we have now identified as the two indicative components of the successor-system. First, in Chapter Seven, comes its integration of knowledge and virtue, which is to say, its transformation of the entire realm of intellect from a this-worldly to an other-worldly enterprise, its treatment of knowing as a matter of enchantment.

The second systemic innovation is the formation of an integrated category of political economy, framed in such a way that at stake in politics and economics alike were value and resource in no way subject to order and rule, but in all ways formed out of the unpredictable resource of *zekhut,* sometimes translated as "merit," but, being a matter of not obligation but supererogatory free will, should be portrayed, I think, as "the heritage of virtue and its consequent entitlements." Between those two conceptions – the Torah as a medium of transformation, the heritage of virtue and its consequent entitlements, which can be gained for oneself and also received from one's ancestors – the received system's this-worldly boundaries were transcended, and the new system encompassed within its framework a supernatural life on earth. And appealing to these two statements of world view, way of life, and social entity, we may as a matter of fact compose a complete description of the definitive traits and indicative systemic concerns of the successor-Judaism.

At the end I formulate the urgent and compelling question that the system proposed to settle in a definitive and self-evidently valid way. I do so by appealing for an analogy to a contemporary of the authorships of the successor-documents, that is, to another principal system builder and framer of the social order, who worked out of religious, rather than philosophical, modes of thought. In the same historical context, addressing comparable issues of gross political change, Augustine set forth his account of the social order, of the city of God, with results remarkably congruent to the design of the social order set forth in the successor-system of Judaism. As we shall soon see, quite specifically and concretely, I find in the pages of the Yerushalmi, Genesis Rabbah, Leviticus Rabbah, and Pesiqta deRab Kahana – but not in the Mishnah and Tosefta – that design of the city of God that Augustine for his part also meant to invent.

IV. Methodological Considerations: Comparing Systems of the Same Religion

As to the method of this book: to show that categorical transformations and reconsiderations have taken place in the systems in transition, I read literary evidence as testament to systemic formation. The evidence for systems of world-construction, such as those with which we deal in the history of Judaism, derives from the correct description and analysis of the surviving writings of the formative age. These provide our evidence of how system-builders chose to express their ideas (rhetoric), conceived that their ideas expressed cogent thought and formed intelligible statements to be shared by others (logic of cogent discourse), and formed the categories through which the facts attained sense and constituted orderly and systematic accounts of the world (topical, propositional program). All three together – the mode of discourse, the media of thought and expression, the message brought to representation through the particular rhetoric and logic at hand – prove accessible when we ask the documentary heritage of the system-builders to point us toward the system expressed therein in detail.

As to proposition, I argue the case for viewing, in the movement from the Mishnah and its companions to the Talmud of the Land of Israel and its companions, the transformation of the Judaic system from philosophical to religious in its basic character. The very raw materials of system-building, which are the formations of categories themselves, undergo transformation. When a philosophical becomes a religious system, the categorical change yields not the reframing or re-formation or re-presentation. What happens is rather the fundamental revaluation of categories, which I call "counterpart categories." Transvaluation and transformation – these comprise the history of religion, so far as history records connections, comparisons, and contrasts, between one thing and something else. The sequence, therefore, is from diachronic comparison to synchronic re-presentation.. But the Judaism that emerges is not merely a reformation of the received system; it is a fundamentally new system, which treats as inert systemically generative categories of the philosophical system, and which frames its own systemically-definitive categories in their place.

Let me now amplify these preliminary remarks. Religions present theories of the social order, framed through the power of their rational thought. By "rational thought" I mean by their capacity to explain all data in a single, cogent, and (to an authorship) self-evidently valid way.

The framers of the religious documents that outline such theories answer urgent questions, posed in the language that in that context speaks of public policy in society and politics, economics, and philosophy or science. In that way they produce answers deemed self-evidently valid by those whom they mean to address in the formation of their system. When documents such as the Mishnah and Scripture and the successor-writings, the Talmud of the Land of Israel and Midrash-compilations, turn out to set forth, in an odd idiom to be sure, the principal parts of the social structure and system, they permit us to describe, analyze, and interpret not merely the documentary statements, but the social implications of those statements. In these pages we see how the system attested in earlier writings, the Mishnah and its related Midrash-compilations, is received and revised by the authorships of later writings that point toward a successor-system.

Throughout these pages, the word "system" recurs. Let me define it before proceeding. Writings that are meant (even after the fact) to be read all together, such as those of the unfolding canon of Judaism in late antiquity, are held to make a cogent and important statement. I call that encompassing, canonical picture a "system," a theory of the social order, when it is composed of these three necessary components: an account of a world-view, a prescription of a corresponding way of life, and a definition of the social entity that finds definition in the one and description in the other. When those three fundamental components fit together, they sustain one another in explaining the whole of a social order, hence constituting the theoretical account of a system.

Defined in this way, systems comprise for their framers a cogent picture of *how* things are correctly to be sorted out and fitted together, of *why* things are done in one way, rather than in some other, and of *who* they are that do and understand matters in this particular way. When, as is commonly the case, people invoke God as the foundation for their world-view, maintaining that their way of life corresponds to what God wants of them, projecting their social entity in a particular relationship to God, then we have a religious system. When, finally, a religious system appeals as an important part of its authoritative literature or canon to the Hebrew Scriptures of ancient Israel ("Old Testament"), we have a Judaism. That is why I maintain that, in these pages we deal with two such Judaic systems or Judaisms, one philosophical, the next and successor, religious, in classification.

My intent is to set forth a theory of the comparison of religions, specifically, an account of category-formation and re-formation. Then I explain why I think the successor-system is fundamentally new in categorical definition and structure, and I place the new Judaism into the context of religion by showing the character of its category-formation to

Introduction

be religious: not analytical and differentiating but integrative. I further identify what I conceive to be the urgent question and compelling answer that makes the system single and whole, and in a few brief and, of necessity superficial, observations, I place the Judaic system side-by-side in its salient systemic traits (but not in its doctrinal ones!) with a contemporary system that seems to me to have asked the same question – the one of world-historical calamity, the utter ruin of the old order – and to have gone about answering it in a manner that was remarkably congruent: system-building.

By this example I offer a theory of systemic comparison, with special attention to two religious systems formed within a single religion or religious tradition and therefore connected in important ways with one another.[19] True, my theory of how the work is to be done is worked out wholly in terms of a single example, the comparison of two Judaisms, that is, two Judaic systems, with only the most casual allusion to an external system of a similar sort. But other religious systems can be compared by appeal to the same considerations of category-formation and redefinition of categories.

The basis of comparison and contrast between (and among) systems depends upon the imputed relationships among them. For these classifications of relationships signal the contrast between the first system and its successor. Such religious systems, addressing what is conceived to be a single, continuous social entity,[20] may relate to others in context in one of three ways. They may be [1] autonomous of one another, [2] connected with one another, or [3] continuous with one another. The classification of relationship depends upon our observation of the character of the literary evidence: free-standing, contingent, utterly undifferentiated, respectively. In the case at hand we invoke two of those three possible relationships, the first and the second.[21] The first of

---

[19] Important for reasons explained just now.

[20] I say "conceived to be" since we deal with evidence deriving not from observation or field study but from literary, and only literary, statements. In my *Judaism and its Social Metaphors* (Cambridge and New York, 1989: Cambridge University Press), I show the uses of the word "Israel" that diverse Judaisms have made. There is no possibility of simply using a word such as "Israel" or "people," "nation," "family," or "community." At hand are what in anthropology are called "imagined communities," and the nature of our evidence – every line of it a much-reflected upon cultural artifact – attests only to the shared imagination of the persons who wrote the documents, preserved them, and imputed to them definitive authority. But, in the case at hand, we deal with later documents that appeal to earlier ones – hence my claim to speak of what is conceived to be a single, continuous social entity.

[21] The relationship of continuity among systems occupies my thought, since I do not understand how out of autonomous or connected systems a continuous

the two systems is autonomous, the second, connected to the first but free-standing, and the comparison of the second to the first yields the method of systemic comparison that I mean to set forth here.

My specific contribution to the problem of theory and method, expressed in a concrete case bearing ample generalization as to method, is in three parts. The first is to accomplish, so far as I know for the first time in the study of the history of religion, the comparison of religious systems that are both connected to one another but also distinct from one another.[22] In this way I take account of the important variations that distinguish formations within a single religious tradition, no longer harmonizing or merely ignoring important differences but utilizing them in the description, analysis, and interpretation of the diverse systems that a given tradition over time puts forth. To do so I begin with the description of the generative categories of the initial system and then ask how the successor-system has dealt with these categories.

That comparison leads to my second methodological innovation. It is to identify categorical revision so far-reaching as to require the invention of a new classification of systemic category, which I have called the counterpart-category, a term defined in context. I show how the formation of a counterpart-category emerges from the comparison of the way distinct systemic structures frame the same category. I have

---

system is composed. But, it seems to me quite obvious, the framers of the Talmud of Babylonia accomplished precisely that when they set forth a single and coherent Judaism, comprising all that had come down to them and defining all that would succeed after them. Obviously, the work must begin with the literary problems and proceed outward from there, that is, from text, to matrix, to context.

[22]In general, by comparative religion, people mean the comparison of two or more utterly unrelated religions, e.g., Buddhism and Christianity. But these categories, Christianity and Buddhism, are hopeless constructs, because they homogenize vast and complex sets of religious systems and treat as one what are many things. "Judaism," through time and change, and "Christianity," in all of "its" formulations, cannot be compared because neither the -ism nor the -ity ever existed in social reality; there have been only Judaisms and Christianities, and the work of comparison and contrast must entail the study of the differences between two things that are like, not the contrast of two things that are not like to begin with; only in likeness do we find the possibility of establishing the context for difference. That is the burden of the exchange between Jonathan Z. Smith and myself in Jacob Neusner, ed., *Take Judaism, for Example. Studies toward the Comparison of Religions* (Chicago, 1983: University of Chicago Press). It has taken me eight years from the time of the conversations that yielded that book to find for myself a contribution to that dialogue, and this book constitutes my reply to Smith's wonderful challenge. Whether it is a suitable and even an adequate reply I cannot claim to know.

invented the language, "counterpart-category," to serve my method of systemic comparison.

The third is to set forth how a fresh system addresses fundamental problems its framers discerned in a received system, and this is in the two principal parts which together define the new system as coherent: a new theory of the systemic power of the system's world view, and a new coherence imputed to the systemic components of way of life and social entity. I characterize the initial system as philosophical, the successor-one as religious, and I further show how the religious system has (re)integrated the received categories within the counterpart ones in what is an essentially and fundamentally fresh statement of its own: a Judaism, a system connected with the former but quite clearly intended to deliver its own answers to its own questions.

Let me specify what I conceive to be at stake in this work. This work derives wholly from the analysis of texts, and what I am attempting to do is to find out how to describe that "Judaism" beyond the specific texts, moving beyond the text and the context and toward the matrix of all of the canonical texts. What is it that each document takes for granted but no document spells out? To answer that question I have to describe the processes of category-formation, to specify the categorical imperative in the description of a Judaism. That accounts for the focus of this book on the re-formation of received categories and the formation of new ones, wholly congruent to the received ones but also entirely fresh.

1

Learning and the Category, "Torah"

In the Mishnah's system Torah served as a taxic indicator, that is, the status of Torah as distinct from other (lower) status, hence, Torah-teaching in contra-distinction to scribal-teaching.[1] The category-formation attested in the successor-documents, by contrast, conceived that what the sage said was in the status of the Torah It was Torah *because the sage was Torah incarnate.* Knowledge of the Torah yields power over this world and the next, capacity to coerce to the sage's will the natural and supernatural worlds alike, on that account. The Torah is thus transformed from a philosophical enterprise of the sifting and classification of the facts of this world into a gnostic process of changing persons through knowledge. It is on that basis that in the Yerushalmi and related writings I find in the Torah the counterpart-category to philosophy in the Mishnah.

Now we deal with a new intellectual category: Torah, meaning, religious learning *in place of* philosophical learning. What is the difference between the one and the other? First comes appeal to

---

[1] In the present matter I see Abot as an intermediate document, but not as a mediating or transitional one. In Abot the Torah indicated who was a sage and who was not. Accordingly, the apology of Abot for the Mishnah was that the Mishnah contained things sages had said. What sages said formed a chain of tradition extending back to Sinai. Hence it was equivalent to the Torah. The upshot is that words of sages enjoyed the status of the Torah. The small step beyond, I think, was to claim that what sages said was Torah, as much as what Scripture said was Torah. And, a further small step (and the steps need not have been taken separately or in the order here suggested) moved matters to the position that there were two forms in which the Torah reached Israel: one [Torah] in writing, the other [Torah] handed on orally, that is, in memory.

revealed truth as against perceived facts of nature and their regularities, second, the conception of an other-worldly source of explanation and the development of a propositional program focused upon not nature but Scripture, not the nations in general but Israel in particular, and third, the gnosticization of knowledge in the conception that knowing works salvation.

The philosophical modes of thought characteristic of the Mishnah, with list-making as a medium for discovering the rules of classification of data yielding the hierarchical classification of all things, also characterize the logical and even rhetorical program of the documents that set forth the successor-system. What was to change, therefore, was not the mode of thought. *Listenwissenschaft*, after all, had characterized intellectual life in the Near and Middle East for three thousand years, reaching its apex with Aristotle's natural philosophy.[2] What was new, rather, was the propositions to be demonstrated philosophically, and what made these propositions new was the focus of interest, on the one side, and data assembled by way of demonstrating them, on the other. From a philosophical proposition within the framework of free-standing philosophy of religion and metaphysics that, we saw, the Mishnah's system aimed to establish, we move to religious and even theological propositions within the setting of contingent exegesis of Scripture.

Then how do we know that what was changing was not merely topical and propositional but *categorical* in character? The answer lies in the symbolic vocabulary that would be commonly used in the late fourth and fifth century writings but not at all, or not in the same way, in the late second century ones. When people select data not formerly taken into account and represent the data by appeal to symbols not formerly found evocative or expressive, or not utilized in the way in which they later on were used, then – so I claim – we are

---

[2] I repeat what I have already emphasized, lest my proposition be misinterpreted. The intellectuals whose system(s) we here analyze did not live in the great metropolitan centers of intellectual life and cannot be expected, in the back country, fundamentally to have rethought the very processes of thought that were the givens of intellect from Sumerian times onward. Among them was no one who, like Kant, could address in the abstract the most abstract questions of intellect. Such utter independence of mind, moreover, lay beyond the social circumstances of clerks and petty administrators. Quite to the contrary, I find genuinely awesome the capacity of these rather minor figures to undertake the world-construction that we are now going to examine. The category-formation they inherited, with all its prestige and force of mind, did not inhibit their own enterprise of category-reformation – or even very much influence it. That power of independent thought seems to me to form a counterpart to Kant's.

justified in raising questions about category-formation and the development of new categories alongside, or instead, of the received ones. In the case at hand, the character of the transformation we witness is shown by the formation of a symbol serving to represent a category. And that is not a matter of subjective judgment, for we shall find right on the surface the explicit substitution of one category for another category, symbol for symbol.

To signal what is to come, we shall find the quite bald statement that, in the weighing of the comparative value of capital, which in this time and place meant land or real property, and Torah, Torah was worthwhile, and land was not – a symbolic syllogism that is explicit, concrete, repeated, and utterly fresh for the documents we consider. On the basis of that quite explicit symbolic comparison I speak of transformation – symbolic and therefore *categorical* transformation, not merely thematic shifts in emphasis or even propositional change. And that is why I hold that we witness in the successor-writings the formation of a system connected with, but asymmetrical to, the initial, philosophical one. Then for the world-view of the transformed Judaism, the counterpart-category to philosophy is formulated by appeal to the symbolic medium for the theological message, and it is the category, the Torah, expressed, as a matter of fact, by the symbol of *Torah*.[3]

Let us deal first with what continued, since the continuities justify our interpretation of phenomena as transformation of a received system and structure, not invention of a new one altogether. That the Yerushalmi, Genesis Rabbah, Leviticus Rabbah, and Pesiqta deRab Kahana carried forward and maintained connections with the initial ones, the Mishnah and the Tosefta, is shown not merely by the literary character of the later writings, framed as they were as commentaries on earlier ones. Much more important, connection is established by the paramount role of philosophical modes of thought in them. The successor-documents, specifically, continued the work of the comparison and contrast of species in quest of the genus and the rule governing that genus. But their inquiry led them in directions not contemplated by the framers of the system portrayed in part by the Mishnah – at least, so far as the Mishnah, their end-product, tells us. It moreover produced results concerning a set of issues not considered in the Mishnah and its related writings. The persistence of list-making shows us how the intellects whose

---

[3]Much that is said here alludes to the results of my *Torah: From Scroll to Symbol in Formative Judaism* (Philadelphia, 1985: Fortress; second printing: Atlanta, 1989: Scholars Press for Brown Judaic Studies).

system is adumbrated in the Yerushalmi, Genesis Rabbah, Leviticus Rabbah, and Pesiqta deRab Kahana, remained well within the received modes of thought.[4] But what they learned about how to think did not dictate to them the program for reflection. The propositions of their documents, shown in particular in the Midrash-compilations, will lead us to the conclusion that the formation of a category counterpart to the philosophical one had gotten underway.

Proceeding from modes of thought to message and only then to the categorical formation at hand, we start with the matter of list-making. List-making, which places on display the data of the like and the unlike and implicitly (ordinarily, not explicitly) then conveys the rule. Once a series is established, the authorship assumes, the governing rule will be perceived. That explains why, in exposing the interior logic of its authorship's intellect, the Mishnah had to be a book of lists, with the implicit order, the nomothetic traits of a monothetic order, dictating the ordinarily unstated general and encompassing rule. The purpose of list-making in the Mishnah is in order to make a single statement, endless times over, and to repeat in a mass of tangled detail precisely the same fundamental judgment. To form their lists, the framers of the Mishnah appeal solely to the traits of things. Establishing a set of shared traits that form a rule which compels us to reach a given conclusion, Mishnaic list-making assembled probative facts to derive from the classification of data whatever conclusion they reached.

Taking Leviticus Rabbah as our example of the mode of thought characteristic of the writings of the successor-system, we find argument in behalf of a given proposition through a syllogism set forth by a sequence of examples. These examples, drawn from Scripture, form the counterpart to the facts concerning the natural world that yield, in the Mishnah, the propositions of hierarchical classification ascending toward the One [God] that dominate in the Mishnah. Lists of examples, deriving from Scripture, provide an entirely logical, because factual, demonstration. The proposition is a simple one: if X, then Y; if not X, then not Y. If Israel carries out its obligations, then God will redeem Israel; if not, then God will not

---

[4]But list-making would change in form and I think in character; I do not mean to take for granted *Listenwissenschaft* beginning to end was everywhere and always pretty much the same thing. In my treatment of "another matter," I show both that Listenwissenschaft defined the method of the late Midrash-compilations and also that that method underwent considerable revision for the purposes of the compilers of those documents. I refer specifically to *From Literature to Theology in Formative Judaism. Three Preliminary Studies.* Atlanta, 1989: Scholars Press for Brown Judaic Studies.

Learning and the Category, "Torah"

redeem but will punish Israel. That simple commonplace is given numerous illustrations.

An example of the syllogism demonstrated by example is that Israel in times past repented, so God saved them. Israel in times past sinned, so God punished them. Another proposition is that God loves the humble and despises the haughty. Therefore God saves the humble and punishes the haughty. Let me give one example of the way in which, in the Midrash-compilations of the late fourth and fifth centuries, the mode of compiling lists of data that bear shared taxonomic traits serves to demonstrate propositions. What we wish to prove in the following composition is that the third day marks the salvific occasion, with the further implication that salvation comes in the end of a series of three. The mode of argument, which is what is pertinent here, is the familiar one of presenting a variety of facts that point to the same conclusion, and, in context, only to that conclusion.

Genesis Rabbah LVI:I

1. A. "On the third day Abraham lifted up his eyes and saw the place afar off" (Gen. 22:4):
   B. "After two days he will revive us, on the third day he will raise us up, that we may live in his presence" (Hos. 16:2).
   C. On the third day of the tribes: "And Joseph said to them on the third day, 'This do and live'" (Gen. 42:18).
   D. On the third day of the giving of the Torah: "And it came to pass on the third day when it was morning" (Ex. 19:16).
   E. On the third day of the spies: "And hide yourselves there for three days" (Josh 2:16).
   F. On the third day of Jonah: "And Jonah was in the belly of the fish three days and three nights" (Jonah 2:1).
   G. On the third day of the return from the Exile: "And we abode there three days" (Ezra 8:32).
   H. On the third day of the resurrection of the dead: "After two days he will revive us, on the third day he will raise us up, that we may live in his presence" (Hos. 16:2).
   I. On the third day of Esther: "Now it came to pass on the third day that Esther put on her royal apparel" (Est. 5:1).
   J. She put on the monarchy of the house of her fathers.
   K. On account of what sort of merit?
   L. Rabbis say, "On account of the third day of the giving of the Torah."
   M. R. Levi said, "It is on account of the merit of the third day of Abraham: 'On the third day Abraham lifted up his eyes and saw the place afar off' (Gen. 22:4)."
2. A. "...lifted up his eyes and saw the place afar off" (Gen. 22:4):
   B. What did he see? He saw a cloud attached to the mountain. He said, "It would appear that that is the place concerning which the Holy One, blessed be He, told me to offer up my son."

The third day marks the fulfillment of the promise, at the end of time of the resurrection of the dead, and, at appropriate moments, of Israel's redemption. The reference to the third day at Gen. 22:2 then invokes the entire panoply of Israel's history.

Another commonplace mode of argument may be noted. If one condition is met, the other will come about. This, too, is set forth with its corpus of examples, which, in context, form demonstrations. And the whole is given the form of the list, that is, example after example of a single proposition. The thirty-seven parashiyyot of Leviticus Rabbah then form the counterpart to the making of lists that defined the labor of the philosophers of the Mishnah. A nomothetic definitive trait then serves to demonstrate the rules that apply throughout. True, in the present instance, the rules concern the social life, rather than the natural world upon which so much of the Mishnah (for example, the Division of Purities) concentrates. But the mode of thought is consistent. That shared method, for the Midrash-compilations, appeals to the rhetoric of joining distinct examples by the use of "another matter" (in Hebrew, davar-aher, hence, the davar-aher-construction). Sequences of comments on the same verse, joined by "another matter," mean to establish compositions of taxically-joined facts, that is to say, lists. And, as is now clear, as soon as we recognize that obvious fact, we are drawn back to the Mishnah's method, which is that of list-making as well.

Now, it is clear, that mode of thought common to both the Mishnah and the Midrash-compilations later on hardly leads us to anticipate the formation of a counterpart-category, one quite different in not only message and medium but also, and especially, in its symbolic formulation, from the philosophical category that the Mishnah sets forth. And as a matter of fact, evidence for the formation of that counterpart-category comes, to begin with, from vast differences in propositional program; only at the end shall we turn out attention to the symbolic formulation of the counterpart category. The results of learning accomplished through list-making, that is, *Listenwissenschaft,* in the philosophical setting of the Mishnah vastly differ from those of the same method of learning worked out in the theological setting of the Midrash-compilations of the fourth and fifth centuries. So let us now ask how, in the successor-documents, familiar methods yielded a new message. And, not forgetting our thesis, on what basis do I characterize that new message as not philosophical but religious?

In the Mishnah, philosophy sets forth a system concerning the orderly classification of things, while in the Midrash-compilations the same philosophical modes of thought yields propositions of fixed truth about God and God's relationship with Israel. However diverse the language and however original the arrangement of the data, drawn from Scripture rather than nature, that convey that message, the message is uniform throughout, and the articulation is essentially through the repetition in marginally different theological "things" of the same thing: *davar-aher* really does stand for "another matter" that is in fact the same matter. So the same method of learning is used for different purposes, the one philosophical, systematizing the evidence of nature, the other religious in substance, if not theological in structure,[5] recapitulating the evidence of supernature revealed by God in the Torah.[6]

The propositional programs of Leviticus Rabbah, Genesis Rabbah, and Pesiqta deRab Kahana set forth on the basis of the facts of not nature but Scripture propositions of a religious, rather than a philosophical, character. Why the difference? Philosophy generalizes and aims at classification of all data in a single way, accounting to be sure for exceptions, but only by appeal to appropriate rules to explain exceptions. But religion – at least in the present case – concerns itself with integrating the traits of a single category, for example, a unique social entity, a holy, therefore separate and different, way of life, a revealed world view not to be discovered within the facts of nature but only through the data of supernature, supernaturally revealed (in the case of a Judaism). Accordingly, these not philosophical and general but religious and particular propositions deal with not the nature of things but the special traits of Israel, setting forth not how humanity in general conducts itself or how nature in general is structured but the rules particular to the holy people in its holy way of life. The world-view that emerges then pertains to only the theologically-identified social entity, Israel, and it follows, Israel now stands for not a taxic indicator that distinguishes diverse species of a common genus, but as a social entity that is simply *sui generis*.[7] Let me now rapidly survey the

---

[5]The distinction made here will form the problematic of the study of the transformation of a religious into a theological system.

[6]I have vastly elaborated on this conception of The Torah in my *Uniting the Dual Torah: Sifra and the Problem of the Mishnah* (Cambridge, 1989: Cambridge University Press). There is no need to recapitulate that argument here.

[7]In my *Judaism and its Social Metaphors* (Cambridge and New York, 1989: Cambridge University Press) I have set forth the standing of "Israel" in the Mishnah as a taxic indicator, by contrast to the uses of "Israel" in the successor-documents as referring to a genus with no counterpart, Israel as sui generis in one of two ways: a family different from all other families and unrelated to them; or a holy society bearing no points in common with any

propositions that a synthetic reading of the several documents may yield.

Philosophy sought the generalizations that cases might yield. So, too, did religion (and, in due course, theology would too). But the range of generalization vastly differed. Philosophy spoke of the nature of things, while theology represented the special nature of Israel in particular. Philosophy then appealed to the traits of things, while theology to the special indicative qualities of Israel. In Leviticus Rabbah, for example, the framers systematically adopted for themselves and adapted to their own circumstance the reality of the Scripture, its history and doctrines. They transformed that history from a sequence of one-time events, leading from one place to some other, into the fixtures of the enduring tableau of an ever-present mythic world. That is what I mean by generalizing on the basis of particular cases. Thus persons who lived once now operate forever; events take on that trait of recurrence, circularity, or replicability, that allows them to happen again and again, every day. That is because events now are seen to yield rules, and the rules apply throughout: philosophical mode of thought, but religious proposition.

No longer was there one Moses, one David, one set of happenings of a distinctive and never-to-be-repeated character. Now whatever happens, of which the thinkers propose to take account, must enter and be absorbed into that established and ubiquitous pattern and structure founded in Scripture. One-time history is therefore transformed into all-time social structure. It is not that biblical history repeats itself or is turned from a one-way path to a cyclical system. Rather, biblical history no longer constitutes history as a story of things that happened once, long ago, and pointed to some one moment in the future. Rather it becomes an account of things that happen every day – hence, an ever-present mythic world, or, in anachronistic terms, history is turned into social science.

The organizing rhetoric carries the same message. The verses that are quoted ordinarily shift from the meanings they convey to the implications they contain, speaking about something, anything, other than what they seem to be saying. What the sages of the system adumbrated by Leviticus Rabbah now proposed was a reconstruction of existence along the lines of the ancient design – the social rules – of Scripture as they read it. What that meant was that, from a sequence of one-time and linear events, everything that

---

other society, being in fact of a different genus from societies in general. That is the basis for the statement made here.

Learning and the Category, "Torah" 39

happened was turned into a repetition of known and already experienced paradigms, hence, once more, a mythic being. The source and core of the myth, of course, derive from Scripture – Scripture reread, renewed, reconstructed along with the society that revered Scripture. In an exact sense, they were engaged in a labor of natural history: classification of data, formation of species and reformation of species into genera. Counterpart to the natural philosophy of the Mishnah, the successor-system produced a kind of natural history, by treating history as social science. That explained the movement to Scripture as the organizing structure, for Scripture was history and dictated the contents of history, laying forth the structures of time, the rules that prevailed and were made known in events.

A category requires structure and order. Can we identifies the lines of structure of the counterpart-category in process? The principal lines of structure flow along the borders with the world beyond: Israel's relationships with others. These are horizontal, with the nations, and vertical, with God. But, from the viewpoint of the framers of the document, the relationships form a single, seamless web, for Israel's vertical relationships dictate the horizontals as well; when God wishes to punish Israel, the nations come to do the work. When we contrast philosophy, with its concern for generalization and classification of everything in some one way and its reading of "Israel" as a taxic indicator, with religion, with its interest in the distinctive, the specific, and the special, this is precisely the result we should anticipate: the turning from a horizontal perspective on everybody in the same way to a vertical vision of Israel seen from above, all by itself.

The relationships that define Israel, moreover, prove dynamic, not static, in that they respond to the movement of the Torah through Israel's history. When the Torah governs, then the vertical relationship is stable and felicitous, the horizontal one secure, and, when not, God obeys the rules and the nations obey God. So the first and paramount, category takes shape within the themes associated with the national life of Israel. The principal lines of structure flow along the fringe, Israel's relationships with others. The relationships form a single, seamless web, for Israel's vertical relationships dictate the horizontals as well; when God wishes to punish Israel, the nations come to do the work. The relationships that define Israel, moreover, prove dynamic, not static, in that they respond to the movement of the Torah through Israel's history. When the Torah governs, then the vertical relationship is stable and felicitous, the horizontal one secure, and, when not, God obeys the rules and the nations obey God.

What of the propositional program that the document sets forth? The philosophical proposition of the Mishnah demonstrated from the facts and traits of things the hierarchical order of all being, with the obvious if merely implicit proposition that God stands at the head of the social order. The religious propositions of the successor-documents speak in other words of other things, having simply nothing in common with the propositional program of the Mishnah's philosophy. For Leviticus Rabbah, for example, the principal propositions are these: God loves Israel, so gave them the Torah, which defines their life and governs their welfare. Israel is alone in its category (*sui generis*), so what is a virtue to Israel is a vice to the nation, life-giving to Israel, poison to the gentiles. True, Israel sins, but God forgives that sin, having punished the nation on account of it. Such a process has yet to come to an end, but it will culminate in Israel's complete regeneration. Meanwhile, Israel's assurance of God's love lies in the many expressions of special concern, for even the humblest and most ordinary aspects of the national life: the food the nation eats, the sexual practices by which it procreates. These life-sustaining, life-transmitting activities draw God's special interest, as a mark of his general love for Israel. Israel then is supposed to achieve its life in conformity with the marks of God's love. These indications moreover signify also the character of Israel's difficulty, namely, subordination to the nations in general, but to the fourth kingdom, Rome, in particular. Both food laws and skin diseases stand for the nations. There is yet another category of sin, also collective and generative of collective punishment, and that is social. The moral character of Israel's life, the treatment of people by one another, the practice of gossip and small-scale thuggery – these, too, draw down divine penalty. The nation's fate therefore corresponds to its moral condition. The moral condition, however, emerges not only from the current generation. Israel's richest hope lies in the merit of the ancestors, thus in the Scriptural record of the merits attained by the founders of the nation, those who originally brought it into being and gave it life.

The world to come is so portrayed as to restate these same propositions. Merit overcomes sin, and doing religious duties or supererogatory acts of kindness will win merit for the nation that does them. Israel will be saved at the end of time, and the age, or world, to follow will be exactly the opposite of this one. Much that we find in the account of Israel's national life, worked out through the definition of the liminal relationships, recurs in slightly altered form in the picture of the world to come. The world to come will right all presently unbalanced relationships. What is good will go forward, what is bad will come to an end. The simple message is that the things people revere, the cult and its majestic course through the year, will go on; Jerusalem will come back, so, too, the Temple, in all their glory. Israel will be saved through the merit of the ancestors, atonement, study of Torah, practice of religious duties. The prevalence of the eschatological dimension at the formal structures, with its messianic and other expressions, here finds its counterpart in the repetition of the same few symbols in the expression of doctrine. The theme of the moral life of Israel produces propositions concerning not only the individual but, more important, the social virtues that the community as a whole must exhibit.

This brings us to the laws of society for Israel's holy community as the authorship of Leviticus Rabbah sets forth those laws. The message to the individual constitutes a revision, for this context, of the address to the nation: humility as against arrogance, obedience as against sin, constant concern not to follow one's natural inclination to do evil or to overcome the natural limitations of the human condition. Israel must accept its fate, obey and rely on the merits accrued through the ages and God's special love. The individual must conform, in ordinary affairs, to this same paradigm of patience and submission. Great men and women, that is, individual heroes within the established paradigm, conform to that same pattern, exemplifying the national virtues. Among these, of course, Moses stands out; he has no equal. The special position of the humble Moses is complemented by the patriarchs and by David, all of whom knew how to please God and left as an inheritance to Israel the merit they had thereby attained.

If we now ask about further recurring themes or topics, there is one so commonplace that we should have to list the majority of paragraphs of discourse in order to provide a complete list. It is an exercise in *Listenwissenschaft,* such as the Mishnah has led us to anticipate, but what is listed is not a taxonomy of traits of the natural world but rather the catalogue of events in Israel's history, meaning, in this context, Israel's history solely in scriptural times, down through the return to Zion. The one-time events of the generation of the flood, Sodom and Gomorrah, the patriarchs and the sojourn in Egypt, the exodus, the revelation of the Torah at Sinai, the golden calf, the Davidic monarchy and the building of the Temple, Sennacherib, Hezekiah, and the destruction of northern Israel, Nebuchadnezzar and the destruction of the Temple in 586 B. C., the life of Israel in Babylonian captivity, Daniel and his associates, Mordecai and Haman – these events occur over and over again. They turn out to serve as paradigms of sin and atonement, steadfastness and divine intervention, and equivalent lessons. We find, in fact, a fairly standard repertoire of scriptural heroes or villains, on the one side, and conventional lists of Israel's enemies and their actions and downfall, on the other. The boastful, for instance, include the generation of the flood, Sodom and Gomorrah, Pharaoh, Sisera, Sennacherib, Nebuchadnezzar, the wicked empire (Rome) – contrasted to Israel, "despised and humble in this world." The four kingdoms recur again and again, always ending, of course, with Rome, with the repeated message that after Rome will come Israel. But Israel has to make this happen through its faith and submission to God's will. Lists of enemies repeatedly refer to Cain, the Sodomites, Pharaoh, Sennacherib, Nebuchadnezzar, Haman.

Accordingly, the mode of thought brought to bear upon the theme of history remains exactly the same as before: list making, with data exhibiting similar taxonomic traits drawn together into lists based on common monothetic traits or definitions. In the Mishnah *Listenwissenschaft* yielded a composition of natural philosophy; in the successor-documents, one of natural history. For these lists in Leviticus Rabbah, our exemplary case, then through the power of repetition make a single enormous point. They prove a social law of history. The catalogues of exemplary heroes and historical events serve a further purpose. They provide a model of how contemporary events are to be absorbed into the biblical paradigm. Since biblical events exemplify recurrent happenings, sin and redemption, forgiveness and atonement, they lose their one-time character. At the same time and in the same way, current events find a place within the ancient, but eternally present, paradigmatic scheme. So no new historical events, other than exemplary episodes in lives of heroes, demand narration because, through what is said about the past, what was happening in the times of the framers of Leviticus Rabbah would also come under consideration. This mode of dealing with biblical history and contemporary events produces two reciprocal effects. The first is the mythicization of biblical stories, their removal from the framework of ongoing, unique patterns of history and sequences of events and their transformation into accounts of things that happen all the time. The second is that contemporary events, too, lose all of their specificity and enter the paradigmatic framework of established mythic existence. So (1) the Scripture's myth happens every day, and (2) every day produces reenactment of the Scripture's myth.

Israel is God's special love. That love is shown in a simple way. Israel's present condition of subordination derives from its own deeds. It follows that God cares, so Israel may look forward to redemption on God's part in response to Israel's own regeneration through repentance. When the exegetes proceeded to open the scroll of Leviticus, they found numerous occasions to state that proposition in concrete terms and specific contexts. The sinner brings on his own sickness. But God heals through that very ailment. The nations of the world govern in heavy succession, but Israel's lack of faith guaranteed their rule and its moment of renewal will end it. Israel's leaders – priests, prophets, kings – fall into an entirely different category from those of the nations, as much as does Israel. In these and other concrete allegations, the same classical message comes forth. Accordingly, at the foundations of the pretense lies the long-standing biblical-Jewish insistence that Israel's sorry condition in no way testifies to Israel's true worth – the grandest pretense of all. All of the little evasions of the primary sense in favor of some other testify to this, the great denial that what is, is what counts. Leviticus Rabbah makes that statement with art and imagination. But it is never subtle about saying so.

Salvation and sanctification join together in Leviticus Rabbah. The laws of the book of Leviticus, focused as they are on the sanctification of the nation through its cult, in Leviticus Rabbah indicate the rules of salvation as well. The message of Leviticus Rabbah attaches itself to the book of Leviticus, as if that book had come from prophecy and addressed the issue of the meaning of history and Israel's salvation. But the book of Leviticus came from the priesthood and spoke of sanctification. The paradoxical syllogism – the as-if reading, the opposite of how things seem – of the composers of Leviticus Rabbah therefore reaches simple formulation. In the very setting of sanctification we find the promise of salvation. In the topics of the cult and the priesthood we uncover the national and social issues of the moral life and redemptive hope of Israel. The repeated comparison and contrast of priesthood and prophecy, sanctification and salvation, turn out to produce a complement, which comes to most perfect union in the text at hand.

The focus of Leviticus Rabbah and its laws of history is upon the society of Israel, its national fate and moral condition. Indeed, nearly all of the *parashiyyot* of Leviticus Rabbah turn out to deal with the national, social condition of Israel, and this in three contexts: (1) Israel's setting in the history of the nations, (2) the sanctified character of the inner life of Israel itself, (3) the future, salvific history of Israel. So the biblical book that deals with the holy Temple now is shown to address the holy people. Leviticus really discusses not the consecration of the cult but the sanctification of the nation – its conformity to God's will laid forth in the Torah, and God's rules. So when we review the document as a whole and ask what is that something else that the base text is supposed to address, it turns out that the sanctification of the cult stands for the salvation of the nation. So the nation now is like the cult then, the ordinary Israelite now like the priest then. The holy way of life lived now, through acts to which merit accrues, corresponds to the holy rites then. The process of metamorphosis is full, rich, complete. When everything stands for something else, the something else repeatedly turns out to be the nation. This is what Leviticus Rabbah spells out in exquisite detail, yet never missing the main point. It is in the context of that highly cogent message that we shall ask whether Sifra sets forth any propositions, let alone a cogent and stunning judgment so powerfully laid out in Leviticus Rabbah. But first we shall have to make certain that the treatment of the book of Leviticus by the authorship of Leviticus Rabbah is particular and significant, not simply a repetition of generally prevailing propositions in a singular context.

Lest readers suppose I present them with a series of one, I have now to ask, what of the other documents that point toward the shape and structure of the successor-system, Genesis Rabbah and Pesiqta deRab Kahana? The mode of thought paramount in Leviticus Rabbah proves entirely congruent with the manner of reflection characteristic of Genesis Rabbah, and the propositions concerning history and the social laws of Israel are the same. If I had to point to the single most important proposition of Genesis Rabbah, it is that, in the story of the beginnings of creation, humanity, and Israel, we find the message of the meaning and end of the life of the Jewish people. This appeal to not history but rule-making precedent runs parallel to the equivalent interest in regularities in Leviticus Rabbah. Where the authorship of Genesis Rabbah differs is the choice of the paradigm, which is now the age of beginnings; but that choice leads to quite distinctive propositions, which, to be sure, prove quite congruent to those important in Leviticus Rabbah.

As the rules of Leviticus set forth the social laws of Israel's history in Leviticus Rabbah, so the particular tales of Genesis are turned into paradigms of social laws in Genesis Rabbah.[8] The deeds

---

[8]The parallel mode of thought in Sifré to Deuteronomy and in Sifra is the exercise of inclusion and exclusion, which turns a case or an example into a law with clear-cut application or exclusion. That mode of generalizing law forms the counterpart to the interest in generalizing laws from incidents or anecdotes that is characteristic of Genesis Rabbah. In both cases we observe the move from an *ad hoc* and episodic mode of thinking to a philosophical and scientific one. The profound interest in generalization, rather than

Learning and the Category, "Torah" 45

of the founders supply signals for the children about what is going to come in the future. So the biography of Abraham, Isaac, and Jacob also constitutes the paradigm by which to interpret the history of Israel later on. If the sages could announce a single syllogism and argue it systematically, that is the proposition on which they would insist. The sages understood that stories about the progenitors, presented in the book of Genesis, define the human condition and proper conduct for their children, Israel in time to come. Accordingly, they systematically asked Scripture to tell them how they were supposed to conduct themselves at the critical turnings of life. In a few words let me restate what I conceive to be the conviction of the framers of Genesis Rabbah about the message and meaning of the book of Genesis:

> "We now know what will be in the future. How do we know it? Just as Jacob had told his sons what would happen in time to come, just as Moses told the tribes their future, so we may understand the laws of history if we study the Torah. And in the Torah, we turn to beginnings: the rules as they were laid out at the very start of human history. These we find in the book of Genesis, the story of the origins of the world and of Israel. The Torah tells us not only what happened but why. The Torah permits us to discover the laws of history. Once we know those laws, we may also peer into the future and come to an assessment of what is going to happen to us – and, especially, of how we shall be saved from our present existence. Because everything exists under the aspect of a timeless will, God's will, and all things express one thing, God's program and plan, in the Torah we uncover the workings of God's will. Our task as Israel is to accept, endure, submit, and celebrate."

In Genesis Rabbah the entire narrative of Genesis is so formed as to point toward the sacred history of Israel, the Jewish people: its slavery and redemption; its coming Temple in Jerusalem; its exile and salvation at the end of time. The powerful message of Genesis in Genesis Rabbah proclaims that the world's creation commenced a

---

merely precedent or ad hoc observation, characteristic of the authorships of Sifra and Sifré to Deuteronomy, for law, and of Leviticus Rabbah and Genesis Rabbah, for history, seems to me one of the deepest and most indicative traits of mind of the Judaism of the Dual Torah in its intellectual origin and marks that Judaism as deeply philosophical. No student of the writings of the Church fathers can find that fact surprising, even though the idiom of the formative intellects of the Judaism of the Dual Torah is less accessible, within the philosophical mode, than that of the formative intellects of Christianity, particularly Catholic (not Gnostic) Christianity. But the gnostic side to the successor-system will presently emerge as a principal characteristic.

single, straight line of events, leading in the end to the salvation of Israel and through Israel all humanity. Israel's history constitutes the counterpart of creation, and the laws of Israel's salvation form the foundation of creation. Therefore a given story out of Genesis, about creation, events from Adam to Noah and Noah to Abraham, the domestic affairs of the patriarchs, or Joseph, will bear a deeper message about what it means to be Israel, on the one side, and what in the end of days will happen to Israel, on the other.

So the persistent program of religious inquiry into God's place in Israel's history requires sages' to search in Scripture for meaning for their own circumstance and for the condition of their people. In the story of the beginnings of creation, humanity, and Israel, we find the message of the meaning and end of the life of the Jewish people. The deeds of the founders supply signals for the children about what is going to come in the future. The biography of Abraham, Isaac, and Jacob also constitutes a protracted account of the history of Israel later on. If the sages could announce a single syllogism and argue it systematically, that is the proposition upon which they would insist. Sages read the book of Genesis as if it portrayed the history of Israel and Rome. Why Rome in the form it takes in Genesis Rabbah? And how come the obsessive character of sages disposition of the theme of Rome?

Were their picture merely of Rome as tyrant and destroyer of the Temple, we should have no reason to link the text to the problems of the age of redaction and closure. But now it is Rome as Israel's brother, counterpart, and nemesis, Rome as the one thing standing in the way of Israel's, and the world's, ultimate salvation. So the stakes are different, and much higher. It is not a political Rome but a Christian and messianic Rome that is at issue: Rome as surrogate for Israel, Rome as obstacle to Israel. Why? It is because Rome now confronts Israel with a crisis, and, I argue, the program of Genesis Rabbah constitutes a response to that crisis. Rome in the fourth century became Christian. Sages respond by facing that fact quite squarely and saying, "Indeed, it is as you say, a kind of Israel, an heir of Abraham as your texts explicitly claim. But we remain the sole legitimate Israel, the bearer of the birthright – we and not you. So you are our brother: Esau, Ishmael, Edom." And the rest follows.

The authorship of Genesis Rabbah focuses its discourse on the proposition that the book of Genesis speaks to the life and historical condition of Israel, the Jewish people. The entire narrative of Genesis is so formed as to point toward the sacred history of Israel, the Jewish people: its slavery and redemption; its coming Temple in Jerusalem; its exile and salvation at the end of time. The powerful message of Genesis in the pages of Genesis Rabbah proclaims that the world's creation commenced a single, straight line of events, leading in the end to the salvation of Israel and through Israel all humanity. Therefore a given story will bear a deeper message about what it means to be Israel, on the one side, and what in the end of days will happen to Israel, on the other. And that is precisely the proposition endlessly represented by the authorship of Leviticus Rabbah. The subjects change, the point remains the same. The third compilation of Midrash-exegeses adduced as evidence of the successor-system, Pesiqta deRab Kahana, now requires inclusion into this account of the propositional program subject to development by our system-builders.

Closely related to Leviticus Rabbah in that its authorship has borrowed five *parashiyyot* from the earlier writing, the framers of Pesiqta deRab Kahana moved beyond the appeal to scriptural history (as in Genesis Rabbah) or to scriptural case-law (as in Leviticus Rabbah). Rather they set forth propositions entirely independent of the received Scripture and so produced the most sustainedly theological compilation, worked out in the modes of argument of philosophy and in the idiom of scriptural exegesis, of midrash-exegeses that derives from late antiquity. In Pesiqta deRab Kahana I see three propositions, all of them religious, none of them philosophical within the definitions now set forth.

The first is that God loves Israel, that love is unconditional, and Israel's response to God must be obedience to the religious duties that God has assigned, which will produce merit. Much of the argument for this proposition draws upon the proof of history as laid out in Scripture and appeals to history transformed into paradigm. Israel's obedience to God is what will save Israel. That means doing the religious duties as required by the Torah, which is the mark of God's love for – and regeneration of – Israel. The tabernacle symbolizes the union of Israel and God. When Israel does what God asks above, Israel will prosper down below. If Israel remembers Amalek down below, God will remember Amalek up above and will wipe him out. A mark of Israel's loyalty to God is remembering Amalek. God does not require the animals that are sacrificed, since man could never match God's appetite, if that were the issue. But the savor pleases God [as a mark of Israel's loyalty and obedience]. The first sheaf returns to God God's fair share of the gifts that God bestows on Israel, and those who give it benefit, while those who hold it back suffer. Observing religious duties, typified by the rites of The Festival, brings a great reward of that merit that ultimately leads to redemption. God's ways are just, righteous and merciful, as shown by God's concern that the offspring remain with the mother for seven days. God's love for Israel is so intense that he wants to hold them back for an extra day after The Festival in order to spend more time with them, because, unlike the nations of the world, Israel knows how to please God. This is a mark of God's love for Israel.

The second proposition moves us from the ontology to the history of that *sui generis* social entity that is Israel. It is that God is reasonable and when Israel has been punished, it is in accord with God's rules. God forgives penitent Israel and is abundant in mercy. The good and the wicked die in exactly the same circumstance or condition. Laughter is vain because it is mixed with grief. A wise person will not expect too much joy. But when people suffer, there ordinarily is a good reason for it. That is only one sign that God is reasonable and God never did anything lawless and wrong to Israel or made unreasonable demands, and there was, therefore, no reason for Israel to lose confidence in God or to abandon him. God punished Israel to be sure. But this was done with reason. Nothing happened to Israel of which God did not give fair warning in advance, and Israel's failure to heed the prophets brought about her fall. And God will forgive a faithful Israel. Even though the Israelites sinned by making the golden calf, God forgave them and raised them up. On the New Year, God executes justice, but the justice is tempered with mercy. The rites of the New Year bring about divine judgment and also forgiveness because of the merit of the fathers. Israel must repent and return to the Lord, who is merciful and will forgive them for their sins. The penitential season of the New Year and Day of Atonement is the right time for confession and penitence, and God is sure to accept penitence. By exercising his power of mercy, the already-merciful God grows still stronger in mercy.

The third proposition is that God will save Israel personally at a time and circumstance of his own choosing. While I take for granted that the hope for future redemption animates the other compilations, we look in vain in some of them, Sifra for a prime example, for an equivalent obsession with messianic questions. Israel may know what the future redemption will be like, because of the redemption from Egypt. The paradox of the red cow, that what imparts uncleanness, namely touching the ashes of the red cow, produces cleanness is part of God's ineffable wisdom, which man cannot fathom. Only God can know the precise moment of Israel's redemption. That is something man cannot find out on his own. But God will certainly fulfill the predictions of the prophets about Israel's coming redemption. The Exodus from Egypt is the paradigm of the coming redemption. Israel has lost Eden – but can come home, and, with God's help, will. God's unique power is shown through Israel's unique suffering. In God's own time, he will redeem Israel. The lunar calendar, particular to Israel, marks Israel as favored by God, for the new moon signals the coming of Israel's redemption, and the particular new moon that will mark the actual event is that of Nisan. When God chooses to redeem Israel, Israel's enemies will have no power to stop him, because God will force Israel's enemies to serve Israel, because of Israel's purity and loyalty to God. Israel's enemies are punished, and what they propose to do to Israel, God does to them. Both directly and through the prophets, God is the source of true comfort, which he will bring to Israel. Israel thinks that God has forsaken them. But it is Israel who forsook God, God's love has never failed, and will never fail. Even though he has been angry, his mercy still is near and God has the power and will to save Israel. God has designated the godly for himself and has already promised to redeem them. He will assuredly do so. God personally is the one who will comfort Israel. While Israel says there is no comfort, in fact, God will comfort Israel. Zion/Israel is like a barren woman, but Zion will bring forth children, and Israel will be comforted. Both God and Israel will bring light to Zion, which will give light to the world. The rebuilding of Zion will be a source of joy for the entire world, not for Israel alone. God will rejoice in Israel, Israel in God, like bride and groom.

There is a profoundly cogent statement made through the composition of this document, and this is the message of Pesiqta deRab Kahana: God loves Israel, that love is unconditional, and Israel's response to God must be obedience to the religious duties that God has assigned, which will produce merit. God is reasonable and when Israel has been punished, it is in accord with God's rules. God forgives penitent Israel and is abundant in mercy. God will save Israel personally at a time and circumstance of his own choosing. Israel may know what the future redemption will be like, because of the redemption from Egypt. Pesiqta deRab Kahana therefore has been so assembled as to exhibit a viewpoint, a purpose of its particular authorship, one quite distinctive, in its own context (if not in a single one of its propositions!) to its framers or collectors and arrangers. Why the authorship of Leviticus Rabbah will not have concurred in a general way I cannot say. But I also cannot find these propositions in Leviticus Rabbah, which presents its own points.[9]

---

[9] I immediately qualify that there are chapters of Pesiqta deRab Kahana which originate in Leviticus Rabbah. In form and in polemic, in plan and in program, the materials assembled in Pesiqta deRab Kahana cohere, to such a

And when these particular propositions do make an appearance in Leviticus Rabbah or in Genesis Rabbah, they do not receive that emphasis that characterizes Pesiqta deRab Kahana's authorships presentation of them. Both documents address issues of salvation, but I find Pesiqta deRab Kahana's message of salvation couched in explicitly messianic terms, which is not the case in Leviticus Rabbah. And, as we move toward Sifré to Deuteronomy, Sifré to Numbers, and Sifra, we shall find noteworthy the centrality in the Rabbah-compilations of historical-salvific issues, for, in the other family of midrash-compilations, people focus upon other matters entirely.

Enough has been said to show how the three Midrash-compilations present propositions that, while surely consistent with the range of positions and attitudes of the Mishnah and the Tosefta, simply play no role whatsoever in those expressions of the initial system. And by appeal to our initial definition of the difference between a philosophical and a religious system, we may bypass extensive reiteration of an obvious point. It is that the successor-writings concern themselves with not natural philosophy yielding philosophy of religion but revealed truths, appealing to Scripture in particular, yielding a religious account of the social order. It suffices to say simply that the single definitive point of difference between the philosophical system adumbrated by the Mishnah and the religious system to which the Midrash-compilations before us attest lies in the rhetorical form, constant appeal to Scripture, and the propositional result, rules that derive not from the nature of things and apply without differentiation to all of nature, but laws that derive from the history of Israel and pertain solely to Israel. Now my claim concerning the formation of a counterpart-category, one that serves to portray a world-view just as philosophy does, but that forms a category essentially different from the philosophical one, requires sustained attention.

If I ask the Mishnah for a verbal symbol for philosophy, the document remains dumb. Philosophy for the Mishnah serves as source of method and taxon of proposition. But the Mishnah's framers have no word for philosophy, nor for natural science, nor for learning, nor for system, nor for any of my other analytical categories.[10] Nor, despite their formidable powers of abstraction in thought and expression do they even set forth the abstract proposition concerning the hierarchical unity of being that in point of fact is their principal result. Certainly, in the Mishnah the symbol, Torah, like "Israel," serves as a taxic indicator and does not convey more than it expresses; "Torah", with or without the definite article, with or without a capital T, serves no symbolic functions; bears no symbolic valence. And there is, in the Mishnah, no other. Whatever single symbol captures the entirety of the Mishnah's message in the Mishnah's own language, it is not the symbol of Torah.[11]

By contrast, if I ask the Midrash-compilations associated with the Yerushalmi to express, in a single word, the medium and the message that constitute their world-view, they have that word and

---

degree that on the basis of traits of cogency we can differentiate materials in Pesiqta deRab Kahana that are original to Leviticus Rabbah from those distinctive to Pesiqta deRab Kahana.

[10] And that fact has rightly impressed those who have not recognized the philosophical character of the document; there is no philological evidence that suggests knowledge of any concrete philosophical modes of thought, let alone propositions.

[11] The truth is, I can think of no single symbol that serves the entirety of the Mishnah as a medium of expressing the whole or evoking it. Surely, in tractate Avot, fifty years or so later, we may readily point to "Torah" as that symbol, referring to not a document but a status, but vividly so and not merely (as with the Mishnah) as a medium of taxonomic thought. That is to say, in tractate Avot we can point to the object, Torah, speak of words of Torah, identify the status of a person or a gesture or action within the classification of Torah, and so in a single symbol speak of the whole and state the message of the whole. In the Mishnah, by contrast, I find no such symbolic centerpiece. I could make the case that the symbolic system of the Mishnah comes to expression not pictorially or visually or verbally (as with the object "Torah") but rather in what is as recurrent in the Mishnah as Torah is in tractate Avot, and that is, the deepest structures of syntax, the orderly formation of thought in well-patterned language. But if I can find in any few sentences of the Mishnah the whole of the Mishnah in its syntactic structure (and, I have claimed, also its message as well, as in my *A History of the Mishnaic Law of Purities*. (Leiden, 1977: Brill) XXI. *The Redaction and Formulation of the Order of Purities in the Mishnah and Tosefta*., that does not seem to me to be the same thing as a symbol of the order of Torah or The Torah. But then, it seems fair to claim, philosophers in that context did not convey their messages through symbolic but rather through verbal discourse and argument, and the Mishnah's very philosophicality explains its failure to give us in a single way a medium for saying many things. Then, to take a step further, the formation of the counterpart-category for world-view, Torah, which is religious, for philosophy, in medium and message alike, is signalled by the symbolic transaction represented by the word Torah.

use it constantly, and it is the word, *Torah*. It is the Torah that conveys the generative facts of learning; it is Torah, losing its definite article, that defines the range of truth. When we grasp the re-presentation of Torah, and of *the* Torah, in the successor-writings, we can follow the outlines of the counterpart category that serves in the new system to set forth the world-view in the way in which, in the received one, philosophy today. The very symbolization of learning, of philosophy, in the word Torah (and in such visual symbols as the Torah can have generated in context) alerts us to the formation of the new category, or, in slightly different language, the categorical formation and reformation that is taking place.

Let me give a single example of the generative symbol, Torah, and its concretization in *the* Torah, that characterizes the successor-system. In what follows, the Torah turns out to form not the post facto description of the facts of the world, but the design of the world that God followed in creation. The Torah comes prior to reality, that of nature as much as that of history, and its rules prove descriptive of how later on things were made – a stunning reversal of the order of nature and a clear and decisive proof that a categorical reformation is before us. The Mishnah's source of truth was nature, the successor-documents' source of truth, the Torah: clear evidence for the formation of a counterpart category indeed! The following expresses this the proposition of the priority of the Torah:

Genesis Rabbah I:I.1.

1. A. "In the beginning God created" (Gen. 1:1):
   B. R. Oshaia commenced [discourse by citing the following verse:] "'Then I was beside him like a little child, and I was daily his delight [rejoicing before him always, rejoicing in his inhabited world, and delighting in the sons of men]' (Prov. 8:30-31).
   C. "The word for 'child' uses consonants that may also stand for 'teacher,' 'covered over,' and 'hidden away.'
   D. "Some hold that the word also means 'great.'
   E. "The word means 'teacher,' in line with the following: 'As a teacher carries the suckling child' (Num. 11:12).
   F. "The word means 'covered over,' as in the following: 'Those who were covered over in scarlet' (Lam. 4:5).
   G. "The word means 'hidden,' as in the verse, 'And he hid Hadassah ' (Est. 2:7).
   H. "The word means 'great,' in line with the verse, 'Are you better than No-Ammon?' (Nah. 3:8). This we translate, 'Are you better than Alexandria the Great, which is located between rivers.'"
2. A. Another matter:
   B. The word means "workman."

C.	[In the cited verse] the Torah speaks, "I was the work-plan of the Holy One, blessed be He."
D.	In the accepted practice of the world, when a mortal king builds a palace, he does not build it out of his own head, but he follows a work-plan.
E.	And [the one who supplies] the work-plan does not build out of his own head, but he has designs and diagrams, so as to know how to situate the rooms and the doorways.
F.	Thus the Holy One, blessed be He, consulted the Torah when he created the world.
G.	So the Torah stated, "By means of 'the beginning' [that is to say, the Torah] did God create..." (Gen. 1:1).
H.	And the word for "beginning" refers only to the Torah, as Scripture says, "The Lord made me as the beginning of his way" (Prov. 8:22).

The list before us – the initial proposition, then "another matter" – makes the simple point that the Torah comes prior to creation and reveals the plan of creation. If people appeal to the facts of nature, therefore, they err, because it is in the Torah, not in natural philosophy, that we find out how things are meant to be and actually are. Now we see the link between the Torah and Israel, which explains why the special rules governing Israel derive from the Torah in particular.

There are then two sets of facts, those of nature pertaining to the world in general, those of Scripture, dealing with Israel in particular.

Genesis Rabbah I:IV.1

A.	["In the beginning God created" (Gen. 1:1):] Six things came before the creation of the world, some created, some at least considered as candidates for creation.
B.	The Torah and the throne of glory were created [before the creation of the world].
C.	The Torah, as it is written, "The Lord made me as the beginning of his way, prior to his works of old" (Prov. 8:22).
D.	The throne of glory, as it is written, "Your throne is established of old" (Ps. 93:2).
E.	The patriarchs were considered as candidates for creation, as it is written, "I saw your fathers as the first-ripe in the fig tree at her first season" (Hos. 9:10).
F.	Israel was considered [as a candidate for creation], as it is written, "Remember your congregation, which you got aforetime" (Ps. 74:2).
G.	The Temple was considered as a candidate for creation], as it is written, "You, throne of glory, on high from the beginning, the place of our sanctuary" (Jer. 17:12).
H.	The name of the Messiah was kept in mind, as it is written, "His name exists before the sun" (Ps. 72:17).

	I.	R. Ahbah bar Zeira said, "Also [the power of] repentance.
	J.	"That is in line with the following verse of Scripture: 'Before the mountains were brought forth' (Ps. 90:2). From that hour: 'You turn man to contrition and say, Repent, you children of men' (Ps. 90:3)."
	K.	Nonetheless, I do not know which of these came first, that is, whether the Torah was prior to the throne of glory, or the throne of glory to the Torah.
	L.	Said R. Abba bar Kahana, "The Torah came first, prior to the throne of glory.
	M.	"For it is said, 'The Lord made me as the beginning of his way, before his works of old' (Prov. 8:22).
	N.	"It came prior to that concerning which it is written, 'For your throne is established of old' (Ps. 93:2)."
2.	A.	R. Huna, R. Jeremiah in the name of R. Samuel b. R. Isaac: "Intention concerning the creation of Israel came before all else.
	B.	"The matter may be compared to the case of a king who married a noble lady but had no son with her. One time the king turned up in the market place, saying, 'Buy this ink, inkwell, and pen on account of my son.'
	C.	"People said, 'He has no son. Why does he need ink, inkwell, and pen?'
	D.	"But then people went and said, 'The king is an astrologer, so he sees into the future and he therefore is expecting to produce a son!'
	E.	"Along these same lines, if the Holy One, blessed be He, had not foreseen that, after twenty-six generations, the Israelites would be destined to accept the Torah, he would never have written in it, 'Command the children of Israel.' [This proves that God foresaw Israel and created the world on that account.]"
3.	A.	Said. R. Benaiah, "The world and everything in it were created only on account of the merit of the Torah.
	B.	"'The Lord for the sake of wisdom [Torah] founded the earth' (Prov. 3:19)."
	C.	R. Berekhiah said, "It was for the merit of Moses.
	D.	"'And he saw the beginning for himself, for there a portion of a ruler [Moses] was reserved' (Deut. 33:21)."

The power of the exposition is to forge a link between the natural world of creation and the historical world of Israel, its life and salvation. The world was created because of Israel. That simple proposition lays down a judgment that will lead the exegete to join details of creation and of the stories of the patriarchs to details of the history of Israel, with the gross effect of showing the correspondence between Israel's salvific existence and the natural order of the world. We have a set piece exposition of the opening proposition, that is, the six things preceding the creation of the world. That topic, and not the exposition of Gen. 1:1, explains the composition at hand. We begin with the necessary catalogue of the

Learning and the Category, "Torah"

six things and proceed at No. 2 to a secondary exposition of the same matter. Then we introduce creation for the sake of the Torah, followed by a complementary proposition on other things for the sake of which the world was created. Here is the point at which Gen. 1:1 serves as a proof-text.

This protracted representation of matters through abstracts should not obscure the simple point the citations are meant to make. Let me state the point with emphasis: *the Torah now defines the category, world-view.* As a symbol, the Torah no longer denotes a particular book, let alone the contents of such a book. In the Talmud of the Land of Israel and its associated writings, as a matter of fact, the Torah, with or without its definite article, and, with or without a capital t, connotes a broad range of clearly distinct categories of noun and verb, concrete fact and abstract relationship alike.[12] "Torah" stands for a kind of human being. It connotes a social status and a sort of social group. It refers to a type of social relationship. It further denotes a legal status and differentiates among legal norms. As symbolic abstraction, the word encompasses things and persons, actions and status, points of social differentiation and legal and normative standing, as well as "revealed truth."

The main points of insistence of the whole of Israel's life and history come to full symbolic expression in that single word. If people wanted to explain how they would be saved, they would use the word Torah. If they wished to sort out their parlous relationships with gentiles, they would use the world Torah. Torah stood for salvation and accounted for Israel's this-worldly condition and the hope, for both individual and national alike, of life in the world to come. For the successor-system, therefore, the word Torah stood for everything. The Torah symbolized the whole, at once and entire. There is no counterpart in the Mishnah, a symbol that captures in itself the entire sense of "world-view," the whole weight of what we must now categorize as "knowledge," "learning," and "science" in the broadest sense. The generative symbol, the total, exhaustive expression of the system as a whole, the Torah stood for these things then: knowledge, learning, and science.

A brief catalogue of the senses of the word Torah suffices for the present purpose. When the Torah refers to a particular thing, it is to a scroll containing divinely revealed words. The Torah may further refer to revelation, not as an object but as a corpus of doctrine. When one "does Torah" the disciple "studies" or "learns," and the master

---

[12]The basis of these statements again is in my *Torah: From Scroll to Symbol in Formative Judaism.*

"teaches," Torah. Hence while the word Torah never appears as a verb, it does refer to an act. The word also bears a quite separate sense, *torah* as category or classification or corpus of rules, for example, "the torah of driving a car" is a usage entirely acceptable to some documents. This generic usage of the word does occur. The word Torah very commonly refers to a status, distinct from and above another status, as "teachings of Torah" as against "teachings of scribes." For the two Talmuds that distinction is absolutely critical to the entire hermeneutic enterprise. But it is important even in the Mishnah. Finally, the word Torah refers to a source of salvation, often fully worked out in stories about how the individual and the nation will be saved through Torah. In general, the sense of the word "salvation" is not complicated. It is simply salvation in the way in which Deuteronomy and the Deuteronomic historians understand it: kings who do what God wants win battles, those who do not, lose. So, too, here, people who study and do Torah are saved from sickness and death, and the way Israel can save itself from its condition of degradation also is through Torah.

This range of meanings imputed to *Torah*, the word now made into a symbol, vastly exceeds the limits of the word, not treated as a symbol, in the Mishnah. What is critical to the symbol, Torah, as worked out in the successor-symbol is the literary definition of Torah as encompassing an oral component beginning with the Mishnah. And to show the categorical novelty of Torah, we may simply note that the framers of the Mishnah nowhere claim, implicitly or explicitly, that what they have written forms part of the Torah, enjoys the status of God's revelation to Moses at Sinai, or even systematically carries forward secondary exposition and application of what Moses wrote down in the wilderness. But the symbol of Torah takes on mythic expression, by contrast, with the position of the Yerushalmi that God's revelation of the Torah at Sinai encompassed the Mishnah as much as Scripture. Second, the Mishnah was handed on through oral formulation and oral transmission from Sinai to the framers of the document as we have it. These two convictions, fully exposed in the ninth-century letter of Sherira, in fact emerge from the references of both Talmuds to the Dual Torah. One part is in writing. The other was oral and now is in the Mishnah.

Proof that the Mishnah and its associated writings know nothing of the symbol – therefore the category – of Torah as it would take shape in the successor-system is readily adduced. The Mishnah contains not a hint that anyone has heard any such a myth. The earliest apologists for the Mishnah, represented in Abot and the Tosefta alike, know nothing of the fully realized myth of the Dual

Torah of Sinai of which the Mishnah as a document forms a principal component The Yerushalmi marks the change.

True, the Mishnah places a high value upon studying the Torah and upon the status of the sage. A "*mamzer* – disciple of a sage takes priority over a high-priest-*am-haares*," as at M. Hor. 3:8. So the rights of caste-position are set aside – but the caste-status is unchanged. But that judgment, distinctive though it is, cannot settle the question. All it shows is that the Mishnah pays due honor to the sage. But if the Mishnah does not claim to constitute part of the Torah, then what makes a sage a sage is not mastery of the Mishnah in particular. What we have in hand merely continues the established and familiar position of the wisdom writers of old. Wisdom is important. Knowledge of the Torah is definitive. But to maintain that position, one need hardly profess the fully articulated Torah-myth of rabbinic Judaism. Proof of that fact, after all, is the character of the entire wisdom literature prior to the Mishnah itself.

Abot draws into the orbit of Torah-talk the names of authorities of the Mishnah. But Abot does not claim that the Mishnah forms part of the Torah. Nor, obviously, does the tractate know the doctrine of the two Torahs. Only in the Talmuds do we begin to find clear and ample evidence of that doctrine. Abot, moreover, does not understand by the word Torah much more than the framers of the Mishnah do. Not only does the established classification scheme remain intact, but the sense essentially replicates already familiar usages, producing no innovation. On the contrary, I find a diminution in the range of meanings.[13] In Abot, Torah is instrumental. The figure of the sage, his ideals and conduct, forms the goal, focus and center. To state matters simply: Abot regards study of Torah as what a sage does. The substance of Torah is what a sage says. That is so whether or not the saying relates to scriptural revelation. The content of the sayings attributed to sages endows those sayings with self-validating status. The sages usually do not quote verses of Scripture and explain them, nor do they speak in God's name. Yet, it is clear, sages talk Torah. If a sage says something, what he says is Torah. More accurately, what he says falls into the classification of

---

[13] Yet Abot in the aggregate does differ from the Mishnah. The difference has to do with the topic at hand. The other sixty-two tractates of the Mishnah contain Torah-sayings here and there. But they do not fall within the framework of Torah-discourse. They speak about other matters entirely. The consideration of the status of Torah rarely pertains to that speech. Abot, by contrast, says a great deal about Torah-study. The claim that Torah-study produces direct encounter with God forms part of Abot's thesis about the Torah.

Torah. "Torah" then forms a taxic indicator, as much as it does in the Mishnah.

The Yerushalmi is the first document in the canon of the Judaism of the Dual Torah to represent the Mishnah as equivalent to Scripture (Y. Hor. 3:5). And once the Mishnah entered the status of Scripture, it would take but a short step to a theory of the Mishnah as part of the revelation at Sinai – hence, Oral Torah. Here we find the first glimmerings of an effort to theorize in general, not merely in detail, about how specific teachings of Mishnah relate to specific teachings of Scripture. The citing of scriptural proof-texts for Mishnah propositions would not have caused much surprise to the framers of the Mishnah; they themselves included such passages, though not often. But what conception of the Torah underlies such initiatives, and how to Yerushalmi sages propose to explain the phenomenon of the Mishnah as a whole? The following passage gives us one statement. Y. Hagigah 1:7 refers to the assertion at M. Hag. 1:8D that the laws on cultic cleanness presented in the Mishnah rest on deep and solid foundations in the Scripture.

> [B] R. Zeira in the name of R. Yohanan: "If a law comes to hand and you do not know its nature, do not discard it for another one, for lo, many laws were stated to Moses at Sinai, and all of them have been embedded in the Mishnah."

The Mishnah now is claimed to contain statements made by God to Moses. Just how these statements found their way into the Mishnah, and which passages of the Mishnah contain them, we do not know. That is hardly important, given the fundamental assertion at hand. The passage proceeds to a further, and far more consequential, proposition. It asserts that part of the Torah was written down, and part was preserved in memory and transmitted orally. In context, moreover, that distinction must encompass the Mishnah, thus explaining its origin as part of the Torah. Here is a clear and unmistakable expression of the distinction between two forms in which a single Torah was revealed and handed on at Mount Sinai, part in writing, part orally.

Short of explicit allusion to Torah-in-writing and Torah-by-memory, which (so far as I am able to discern) we find mainly in the Talmud of Babylonia, the ultimate theory of Torah of formative Judaism is at hand in what follows:

Yerushalmi Hagigah 1:7.V

> [D] R. Zeirah in the name of R. Eleazar: "'Were I to write for him my laws by ten thousands, they would be regarded as a strange thing' (Hos. 8:12). Now is the greater part of the Torah written

Learning and the Category, "Torah"

[E] down? [Surely not. The oral part is much greater.] But more abundant are the matters which are derived by exegesis from the written [Torah] than those derived by exegesis from the oral [Torah]."

[E] And is that so?

[F] But more cherished are those matters which rest upon the written [Torah] than those which rest upon the oral [Torah]....

[J] R. Haggai in the name of R. Samuel bar Nahman, "Some teachings were handed on orally, and some things were handed on in writing, and we do not know which of them is the more precious. But on the basis of that which is written, "And the Lord said to Moses, Write these words; in accordance with these words I have made a covenant with you and with Israel' (Ex. 34:27), [we conclude] that the ones which are handed on orally are the more precious."

[K] R. Yohanan and R. Yudan b. R. Simeon — One said, "If you have kept what is preserved orally and also kept what is in writing, I shall make a covenant with you, and if not, I shall not make a covenant with you."

[L] The other said, "If you have kept what is preserved orally and you have kept what is preserved in writing, you shall receive a reward, and if not, you shall not receive a reward."

[M] [With reference to Deut. 9:10: "And on them was written according to all the words which the Lord spoke with you in the mount,"] said R. Joshua b. Levi, "He could have written, 'On them,' but wrote, 'And on them.' He could have written, 'All,' but wrote, 'According to all.' He could have written, 'Words,' but wrote 'The words.' [These then serve as three encompassing clauses, serving to include] Scripture, Mishnah, Talmud, laws, and lore. Even what an experienced student in the future is going to teach before his master already has been stated to Moses at Sinai."

[N] What is the Scriptural basis for this view?

[O] "There is no remembrance of former things, nor will there be any remembrance of later things yet to happen among those who come after" (Qoh. 1:11).

[P] If someone says, "See, this is a new thing," his fellow will answer him, saying to him, "this has been around before us for a long time."

Here we have absolutely explicit evidence that people believed part of the Torah had been preserved not in writing but orally. Linking that part to the Mishnah remains a matter of implication. But it surely comes fairly close to the surface, when we are told that the Mishnah contains Torah-traditions revealed at Sinai. From that view it requires only a small step to the allegation that the Mishnah is part of the Torah, the oral part.

I adduce as evidence of a categorical transformation — that is, in this context, the formation of a counterpart-category — the representation of the worldview as Torah, through the symbol of

Torah because the Torah is now re-presented as a source of salvation.[14] That is a profoundly fresh conception, without consequential antecedent[15] in the Mishnah and related writings.

---

[14] The counterpart-category will be shown to constitute on its own an utterly fresh statement. The conception of knowledge as not merely illuminating but salvific transforms what is at stake in the category, world-view, from philosophical into religious truth.

[15] Given the state of manuscript evidence for all ancient Judaic documents, we cannot claim as decisive the fact that a word or a phrase appears or does not appear in some one piece of writing. The manuscript evidence is too sparse to appeal to the occurrence or absence of a word or a phrase, or to count up the number of occurrences and draw consequences from the result. We can work with large-scale and well-attested aggregates, e.g., the simple fact that all manuscripts of a given document concur on the basic topical program and organization, rhetorical preferences, logical principles of coherent discourse; these do vary from one document to another, and they do represent the choices of the initial authorship of a given document. That is why, as a matter of fact, the state of the evidence does allow us to characterize the fundamental literary structure and intellectual system of documents, since that characterization rests not on details but on the entire evidence in hand. One would have to claim that the Mishnah, for example, yields such diverse manuscript evidence that we can say nothing about its generative conceptions and fixed and formal traits. But it is the simple fact, proven decades ago by Y. N. Epstein in his *Introduction to the Text of the Mishnah* (Jerusalem, 1957), that manuscript variations affect words and phrases. That means the basic structures as to form and topical program are secure. My characterization rests on not details of the non-appearance of a word here or there but rather on the large-scale and secure characteristics of the several documents as a whole. Hence I stress the systemic infrastructure, and the place of a given word or phrase in that infrastructure. If the word "Torah" occurs in a salvific sense, e.g., in the Mishnah, that singleton bears no systemic weight whatsoever in the Mishnah overall. This distinction between the mere appearance or absence of a given word in a document and the systemic importance accorded to the concept represented by that same word in a document is worked out for *zekhut*. There we see that *zekhut* in the sense important later on does occur in documents generally held to have reached closure prior to the Yerushalmi and related Midrash-compilations. But when used earlier, the concept of zekhut is systemically inert, not active and indicative, and this we know because we can identify, in these prior appearances, no systemic burden carried by the word, or concept, of zekhut. In the appearances in the later documents, by contrast, zekhut proves to stand at the very center of discourse, a judgment concerning not the number of times the word occurs, but the place of the concept in the systemic structure. Justification for characterizing the usage in a systemically active and not inert way will be set forth in context. But even here I must underline that, even though the salvific value accorded to Torah, e.g., Torah-study, may appear episodically in some document prior to the ones deemed critical in this book, the place of that concept in the earlier system is not established by an ad hoc usage. That can have been an addition of a later scribe; and it

There (the) Torah forms a taxic indicator. True, knowing the Torah by itself – without caste-status commensurate, without wealth either – imparts status to the one who knows it. But in no way does knowledge – *mere* knowledge – constitute the source of salvation. That profoundly gnostic conception of knowledge, by contrast, in which (merely) knowing something ("the truth") changes the one who knows, comes to the surface time and again in the successor-documents. This power of personal transformation through knowledge of the Torah is a matter to which we shall return.

In the canonical documents up to the Yerushalmi and its companions, we look in vain for sayings or stories that fall into such a category. True, we may take for granted that everyone always believed that, in general, Israel would be saved by obedience to the Torah. That claim surely would not have surprised any Israelite writer from the Deuteronomists of the seventh century B.C. down through the final redactors of the Pentateuch in the time of Ezra and onward through the next seven hundred years. But, in the rabbinical corpus from the Mishnah forward, the specific and concrete assertion that by taking up the scroll of the Torah and standing on the roof of one's house,[16] confronting God in heaven, a sage in particular could take action against the expected invasion – that kind of claim is not located, so far as I know, in any prior composition.[17]

---

also can have been present in the original version of the document (as it can have been in the mind of this one or that one in the circles of sages, and probably was), without making an impact upon the shape and structure of the system attested by the document containing that episodic usage.

[16]This story is cited verbatim at the outset of Chapter Seven.

[17]Precisely what I claim in this "canonical history" of ideas must be made explicit. It is that we deal with a symbolic transaction portrayed in the succession of usages of a given word or symbol as we move from one document to the next. Our survey concerns the description, analysis, and interpretation of successive systems, which I claim were not successor systems. My argument is that knowledge – the intellectual integument of the world-view – in the Mishnah is not Torah and is not salvific, while knowledge in the Yerushalmi and associated writings is Torah and is salvific. I do not know what others, not represented by these writings, were thinking; I cannot even say that systems other than those represented by the successive groups of writings existed. I surely do not claim that the belief that the Torah in the hands of the sage constituted a source of magical, supernatural, and hence salvific power, did not flourish prior, let us say, to ca. 400 C.E. We cannot show it, hence we do not know it (and anyhow, I very much doubt it). All we can say with assurance is that no stories containing such a viewpoint appear in any rabbinical document associated with the Mishnah. So what is critical here is not the generalized category -- the genus -- of conviction that the Torah serves as the source of Israel's salvation. It is the concrete assertion -- the speciation of the genus -- that in the hands of the sage and under

The shift is points not merely toward a revision of a received category, philosophy, but toward the formation of a new category altogether. That is the definition of the counterpart category to philosophy formed by (the) Torah. The new category, conveyed by the symbol, Torah, treated the knowledge represented by the Torah (whether scroll, contents, or act of study) as source and guarantor of salvation. Accordingly, category denoted by the word, Torah, encompasses the centerpiece of a theory of Israel's history, on the one side, and an account of the teleology of the entire system, on the other. Torah indeed has ceased to constitute a specific thing or even a category or classification when stories about studying the Torah yield not a judgment as to status (i.e., praise for the learned man) but promise for supernatural blessing now and salvation in time to come. And the new category, corresponding to philosophy in its mode of thought, counterpart to philosophy in its message, must be classed as a fundamentally religious category, in that knowledge now formed the medium of salvation: knowing the Torah changed the one who knows it, in a way in which, in the Mishnah and related writings, knowing the hierarchical structure and order of things, pointing toward the unity of the natural order, in no way led to the transformation of the one who knew the facts that yielded that knowledge. No wonder then, that, in the Yerushalmi, mastery of Torah transformed the man engaged in Torah-learning into a supernatural figure, who could do things ordinary folk could not do.

So, in all, the transformation of the Judaic worldview encompassed new subjects, a new source of truth, and a new program of learning. How that new program of learning redefined scarce resources and reformed the institutions that carried out the legitimate exercise of violence remains to be seen. We now are prepared to reconsider a simple but fundamental representation of the successor-system, one in which the symbolic transaction is quite concrete: scarce resources, valued things, are now other than they were.

---

conditions specified, the Torah may be utilized in pressing circumstances as Levi, his disciple, and the disciple of his disciple, used it. That is what is new and in my judgment forms decisive evidence for a categorical reformation – in my language, the formation of a counterpart-category) – effected by the system-builders whose views are attested in the documents under study.

2

The Transvaluation of Value

Consideration of the transvaluation of value brings us to the successor-system's counterpart category, that is, the one that in context forms the counterpart to the Mishnah's concrete, this-worldly, material and tangible definition of value in conformity with the familiar, philosophical economics. We have now to ask, what, in place of the received definition of value and the economics thereof, did the new system set forth?

The transformation of economics involved the redefinition of scarce and valued resources in so radical a manner that the concept of value, while remaining material in consequence and character, nonetheless took on a quite different sense altogether.[1] The counterpart category of the successor-system, represented by the authorships responsible for the final composition of the Yerushalmi, Genesis Rabbah, Leviticus Rabbah, and Pesiqta deRab Kahana, concerned themselves with the same questions as did the conventional economics, presenting an economics in function and

---

[1] Let me recapitulate a point made earlier but important here. Does that fact then suggest the new system's theory of the social order set forth no economics at all? After all, there is no reason that a theory of the social order required an economics at all, since a variety of theories of the social order of the same time and place other than Aristotle's and the Mishnah's – Plato's for one, the Gospels' for another, the Essene Community at Qumran's for a third – managed to put forth a compelling theory of society lacking all sustained and systematic, systemically pertinent attention to economics at all. I insist, however, that the successor-system put forth a theory of the way of life that must be characterized as an economics, not as a theology that made reference, by the way, to topics of economic interest but an economics. It was, however, one involving a different value from the ultimate value, real property, characteristic of Aristotle's and the Mishnah's economics.

structure, but one that concerned things of value other than those identified by the initial system. So indeed we deal with an economics, an economics of something other than real estate.

But it was an economics just as profoundly embedded in the social order, just as deeply a political economics, just as pervasively a systemic economics, as the economics of the Mishnah and of Aristotle. Why so? Because issues such as the definition of wealth, the means of production and the meaning of control thereof, the disposition of wealth through distributive or other media, theory of money, reward for labor, and the like – all these issues found their answers in the counterpart-category of economics, as much as in the received and conventional philosophical economics. The new "scarce resource" accomplished what the old did, but it was a different resource, a new currency. At stake in the category meant to address the issues of the way of life of the social entity, therefore, were precisely the same considerations as confront economics in its (to us) conventional and commonplace, philosophical sense. But since the definition of wealth changes from land to Torah, much else would be transformed on that account.

That explains why, in the formation of the counterpart-category of value other than real value but in function and in social meaning value nonetheless, we witness the transformation of a system from philosophy to religion. We err profoundly if we suppose that in contrasting land to Torah and affirming that true value lies in Torah, the framers of the successor-system have formulated an essentially spiritual or otherwise immaterial conception for themselves, that is, a surrogate for economics in the conventional sense. That is not what happened. What we have is an economics that answers the questions economics answers, but that has chosen a different value from real value – real estate – as its definition of that scarce resource that requires a rational policy for preservation and enhancement. Land produced a living; so did Torah. Land formed the foundation of the social entity, so did Torah.

The transvaluation of value was such that an economics concerning the rational management and increase of scarce resources worked itself out in such a way as to answer, for quite different things of value from real property or from capital such as we know as value, precisely the same questions that the received economics addressed in connection with wealth of a real character: land and its produce. Systemic transformation comes to the surface in articulated symbolic change. The utter transvaluation of value finds expression in a jarring juxtaposition, an utter shift of rationality, specifically, the substitution of Torah for real estate. We recall how in a

The Transvaluation of Value

successor-document (but in none prior to the fifth century compilations) Tarfon thought wealth took the form of land, while Aqiba explained to him that wealth takes the form of Torah-learning. That the sense is material and concrete is explicit: land for Torah, Torah for land. Thus, to repeat the matter of how Torah serves as an explicit symbol to convey the systemic worldview, let us note the main point of the now-familiar passage:

Leviticus Rabbah XXXIV:XVI

1. B. R. Tarfon gave to R. Aqiba six silver centenarii, saying to him, "Go, buy us a piece of land, so we can get a living from it and labor in the study of Torah together."
   C. He took the money and handed it over to scribes, Mishnah-teachers, and those who study Torah.
   D. After some time R. Tarfon met him and said to him, "Did you buy the land that I mentioned to you?"
   E. He said to him, "Yes."
   F. He said to him, "Is it any good?"
   G. He said to him, "Yes."
   H. He said to him, "And do you not want to show it to me?"
   I. He took him and showed him the scribes, Mishnah teachers, and people who were studying Torah, and the Torah that they had acquired.
   J. He said to him, "Is there anyone who works for nothing? Where is the deed covering the field?"
   K. He said to him, "It is with King David, concerning whom it is written, 'He has scattered, he has given to the poor, his righteousness endures forever' (Ps. 112:9)."

The successor-system has its own definitions not only for learning, symbolized by the word Torah but also for wealth, expressed in the same symbol. Accordingly, the category-formation for worldview, Torah in place of philosophy, dictates, as a matter of fact, a still more striking category-reformation, in which the entire matter of scarce resources is reconsidered, and a counterpart-category set forth. When "Torah" substitutes for real estate, what, exactly, does the successor-system know as scarce resources, and how is the counterpart-category constructed?

Let us begin with a simple definition of "value." While bearing a variety of inchoate meanings, associated with belief, conviction, ideal, moral preference, and the like, the word to begin with bears an entirely concrete sense. Value means that which people value, under ordinary circumstances, what they hold to be of concrete, tangible, material worth. What is "of value" conventionally is what provides a life of comfort and sustenance and material position. In commonplace language, "value" (as distinct, therefore, from the vague term, "values") refers to those scarce resources to the rational management and increase of which economics devotes its attention: real wealth.[2] This means, in our contemporary context, capital, and in the context of Aristotle's and the Mishnah's economics, real estate.[3] Then when I speak of the transvaluation of value, I mean that the material and concrete things of worth were redefined – even while subjected to an economics functioning in the system as the counterpart to the initial economics of the Mishnah and of Aristotle. In the successor-writings ownership of land, even in the Land of Israel, contrasts with wealth in another form altogether, and the contrast that was drawn was material and concrete, not merely symbolic and spiritual. It was material and tangible and palpable because it produced this-worldly gains, for example, a life of security, comfort, ease, as these, too, found definition in the systemic context of the here and the now.

It follows that, while in the successor system's theory of the component of the social order represented by the way of life, we find an economics, it is an economics of scarce resources defined as something other than particular real estate. Why do I insist that these questions are economic in character? It is because they deal with the rules or theory of the rational management of scarce resources, their preservation and increase, and do so in commonplace terms of philosophical economics, for example, the control of the means of production, the definition of money and of value, the distribution of valued goods and services, whether by appeal to the market or to a theory of distributive economics, the theory of the value of labor and the like. But while the structure remained the same, the contents radically would differ, hence the transvaluation of value. It was as if a new currency were issued to replace the old, then declared of no value, capable of purchasing nothing worth having. In such an economics, there is far more than a currency-reform, but rather a complete economic revolution, a new beginning, as much as a shift from socialism to capitalism. But the transvaluation, in our case, was more thorough-going still, since involved was the very reconsideration of the scarcity of scarce

---

[2] I use "real" in the technical sense, meaning, landed wealth or property, real estate. Any other usage draws me into questions of theology or philosophy, with which economics does not deal. I shall presently argue that there is no spiritualizing or moralizing or philosophizing "value," which bears concrete meanings and material consequences in the documents considered here.

[3] For Aristotle, land could be anywhere; for the Mishnah's economics, the ultimate value was a particular piece of land, which was the Land of Israel occupied by holy Israel.

The Transvaluation of Value

resources. Both elements then underwent transvaluation: the definition of resources of value, the rationality involved in the management of scarcity. In a word, while real estate cannot increase and by definition must always prove scarce, the value represented by Torah could expand without limit. Value could then increase indefinitely, resources that were desired and scarce be made ever more abundant, in the transformed economics of the successor-system.

While responding to the same questions of that same part of the social order with which the received category concerned itself, the economics that emerged in no way proves discontinuous with the received economics. Why not just another economics than the philosophical one we have considered? The reason is that so abrupt and fundamental a reworking will be seen to have taken place that the category – way of life – *while yet an economics* – nonetheless is now a wholly-other economics, one completely without relationship to the inherited definition of way of life (manner of earning a living) as to both structure and system.

For at stake is not merely the spiritualization of wealth, that is to say, the re-presentation of what "wealth" *really* consists of in other-than-material terms.[4] That would represent not an economics but a theology. For example, the familiar saying in tractate Abot, "Who is rich? One who is happy in his lot," simply does not constitute a statement of economics at all. Like sayings in the Gospels that denigrate wealth, this one tells nothing about the rational management (for example, increase) of scarce resources, it merely tells about appropriate moral attitudes of a virtuous order: how life is worth living, not answering an economic question at all. On the other hand, the tale that contrasts wealth in the form of land and its produce with wealth in the form of Torah (whatever is meant by "Torah") does constitute a statement of economics. The reason is that the story-teller invokes precisely the category of wealth – real property – that conventional economics defines as wealth. If I have land, I have wealth, and I can support myself; if I have Torah, I have wealth, and I can support myself. Those form the two components of the contrastive equation before us. But then wealth is disenlandised, and the Torah substituted for real property of all kinds. That forms not a theology, nor an economics in any conventional sense, bur, rather, an anti-economics. The same will be seen to be so in politics.

---

[4] Now the word "real" is used in its non-technical sense, with which sense theologians and philosophers are more at ease.

Take, for example, the as in the following explicit statement that a sentence of the Torah is more valuable than a pearl:

Y Peah 1:1 XVII (trans. by Roger Brooks)

E. Ardavan sent our holy Rabbi a priceless pearl and said to him, "Send me something as valuable as this."

F. He sent him a doorpost-scroll (mezuzah) containing words of Torah].

G. Ardavan said to him, "I sent you an item beyond price, but you send me something worth but a few cents."

H. Rabbi said to him, "Your precious things and my precious things are not equivalent.' You sent me something I have to guard, but I sent something that guards you while you sleep: 'When you walk along, [the words of Torah] will lead you, when you lie down, they will watch over you' (Prov. 6:22)

If I have words of the Torah in hand, there are scarce resources in my possession that I otherwise do not have: security, for example, against whatever demons may want to harm me in my sleep.

Why do I insist that these kinds of stories deal with scarce resources in a concrete sense? Because in both cases cited to this point the upshot of the possession of Torah is this-worldly, concrete, tangible, and palpable. The rewards are not described as "filling treasuries in the heart," nor do they "enrich the soul," nor are they postponed to the world to come (as would be the case in a kind of capitalistic theology of investment on earth for return in heaven). The tale concerning Aqiba and Tarfon, like the one involving Rabbi and Ardavan, insists upon precisely the same *results* of the possession of wealth of value in the form of "Torah" as characterize wealth or value in the form of real estate. The key-language is this: "Go, buy us a piece of land, *so we can get a living from it* and labor in the study of Torah together." Tarfon assumes owning land buys leisure for Torah-study; Aqiba does not contradict that assumption, he steps beyond it.

Then one thing forms the counterpart and opposite of the other – anti-economics, economics, respectively – but both things yield a single result: wealth to sustain leisure, which any reader of Xenophon's handbook on economics (estate management, in his context) will have found an entirely commonplace and obviously true judgment. That explains why the form that wealth in the successor-system now takes – Torah rather than real estate – presents a jarring contrast, one that is, of course, the point of the story. And as a matter of fact, that jarring contrast will have proved unintelligible to any authorship prior to the second stage in the formation of the canonical writings and explicitly contradicts the sense of matters

The Transvaluation of Value

that predominates in the first stage: the Torah is not to be made "a spade to dig with" (whatever that can have meant). In Tarfon's mind, therefore, real (in the theological sense) value is real (in the economic sense) wealth, that is, real estate, because if you own land, you can enjoy the leisure to do what you really want to do, which (as every philosopher understood) is to study (in the sages' case) the Torah together. But to Aqiba, in the tale, that is beside the point, since the real (in the theological sense) value (in the economic sense, that is, what provides a living, food to eat for instance) is Torah (study), and that, in itself, suffices. The sense is, if I have land, I have a living, and if I have Torah, I have a living, which is no different from the living that I have from land – but which, as a matter of fact, is more secure.

Owning land involved control of the means of production, and so did knowing the Torah. But – more to the point – from land people derived a living, and from Torah people derived a living in *precisely* the same sense – that is to say, in the material and concrete sense – in which from land they could do so. That is alleged time and again, and at stake then is not the mere denigration of wealth but the transvaluation of value. Then the transvaluation consisted in [1] the disenlandisement of value, and [2] the transvaluation of (knowing or studying) the Torah, the imputation to Torah of the value formerly associated with land. And that is why it is valid to claim for Torah the status of a counterpart-category: the system's economics, its theory of the way of life of the community and account of the rational disposition of those scarce resources that made everyday material existence possible and even pleasant: an economics of wealth, but of wealth differently defined, while similarly valued and utilized.

For like Aristotle, when the authorship of the Mishnah conducted discourse upon economic questions, they understood wealth in entirely this-worldly terms. The Torah formed a component in the system of hierarchical classification, not a unit of value or a measure of worth. By contrast, in the successor-system portrayed by the Talmud of the Land of Israel, Genesis Rabbah, Leviticus Rabbah, and their companions, the concept of scarce resources was linked to the conception of Torah and so took on altogether fresh meanings, but in exactly the same context and producing exactly the same material consequences, for example, having food to eat and a dwelling for shelter, with the result that we have to redefine that which serves the very category, "economics," altogether. Why is this necessary? It is because of those stunning transvaluations, already cited, of value stated explicitly and baldly in the contrast between land and Torah.

When the successor-documents contrast the received value with the value they recognize, then we must ask about the formation of the counterpart-category and consider how to make sense of that category.

Accordingly, I have now to show that when our authorship spoke of Torah, they addressed the issues of scarce resources in the way in which, when the authorship of the Mishnah or Aristotle spoke of real wealth, they addressed those same issues. Then we require an account of the goods and services assigned the status of "scarce resources," and thence we shall define the theory of rational disposition that in the successor-system constitutes the economics. The questions are the same. But they are addressed to different things of value, different scarce resources altogether, and the systemic goal is to make abundant what has been scarce.[5]

---

[5] Let me briefly recapitulate a fundamental argument. Might one claim that the new system's theory of the social order set forth no economics at all? After all, there is no reason that a theory of the social order required an economics at all, since a variety of theories of the social order of the same time and place other than Aristotle's and the Mishnah's Plato's for one, the Gospels' for another, the Essene Community at Qumran's for a third – managed to put forth a compelling theory of society lacking all sustained and systematic, systemically pertinent attention to economics at all. I insist, however, that the successor-system put forth a theory of the way of life that must be characterized as an economics, not as a theology that made reference, by the way, to topics of economic interest but an economics. It was, however, one involving a different value from the ultimate value, real property, characteristic of Aristotle's and the Mishnah's economics. Why do I maintain that view? It is because the counterpart category of the successor-system, represented by the authorships responsible for the final composition of the Yerushalmi, Genesis Rabbah, Leviticus Rabbah, and Pesiqta deRab Kahana, structurally and functionally concerned themselves with the same questions as did the conventional economics, presenting an economics in function and structure, but one that concerned things of value other than those things of value identified by the initial system. So indeed we deal with an economics, an economics of something other than real estate, but an economics just as profoundly embedded in the social order, just as deeply a political economics, just as pervasively a systemic economics, as the economics of the Mishnah and of Aristotle. Why so? Because issues such as the definition of wealth, the means of production and the meaning of control thereof, the disposition of wealth through distributive or other media, theory of money, reward for labor, and the like – all these issues found their answers in the counterpart-category of economics, as much as in the received and conventional philosophical economics. The new "scarce resource" accomplished what the old did, but it was a different resource, a new currency. At stake in the category meant to address the issues of the way of life of the social entity, therefore, were precisely the same considerations as confront economics in its (to us) conventional and commonplace, philosophical sense. But since the definition of wealth changes, as we have already seen,

The Transvaluation of Value

Since Torah – left undefined for the moment – now forms the definition of wealth,[6] the question immediately confronts us: has that sense of the word really changed so considerably from its representation in the first stratum of the literature that we must impute to the word meanings that are represented as both fresh and simply not considered in the initial economics of the first Judaism? That is to say, was Torah in the Mishnah not that same ultimate value that it became in the successor-system? If it was, then any claim that Torah has replaced real estate as the definition of value and worth – the transvaluation of value in a very concrete sense – is simply beside the point. In the initial system – it may be claimed – Torah stood for something of ultimate worth, right alongside real property and its equivalents, each in its own context, each for its own purpose. I have now therefore to turn back to the issue of the standing and meaning of Torah in the Mishnah and to demonstrate that in the Mishnah, Torah, now to be defined as Torah-learning, in no way functions as a scarce resource; in no way occupies the position, as a statement of real worth and value, that it gained in the successor-system and in the writings that adumbrate it. In the Mishnah, if I know Torah, I enter a certain status, since knowledge of Torah forms part of the taxic structure of the Mishnah's social system. But if I know the Torah, I have still to earn a living, and scarce resources are defined, we already know, by real estate and equivalents.

---

from land to Torah, much else would be transformed on that account. That explains why, in the formation of the counterpart-category of value other than real value but in function and in social meaning value nonetheless, we witness the transformation of a system from philosophy to religion. We err profoundly if we suppose that in contrasting land to Torah and affirming that true value lies in Torah, the framers of the successor-system have formulated an essentially spiritual or otherwise immaterial conception for themselves, that is, a surrogate for economics in the conventional sense. That is not what happened. What we have is an economics that answers the questions economics answers, as I said, but that has chosen a different value from real value – real estate, as we have already seen – as its definition of that scarce resource that requires a rational policy for preservation and enhancement. Land produced a living; so did Torah. Land formed the foundation of the social entity, so did Torah.

[6]Hence the title of this chapter, which alleges that the very category, *value*, is transvalued. In the end of the chapter I explain precisely why I insist that the successor-system does not merely identify a new scarce resource in place of the received one, but that the disenlandisement of value constitutes in this context an utter redefinition of what can be meant by economics, hence, the transvaluation of value.

To make that point stick, I have now to show that, in the Mishnah, Torah stands for status but produces no consequences of a material order, or, as a matter of fact, even for one's caste-status. It is the simple fact that studying the Torah is deemed an action to which accrues unlimited benefit. This is made explicit:

M. Peah. 1:1A-E
(trans. Brooks, in Neusner, *Mishnah*, pp. 14-15).

A. These are things that have no specified measure: the quantity of produce designated as *peah*; the quantity of produce given as firstfruits, the value of the appearance offering, the performance of righteous deeds, and time spent in study of Torah.

B. These are things the benefit of which a person enjoys in this world, while the principal remains for him in the world to come: deeds in honor of father and mother, performance of righteous deeds, and acts which bring peace between a man and his fellow.

C. But the study of Torah is as important as all of them all together

The study of Torah, or knowledge of the Torah, is equivalent to a variety of other meritorious actions, for example, designating produce as "corner of the field" for use by the scheduled castes; bringing an offering of high cost; honoring parents. Among these comparable deeds, study of the Torah enjoys pride of place. But the rewards are not worldly, not material, not palpable. If I know the Torah, I enjoy a higher status than if I do not; but I have still to work for a living.[7]

Knowledge of the Torah did not define the qualifications of the highest offices, for instance, a member of the priestly caste could be high priest and not have mastered the Torah:

M. Yoma 1:6A-D

A. If the high priest was a sage, he expounds the relevant Scriptures of the Day of Atonement, and if not, disciples of sages expound for him. If he was used to reading Scriptures, he read, and if not, they read for him

Not only so, but the Mishnah knows nothing of using holy funds to support disciples of sages, for example, M. Meg. 3:1: Townsfolk who sold a street of a town buy with its proceeds a synagogue, and so on. Mishnah-tractate Sheqalim, with its account of the use of public

---

[7]To be sure, the distinction between *haber* and *am haares* does not encompass Torah study. Only in later strata of the canon would the value of Torah-knowledge contrast with the dis-value (disgrace) of ignorance, distinguishing the *haber* from the *am haares*. And when that distinction would be made, the opposite of am haares would be sage or disciple of a sage.

funds for the Temple, never supposes that disciples of sages associated with the Temple may be paid from the public funds represented by the *sheqel*-tax.

This underlines the simple fact that in the Mishnah it is not assumed that a disciple of a sage gets support on account of his Torah-study, and it also is not assumed that the sages makes his living through Torah-study, or other Torah-activities. Knowledge of the Torah or the act of study enjoys no material value. For instance, an act of betrothal requires an exchange of something of value; among the examples of value the act of study or teaching of the Torah is never offered, for example, "Lo, thou art betrothed to me in exchange for my teaching you [or your brother or your father] a teaching of the Torah" is never suggested as a possibility. So Torah-learning is not material and produces no benefits of a material character. Sages' status may derive from knowledge of Torah, but that status is not confused with the material consideration involved in who may matter whom. In M Qid. 4:1 sages do not form a caste. "Ten castes came up from Babylonia," but the "status" of sage has no bearing upon his caste status. Then what difference does Torah-study or Torah-knowledge make? It is one of taxic consequence and one of status, but with no bearing whatsoever upon one's livelihood. Here are the important statements of the taxic value of knowledge of the Torah, and in them all, what is gained is not of a material or concrete order at all:

M. Baba Mesia 2:11

A. [If he has to choose between seeking] what he has lost and what his father has lost,
B. his own takes precedence.
C. what he has lost and what his master has lost,
D. his own takes precedence.
E. what his father has lost and what his master has lost,
F. that of his master takes precedence.
G. For his father brought him into this world.
H. But his master, who taught him wisdom, will bring him into the life
I. But if his father is a sage, that of his father takes precedence.
J. [If] his father and his master were carrying heavy burdens, he removes that of his master, and afterward removes that of his father.
K. [If] his father and his master were taken captive,
L. he ransoms his master, and afterward he ransoms his father.
M. But if his father is a sage, he ransoms his father, and afterward he ransoms his master.

In this passage Torah-learning has not attained practical consequence. That is to say, there is no theory that, because the master has studied Torah, therefore the master does not have to earn a living ("carrying heavy burdens"). The same is so in the following:

M. Horayot 3:6-8

3:6 A. Whatever is offered more regularly than its fellow takes precedence over its fellow, and whatever is more holy than its fellow takes precedence over its fellow.
B. [If] a bullock of an anointed priest and a bullock of the congregation [M. Hor. 1:5] are standing [awaiting sacrifice] –
C. the bullock of the anointed [high priest] takes precedence over the bullock of the congregation in all rites pertaining to it.

3:7 A. The man takes precedence over the woman in the matter of the saving of life and in the matter of returning lost property.
B. But a woman takes precedence over a man in the matter of [providing] clothing and redemption from captivity.
C. When both of them are standing in danger of defilement, the man takes precedence over the woman.

3:8 A. A priest takes precedence over a Levite, a Levite over an Israelite, an Israelite over a *mamzer*, a *mamzer* over a *Netin*, a *Netin* over a proselyte, a proselyte over a freed slave.
B. Under what circumstances?
C. When all of them are equivalent.
D. But if the *mamzer* was a disciple of a sage and a high priest was an *am haares*, the *mamzer* who is a disciple of a sage takes precedence over a high priest who is an *am haares*.

What is explicit here is that knowledge of the Torah does not change one's caste-status, for example, priest or *mamzer* or *Netin*, and that caste-status does govern whom one may marry, a matter of substantial economic consequence. But it does change one's status as to precedence of another order altogether – one that is curiously unspecific at M. Horayot 3:8. Hierarchical classification for its own sake, lacking all practical consequence, characterizes the Mishnah's system, defining, after all, its purpose and its goal! Along these same lines, the premise of tractate Sanhedrin is that the sage is judge and administrator of the community; knowledge of the Torah qualifies him; but knowledge of the Torah does not provide a living or the equivalent of a living. No provision for supporting the sage as administrator, clerk, or judge is suggested in the tractate.

What about knowledge of Torah as a way of making one's living? In the list of professions by which men make a living we find several positions. First is that of Meir and Simeon:

Mishnah Qiddushin 4:14

E. R. Meir says, "A man should always teach his son a clean and easy trade. And let him pray to him to whom belong riches and possessions.

G. "For there is no trade which does not involve poverty or wealth.

H. " For poverty does not come from one's trade, nor does wealth come from one's trade.

I. "But all is in accord with a man's merit."

J. R. Simeon b. Eleazar says, "Have you ever seen a wild beast or a bird who has a trade? Yet they get along without difficulty. And were they not created only to serve me? And I was created to serve my Master. So is it not logical that I should get along without difficulty? But I have done evil and ruined my living."

One's merit makes the difference between poverty and wealth, or one's sinfulness. A more practical position is that which follows in the continuation of the passage:

K. Abba Gurion of Sidon says in the name of Abba Gurya, "A man should not teach his son to be an ass driver, a camel driver, a barber, a sailor, a herdsman, or a shopkeeper For their trade is the trade of thieves."

L. R. Judah says in his name, "Most ass drivers are evil, most camel drivers are decent, most sailors are saintly, the best among physicians is going to Gehenna, and the best of butchers is a partner of Amalek."

The third view is that of Nehorai, who holds that Torah suffices as a means for making a living:

M. R. Nehorai says, "I should lay aside every trade in the world and teach my son only Torah.

N. "For a man eats its fruits in this world, and the principal remains for the world to come.

O. "But other trades are not that way.

P "When a man gets sick or old or has pains and cannot do his job, lo, he dies of starvation.

Q. "But with Torah it is not that way.

R. "But it keeps him from all evil when he is young, and it gives him a future and a hope when he is old.

S. "Concerning his youth, what does it say? 'They who wait upon the Lord shall renew their strength' (Isa. 40:31). And concerning his old age what does it say? 'They shall still bring forth fruit in old age" (Ps. 92:14).

T. "And so it says with regard to the patriarch Abraham, may he rest in peace, 'And Abraham was old and well along in years, and the Lord blessed Abraham in all things (Gen. 24:1).

U. "We find that the patriarch Abraham kept the entire Torah even before it was revealed, since it says, Since Abraham obeyed my voice and kept my charge, my commandments, my statutes, and my laws (Gen. 26:5)."

Does Nehorai tell us that if we study the Torah, we will have all our worldly needs met, as Aqiba tells Tarfon that Torah is the counterpart of real estate but a more secure investment? I think not. Quite to the contrary, precisely why Torah works as it does is made explicit at R: "It keeps him from evil when he is young." That is to say, the position of Meir and Simeon is repeated, only in a fresh way. If I know the Torah, I will not sin. The conception that, if I study Torah, I automatically get the food I need to eat and the roof I need for shelter is not at issue here, where our concern is with being kept from evil in youth and enjoying God's blessing in old age on account of keeping the Torah – a very different thing.

The first apologia for the Mishnah, tractate Abot, takes the view that one should not make one's living through study of the Torah. That is made explicit in Torah-sayings of tractate Abot, where we find explicit rejection of the theory of Torah-study as a means of avoiding one's obligation to earn a living. Torah-study without a craft is rejected, Torah-study along with labor at a craft is defined as the ideal way of life. The following sayings make that point quite clearly:

M. Abot 2:2 and 3:17

2:2 A. Rabban Gamaliel, a son of Rabbi Judah the Patriarch says: Fitting is learning in the Torah along with a craft, for the labor put into the two of them makes one forget sin. And all learning of the Torah which is not joined with labor is destined to be null and causes sin.

3:17 A. R. Eleazar b. Azariah says, "...If there is no sustenance [lit.: flour], there is no Torah-learning. If there is no Torah-learning, there is no sustenance."

Here there is no contrast between two forms of wealth, one less secure, the other more. The way of virtue lies rather in economic activity in the conventional sense, joined to intellectual or philosophical activity in sages' sense. Again, Xenophon will not have been surprised. The labor in Torah is not an economic activity and produces no solutions to this-worldly problems of getting food, shelter, clothing. To the contrary, labor in Torah defines the purpose of human life; it is the goal; but it is not the medium for maintaining life and avoiding starvation or exposure to the elements. So too, Tosefta's complement to the Mishnah is explicit in connection with M. Gittin 1:7A, "a commandment pertaining to the father concerning the son:"

T. Qiddushin 1:11E-G

It is to circumcise him, redeem him [should he be kidnapped], teach him Torah, teach him a trade, and marry him off to a girl

There clearly is no conception that if one studies Torah, he need not work for a living, nor in the Tosefta's complement to the Mishnah does anyone imagine that merit is gained by supporting those who study the Torah.

Yohanan ben Zakkai speaks of Torah-study as the goal of a human life, on the one side, and a reward paid for Torah study, clearly in a theological sense and context, on the other. That the context of Torah-study is religious and not economic in any sense is shown by Hananiah's saying, which is explicit: if people talk about the Torah, the Presence of God joins them to participate:

M. Abot 2:8, 2:16, 3:2

2:8 A. Rabban Yohanan ben Zakkai received [the Torah] from Hillel and Shammai. He would say: If you have learned much Torah, do not puff yourself up on that account, for it was for that purpose that you were created.

2:16 A. He would say: It's not your job to finish the work, but you are not free to walk away from it. If you have learned much Torah, they will give you a good reward. And your employer can be depended upon to pay your wages for what you do. And know what sort of reward is going to be given to the righteous in the coming time.

3:2 B R. Hananiah b. Teradion says, "[If] two sit together and between them do not pass teachings of the Torah, lo, this is a seat of the scornful, as it is said, Nor sits in the seat of the scornful (Ps. 1:1). But two who are sitting, and words of the Torah do pass between them – the Presence is with them, "as it is said, Then they that feared the Lord spoke with one another, and the Lord hearkened and heard, and a book of remembrance was written before him, for them that feared the Lord and gave thought to his name (Mal 3:16)." I know that this applies to two. How do I know that even if a single person sits and works on the Torah, the Holy One, blessed be He, set aside a reward for him? As it is said, Let him sit alone and keep silent, because he has laid it upon him (Lam. 3:28).

Do worldly benefits accrue to those who study the Torah? The rabbi cited in the following statement maintains that it is entirely inappropriate to utilize Torah-learning to gain either social standing or economic gain:

M. Abot 4:5

B   R. Sadoq says, "Do not make [Torah-teachings] a crown in which to glorify yourself or a spade with which to dig. So did Hillel say, "He who uses the crown perishes. Thus have you learned: Whoever derives worldly benefit from teachings of the Torah takes his life out of this world."

I cannot think of a statement more likely to startle the author of the story involving Aqiba and Tarfon than this one, since Aqiba's position is precisely the one rejected here. It is the simple fact that the bulk of opinion in the Mishnah and in tractate Abot identifies Torah-learning with status within a system of hierarchical classification, not with a medium for earning a living. Admittedly that is not the only position that is represented. The following seems to me to contrast working for a living with studying Torah and to maintain that the latter will provide a living, without recourse to hard labor:

M. Abot 3:15

A.   R. Nehunia b. Haqqaneh says, "From whoever accepts upon himself the yoke of the Torah do they remove the yoke of the state and the yoke of hard labor. And upon whoever removes from himself the yoke of the Torah do they lay the yoke of the state and the yoke of hard labor."

But the prevailing view, represented by the bulk of sayings, treats Torah-study as an activity that competes with economic venture and insists that Torah-study take precedence, even though it is not of economic value in any commonplace sense of the words. That is explicitly imputed to Meir and to Jonathan in the following:

M. Abot 4:10

4:10 A.   R. Meir says, "Keep your business to a minimum and make your business the Torah. And be humble before everybody. And if you treat the Torah as nothing, you will have many treating you as nothing. And if you have labored in the Torah, [the Torah] has a great reward to give you."

4:9 A.   R. Jonathan says, "Whoever keeps the Torah when poor will in the end keep it in wealth. And whoever treats the Torah as nothing when he is wealthy in the end will treat it as nothing in poverty."

Torah-study competes with, rather than replaces, with economic activity. That is the simple position of tractate Abot, extending the conception of matters explicit in the Mishnah. If I had to make a simple statement of the situation prevailing at ca. 250, sages contrast their wealth, which is spiritual and intellectual, with material wealth; they do not deem the one to form the counterpart of the other, but only as the opposite.

And that brings us to consider the re-presentation of wealth in the successor-documents, for I maintain, frames the new economics of the successor system. A system that declares forbidden using the Torah as a spade with which to dig, as a means of making one's living, will have found proof for its position in the numerous allegations in Wisdom literature that the value of wisdom, understood of course as the Torah is beyond price: "Happy is the man who finds wisdom...for the gain from it is better than gain from silver, and its profit better than gold; she is more precious than jewels, and nothing you desire can compare with her...." (Prov. 3:13-15). That and numerous parallels were not understood to mean that if people devoted themselves to the study of the Torah and the teaching thereof, they would not have to work any more. Nor do the praises of wisdom specifically contrast Torah-learning with land-ownership. But in the successor-writings, that is precisely what is commonplace. And the conclusion is drawn that one may derive one's living from study of the Torah: then a spade with which to dig, as much as a real spade served to dig in the earth to make the ground yield a living.

The issue of scarce resources in the context of a society that highly valued honor and despised and feared shame was phrased not only in terms of material wealth but also of worldly repute. Knowledge of the Torah served as did coins, that is, to circulate the name of the holy man or woman (Abraham or Sarah, in this context), all figures to whom, quite naturally, heroic deeds of Torah-learning and -teaching were attributed:

Genesis Rabbah XXXIX:XI.5

A. R. Berekhiah in the name of R. Helbo: "[The promise that God will make Abram great] refers to the fact that his coinage had circulated in the world.

B. "There were four whose coinage circulated in the world.

C. "Abraham: 'And I will make you' (Gen. 12:2). And what image appeared on his coinage? An old man and an old woman on the obverse side, a boy and a girl on the reverse [Abraham, Sarah, Isaac and Rebekkah.

D. "Joshua: 'So the Lord was with Joshua and his fame was in all the land' (Josh. 6:27). That is, his coinage circulated in the world. And what image appeared on his coinage? An ox on the obverse, a wild-ox on the reverse: 'His firstling bullock, majesty is his, and his horns are the horns of a wild ox' (Deut 33:17). [Joshua descended from Joseph.]

E. "David: 'And the fame of David went out into all lands' (1 Chr. 14:17). That is, his coinage circulated in the world. And what image appeared on his coinage? A staff and a wallet on the obverse, a tower on the reverse: 'Your neck is like the tower of David, built with turrets' (Song 4:4).

F. "Mordecai: 'For Mordecai was great in the king's house, and his fame went forth throughout all the provinces' (Est. 9:4). That is, his coinage circulated in the world. And what image appeared on his coinage? Sackcloth and ashes on the obverse, a golden crown on the reverse."

"Coinage" is meant to be jarring, to draw an ironic contrast between true currency, which is the repute that is gained through godly service, and worldly currency; king's use their coins to make their persons and policies known, so do the saints. But this is not, by itself, a saying that assigns to Torah the value equivalent to coins.

But, of course, it cannot make such an assignment, since the value imputed to Torah-study and teaching compares not to (mere) currency, which, in the context of Aristotelian and Mishnaic economics, bore the merely contingent value of a commodity, but only to land. So can we find in the successor-writings clear affirmations, beyond the one now cited concerning Tarfon and Aqiba, that compare land with the Torah? For one thing, the Torah serves as Israel's deed to the land, and, it must follow, knowledge of the Torah is what demonstrates one's right to possess the one resource found worth having:

Genesis Rabbah I.II

1. A. R. Joshua of Sikhnin in the name of R. Levi commenced [discourse by citing the following verse]: "'He has declared to his people the power of his works, in giving them the heritage of the nations' (Ps. 111:6).

   B. "What is the reason that the Holy One, blessed be He, revealed to Israel what was created on the first day and what on the second?

   C. "It was on account of the nations of the world. It was so that they should not ridicule the Israelites, saying to them, 'Are you not a nation of robbers [having stolen the land from the Canaanites]?'

   D. "It allows the Israelites to answer them, 'And as to you, is there no spoil in your hands? For surely: "The Caphtorim, who came forth out of Caphtor, destroyed them and dwelled in their place" (Deut. 2:23)!

   E. "'The world and everything in it belongs to the Holy One, blessed be He. When he wanted, he gave it to you, and when he wanted, he took it from you and gave it to us.'

   F. "That is in line with what is written, '....in giving them the heritage of the nations, he has declared to his people the power of his works' (Ps. 111:6).. [So as to give them the land, he

The Transvaluation of Value

established his right to do so by informing them that he had created it.]

G. "He told them about the beginning: 'In the beginning God created...'" (Gen. 1:1)."

While pertinent, the passage is hardly probative; all we have here is the linkage of Torah to land, but for merely instrumental purposes. Not only so, but the conception of riches in the conventional philosophical sense certainly persisted. "Abram was very rich in cattle" is understood quite literally, interpreted in line with Ps. 105:37: "He brought them forth with silver with gold, and there was none that stumbled among his tribes."[8] Along these same lines, "Jacob's riches" of Gen. 30:43 are understood to be material and concrete: sixty-thousand dogs, for example.[9] One may interpret the story of the disinheritance of Eliezer b. Hyrcanus on account of his running off to study the Torah with Yohanan ben Zakkai as a contrasting tale, therefore. The father intended to disinherit the son from his property because he had gone to study the Torah but then, impressed by his achievements, goes and gives him the whole estate.[10] But that would require us to read into the story a symbolic transaction that is not explicit. So, too, the allegation that "Torah" is represented by bread does not require, and perhaps does not even sustain, the interpretation that Torah-learning forms a scarce resource that provides bread and that is worth bread and that serves as does bread:

Genesis Rabbah LXX:V.1

A. "...will give me bread to eat and clothing to wear:"
B. Aqilas the proselyte came to R. Eliezer and said to him, "Is all the gain that is coming to the proselyte going to be contained in this verse: '...and loves the proselyte, giving him food and clothing' (Deut. 10:18)?"
C. He said to him, "And is something for which the old man [Jacob] beseeched going to be such a small thing in your view namely, '...will give me bread to eat and clothing to wear'? [God] comes and hands it over to [a proselyte] on a reed [and the proselyte does not have to beg for it]."
D. He came to R. Joshua, who commenced by saying words to appease him: "'Bread' refers to Torah, as it is said, 'Come, eat of my bread' (Prov. 9:5). 'Clothing' refers to the cloak of a disciple of sages.
E. "When a person has the merit of studying the Torah, he has the merit of carrying out a religious duty. [So the proselyte

---

[8]Genesis Rabbah XLI:III.1.A-B.
[9]Genesis Rabbah LXXIII:XI.1.D.
[10]Genesis Rabbah XLII:I.1.

F. "And not only so, but his daughters may be chosen for marriage into the priesthood, so that their sons' sons will offer burnt-offerings on the altar. [So the proselyte may also look forward to entry into the priests' caste. That statement will now be spelled out.]
G. "'Bread' refers to the show-bread.'
H. "'Clothing' refers to the garments of the priesthood.'
I. "So lo, we deal with the sanctuary.
J. "How do we know that the same sort of blessing applies in the provinces? 'Bread' speaks of the dough-offering [that is separated in the provinces], 'while 'clothing' refers to the first fleece [handed over to the priest]."

Here too, we may reasonably interpret the passage in a merely symbolic way: "bread" stands for Torah-learning, because just as bread sustains the body, so Torah-learning sustains the soul. That and similar interpretations offer plausible alternatives to the conception that Torah-learning now forms that scarce resource that defines value in the way in which land for Aristotle or Israelite-occupied land in the Land of Israel for the Mishnah forms the final arbiter in the identification of scarce resources.

But there are passages that are quite explicit: land is wealth, or Torah is wealth, but not both; owning land is power and studying Torah permits (re)gaining power. To take the first of the two propositions in its most explicit formulation:

Leviticus Rabbah XXX:I

4. A. R. Yohanan was going up from Tiberias to Sepphoris. R. Hiyya bar Abba was supporting him. They came to a field. He said, "This field once belonged to me, but I sold it in order to acquire merit in the Torah."
B. They came to a vineyard, and he said, "This vineyard once belonged to me, but I sold it in order to acquire merit in the Torah."
C. They came to an olive grove, and he said, "This olive grove once belonged to me, but I sold it in order to acquire merit in the Torah."
D. R. Hiyya began to cry.
E. Said R. Yohanan, "Why are you crying?"
F. He said to him, "It is because you left nothing over to support you in your old age."
G. He said to him, "Hiyya, my disciple, is what I did such a light thing in your view? I sold something which was given in a spell of six days [of creation] and in exchange I acquired something which was given in a spell of forty days [of revelation].

The Transvaluation of Value

    H.   "The entire world and everything in it was created in only six days, as it is written, 'For in six days the Lord made heaven and earth' [Ex. 20:11].

    I.   "But the Torah was given over a period of forty days, as it was said, 'And he was there with the Lord for forty days and forty nights' [Ex. 34:28].

    J.   "And it is written, 'And I remained on the mountain for forty days and forty nights'" (Deut. 9:9).

5. A.   When R. Yohanan died, his generation recited concerning him [the following verse of Scripture]: "If a man should give all the wealth of his house for the love" (Song 8:7), with which R. Yohanan loved the Torah, "he would be utterly destitute" (Song 8:7)....

    C.   When R. Eleazar b. R. Simeon died, his generation recited concerning him [the following verse of Scripture]: "Who is this who comes up out of the wilderness like pillars of smoke, perfumed with myrrh and frankincense, with all the powders of the merchant?" (Song 3:6).

    D.   What is the meaning of the clause, "With all the powders of the merchant"?

    E.   [Like a merchant who carries all sorts of desired powders,] he was a master of Scripture, a repeater of Mishnah traditions, a writer of liturgical supplications, and a liturgical poet.

The sale of land for the acquisition of "merit in the Torah" introduces two principal systemic components, merit and Torah.[11] For our purpose, the importance of the statement lies in the second of the two, which deems land the counterpart – and clearly the opposite – of the Torah.

Now one can sell a field and acquire "Torah," meaning, in the context established by the exchange between Tarfon and Aqiba, the opportunity to gain leisure to (acquire the merit gained by) the study of the Torah. That the sage has left himself nothing for his support in old age makes explicit the material meaning of the statement, and the comparison of the value of land, created in six days, and the Torah, created in forty days, is equally explicit. The comparison of knowledge of Torah to the merchandise of the merchant simply repeats the same point, but in a lower register. So, too, does the this-worldly power of study of the Torah make explicit in another framework the conviction that study of the Torah yields material and concrete benefit, not just spiritual renewal. Thus R. Huna states,

---

[11]In a well-crafted system, of course, principal parts prove interchangeable or closely aligned, and that is surely the case here. But I have already observed that the successor-system is far more tightly constructed than the initial one, in that the politics and the economics flow into one another, in a way in which, in the initial, philosophical system, they do not. The disembedded character of the Mishnah's economics has already impressed us.

"All of the exiles will be gathered together only on account of the study of Mishnah-teachings."[12]

Not only so, but the sage devoted to study of the Torah has to be supported because he can no longer perform physical work. Study of the Torah deprives him of physical strength, and that contrast and counterpart represented by land and working of the land as against Torah and the study of the Torah comes to symbolic expression in yet another way:

Leviticus Rabbah XI:XXII

1. A. R. Eleazar bar Simeon was appointed to impress men and beasts into forced labor [in the corvée]. One time Elijah, of blessed memory, appeared to him in the guise of an old man. Elijah said to him, "Get me a beast of burden."
   B. Eleazar said to him, "What do you have as a cargo [to load on the beast]?"
   C. He said to him, "This old skin-bottle of mine, my cloak, and me as rider."
   D. He said, "Take a look at this old man! I [personally] can take him and carry him to the end of the world, and he says to me to get a beast ready!"
   E. What did he do? He loaded him on his back and carried him up mountains and down valleys and over fields of thorns and fields of thistles.
   F. In the end [Elijah] began to bear down on him. He said to him, "Old man, old man! Make yourself lighter, and if you don't, I'll toss you off."
   G. [Elijah] said to him, "Now do you want to take a bit of a rest?"
   H. He said to him, "Yes."
   I. What did he do? [Elijah] took him to a field and set him down under a tree and gave him food and drink. When he had eaten and drunk, he [Elijah] said to him, "All this running about – what is in it for you? Would it not be better for you to take up the vocation of your fathers?"
   J. He said to him, "And can you teach it to me?"
   K. He said to him, "Yes."
   L. And there are those who say that for thirteen years Elijah of blessed memory taught him until he could recite even Sifra [the exegesis of Leviticus, which is particularly difficult].
   M. But once he could recite that document, [he had so lost his strength that] he could not lift up even a cloak.
2. A. The household of Rabban Gamaliel had a member who could carry forty *seahs* [of grain] to the baker [on his back].
   B. He said to him, "All this vast power do you possess, and you do not devote yourself to the study of Sifra."
   C. When he could recite that document, they say that even a single *seah* of grain he was unable to bear.

---

[12]Pesiqta deRab Kahana VI:III.3.B.

The Transvaluation of Value

D. There are those who say that if someone else did not take it off him, he would not have been able to take it off himself.

These stories about how a mark of the sage is physical weakness are included only because they form part of the (in this instance, secondary) composition on Eleazar b. Simeon. But they do form part of a larger program of contrasting Torah-study with land-ownership, intellectual prowess with physical power, the superiority of the one over the other. No wonder sages would in time claim that their power protected cities, which then needed neither police nor walls. These were concrete claims, affecting the rational utilization of scarce resources as much as the use and distribution of land constituted an expression of a rationality concerning scarce resources, their preservation and increase.

In alleging that the pertinent verses of Proverbs were assigned a quite this-worldly and material sense, so that study of the Torah really was worth more than silver, I say no more than the successor-compilations allege in so many words. Thus we find the following, which faces head-on the fact that masters of the Torah are paid for studying the Torah, so confirming the claim that the Torah now served as a spade with which to dig:

Pesiqta deRab Kahana XXVII:I

1. A. R. Abba bar Kahana commenced [discourse by citing the following verse]: *Take my instruction instead of silver, and knowledge rather than choice gold* (Prov. 8:10)."
   B. Said R. Abba bar Kahana, "*Take the instruction of the Torah instead of silver.*
   C. "*Take the instruction of the Torah and not silver.*
   D. "*Why do you weigh out money? [Because there is no bread]* (Isa. 55:2).
   E. "'*Why do you weigh out money* to the sons of Esau [Rome]? [It is because] *there is no bread*, because you did not sate yourselves with the bread of the Torah.
   F. "*And [why] do you labor? Because there is no satisfaction* (Isa. 55:2).
   G. "*Why do you labor* while the nations of the world enjoy plenty? *Because there is no satisfaction*, that is, because you have not sated yourselves with the bread of the Torah and with the wine of the Torah.
   H. "For it is written, *Come, eat of my bread, and drink of the wine I have mixed* (Prov. 9:5)."
2. A. R. Berekhiah and R. Hiyya, his father, in the name of R. Yosé b. Nehorai: "It is written, *I shall punish all who oppress him* (Jer. 30:20), even those who collect funds for charity [and in doing so, treat people badly], except [for those who collect] the wages to be paid to teachers of Scripture and repeaters of Mishnah traditions.

B. "For they receive [as a salary] only compensation for the loss of their time, [which they devote to teaching and learning rather than to earning a living]."
C. "But as to the wages [for carrying out] a single matter in the Torah, no creature can pay the [appropriate] fee in reward."

The obvious goal, the homily at 1.E, surely stands against my claim that we deal with allegations of concrete and material value: the imputation to the learning of the Torah of the status of "scarce resources." But, as a matter of fact, the whole of No. 2 makes the contrary position explicit: wages are paid to Torah-teachers. The following makes the same point:

Y. Nedarim 4:3.II.

A. It is written, "Behold, I have taught you statutes and ordinances" [Deut. 4:5].
B. Just as I do so without pay, so you must do so without pay.
C. Is it possible that the same rule applies to teaching Scripture and translation [cf. M. Ned. 4:3D]?
D. Scripture says, "Statutes and ordinances."
E. Statutes and ordinances must you teach without pay, but you need not teach Scripture and translation without pay.
F. And yet we see that those who teach Mishnah collect their pay.
G. Said R. Judah b. R. Ishmael, "It is a fee for the use of their time [which they cannot utilize to earn a living for themselves] which they collect."

True, this transformation of Torah-study into something of real worth is rationalized as salary in compensation for loss of time. But the same rationalization clearly did not impress the many masters of the initial system who insisted that one must practice a craft in order to make a living and study the Torah only in one's leisure time. We see the contrast in the two positions quite explicitly in what follows. The contrast between the received position and that before us is found at the following:

Y Peah 1:1.VII.(Brooks)

D It is forbidden to a person to teach his son a trade, in as much as it is written, "And you shall meditate therein day and night" (Joshua 1:8.)
E. But has not R. Ishmael taught, "'You shall choose life" (Deut. 30:19) – this refers to learning [Torah] and practicing a trade as well. [One both studies the Torah and also a trade.]

There is no harmonizing the two views by appeal to the rationalization before us. In fact, study of the Torah substituted for practicing a craft, and it was meant to do so, as A alleges explicitly. In all, therefore, the case in favor of the proposition that Torah has

The Transvaluation of Value

now become a material good, and, further, that Torah has now been transformed into the ultimate scarce resource – explicitly substituting for real estate, even in the Land of Israel – is firmly established.

That ultimate value – Torah-study – surely bears comparison with other foci of value, such as prayer, using money for building synagogues, and the like. It is explicitly stated that spending money on synagogues is a waste of money, while spending money supporting Torah-masters is the right use of scarce resources. Further, we find the claim, synagogues and school houses – communal real estate – in fact form the property of sages and their disciples, who may dispose of them just as they want, as any owner may dispose of his property according to his unfettered will. In Y. Sheqalim we find the former allegation, Y. Megillah the latter:

Y. Sheqalim 5:4.II.

A. R. Hama bar Haninah and R. Hoshaia the Elder were strolling in the synagogues in Lud. Said R. Hama bar Haninah to R. Hoshaia, "How much money did my forefathers invest here [in building these synagogues]!"

B. He said to him, "How many lives did your forefathers invest here! Were there not people who were laboring in Torah [who needed the money more]?"

C. R. Abun made the gates of the great hall [of study]. R. Mana came to him. He said to him, "See what I have made!"

D. He said to him, "'For Israel has forgotten his Maker and built palaces'! (Hos. 8:14). Were there no people laboring in Torah [who needed the money more]?"

Y. Sotah 9:13.VI.

C. A certain rabbi would teach Scripture to his brother in Tyre, and when they came and called him to do business, he would say, "I am not going to take away from my fixed time to study. If the profit is going to come to me, let it come in due course [after my fixed time for study has ended]."

Y. Megillah 3:3:V.

A. R. Joshua b. Levi said, "Synagogues and schoolhouses belong to sages and their disciples."

B. R. Hiyya bar Yosé received [guests] in the synagogue [and lodged them there].

C. R. Immi instructed the scribes, "If someone comes to you with some slight contact with Torah learning, receive him, his asses, and his belongings."

D. R. Berekhiah went to the synagogue in Beisan. He saw someone rinsing his hands and feet in a fountain [in the courtyard of the synagogue]. He said to him, "It is forbidden to you [to do this]."

E. The next day the man saw [Berekhiah] washing his hands and feet in the fountain.

F. He said to him, "Rabbi, is it permitted to you and forbidden to me?"
G. He said to him, "Yes."
H. He said to him, "Why?"
I. He said to him, "Because this is what R. Joshua b. Levi said: 'Synagogues and schoolhouses belong to sages and their disciples.'"

Not all acts of piety, we see, are equal, and the one that takes precedence over all others (just as was alleged at Mishnah-tractate Peah 1:1) is study of the Torah. But the point now is a much more concrete one, and that is, through study of the Torah, sages and their disciples gain possession, as a matter of fact, over communal real estate, which they may utilize in any way they wish; and that is a quite concrete claim indeed, as the same story alleges.

No wonder, then, that people in general are expected to contribute their scarce resources for the support of sages and their disciples. Moreover, society at large was obligated to support sages, and the sages' claim upon others was enforceable by Heaven. Those who gave sages' disciples money so that they would not have to work would get it back from Heaven, and those who did not would lose what they had:

Y. Sotah 7:4.IV.

F. R. Aha in the name of R. Tanhum b. R. Hiyya: "If one has learned, taught, kept, and carried out [the Torah], and has ample means in his possession to strengthen the Torah and has not done so, lo, such a one still is in the category of those who are cursed." [The meaning of "strengthen" here is to support the masters of the Torah.]
G. R. Jeremiah in the name of R. Hiyya bar Ba, "[If] one did not learn, teach, keep, and carry out [the teachings of the Torah], and did not have ample means to strengthen [the masters of the Torah] [but nonetheless did strengthen them], lo, such a one falls into the category of those who are blessed."
H. And R. Hannah, R. Jeremiah in the name of R. Hiyya: "The Holy One, blessed be He, is going to prepare a protection for those who carry out religious duties [of support for masters of Torah] through the protection afforded to the masters of Torah [themselves].
I. "What is the Scriptural basis for that statement? 'For the protection of wisdom is like the protection of money'" (Qoh. 7:12).
J. "And it says, '[The Torah] is a tree of life to those who grasp it; those who hold it fast are called happy'" (Prov. 3:18).

Such contributions form the counterpart to taxes, that is, scarce resources taken away from the owner by force for the purposes of the public good, that is, the ultimate meeting point of economics and politics, the explicit formation of distributive, as against market, economics. Then what is distributed and to whom and by what force forms the centerpiece of the systemic political economy, and the answer is perfectly simple: all sorts of valued things are taken away from people and handed over for the support of sages:

Pesiqta deRab Kahana V:IV.2

A. "A man's gift makes room for him and brings him before great men" (Prov. 18:16).

B. M'SH B: R. Eliezer, R. Joshua, and R. Aqiba went to the harborside of Antioch to collect funds for the support of sages.

C. [In Aramaic:] A certain Abba Yudan lived there.

D. He would carry out his religious duty [of philanthropy] in a liberal spirit, but had lost his money. When he saw our masters, he went home with a sad face. His wife said to him, "What's wrong with you, that you look so sad?"

E. He repeated the tale to her: "Our masters are here, and I don't know what I shall be able to do for them."

F. His wife, who was a truly philanthropic woman – what did she say to him? "You only have one field left. Go, sell half of it and give them the proceeds."

G. He went and did just that. When he was giving them the money, they said to him, "May the Omnipresent make up all your losses."

H. Our masters went their way.

I. He went out to plough. While he was ploughing the half of the field that he had left, the Holy One, blessed be He, opened his eyes. The earth broke open before him, and his cow fell in and broke her leg. He went down to raise her up, and found a treasure beneath her. He said, "It was for my gain that my cow broke her leg."

J. When our masters came back, [in Aramaic:] they asked about a certain Abba Yudan and how he was doing. They said, "Who can gaze on the face of Abba Yudan [which glows with prosperity] – Abba Yudan, the owner of flocks of goats, Abba Yudan, the owner of herds of asses, Abba Yudan, the owner of herds of camels."

K. He came to them and said to them, "Your prayer in my favor has produced returns and returns on the returns."

L. They said to him, "Even though someone else gave more than you did, we wrote your name at the head of the list."

M. Then they took him and sat him next to themselves and recited in his regard the following verse of Scripture: "A man's gift makes room for him and brings him before great men" (Prov. 18:16).

Now what is at stake in the scarce resource represented by Torah-study? It cannot be a (merely) spiritual benefit, when, in consequence of giving money to sages so they will not have to work, I get rich.

Not only so, but the matter of position is equally in play. I get rich and I also enjoy the standing of sages, sitting next to them. So far as social position intersects with wealth, we find in the Torah that wealth that, in this systemic context, serves to tells us what we mean by scarce resources: source of this-worldly gain in practical terms, source of public prestige in social terms, validation of the use of force – in context, psychological force – for taking away scarce (material) resources in favor of a superior value. The entire system comes to expression in this story: its economics, its politics, and, as a matter of fact, its philosophy. But all three are quite different from what they were in the initial structure and system.

No wonder then that sages protect cities. So it is claimed that sages are the guardians of cities, and later on that would yield the further allegation that sages do not have to pay taxes to build walls around cities, since their Torah-study protects the cities:

Pesiqta deRab Kahana XV:V

1. A. R. Abba bar Kahana commenced discourse by citing the following verse: "*Who is the man so wise that he may understand this? To whom has the mouth of the Lord spoken, that he may declare it? Why is the land ruined and laid waste like a wilderness, [so that no one passes through? The Lord said, It is because they forsook my Torah which I set before them; they neither obeyed me nor conformed to it. They followed the promptings of their own stubborn hearts, they followed the Baalim as their forefathers had taught them. Therefore these are the words of the Lord of Hosts the God of Israel: I will feed this people with wormwood and give them bitter poison to drink. I will scatter them among nations whom neither they nor their forefathers have known; I will harry them with the sword until I have made an end of them]* (Jer. 9:16)."
   B. It was taught in the name of R. Simeon b. Yohai, "If you see towns uprooted from their place in the land of Israel, know that [it is because] the people did not pay the salaries of teachers of children and Mishnah-instructors.
   C. "What is the verse of Scripture that indicates it? *Why is the land ruined and laid waste like a wilderness, [so that no one passes through?]* What is written just following? *It is because they forsook my Torah [which I set before them; they neither obeyed me nor conformed to it.]*
2. A. Rabbi sent R. Yosé and R. Ammi to go and survey the towns of the Land of Israel. They would go into a town and say to the people, "Bring me the guardians of the town."
   B. The people would bring out the head of the police and the local guard.
   C. [The sages] would say, "These are not the guardians of the town, they are those who destroy the town. Who are the guardians of the town? They are the teachers of children and Mishnah-

The Transvaluation of Value

		teachers, who keep watch by day and by night, in line with the verse, *And you shall meditate in it day and night* (Josh. 1:8)."
	D.	And so Scripture says, *If the Lord does not build the house, in vain the builders labor* (Ps. 127:1).
7.	A.	Said R. Abba bar Kahana, "No philosophers in the world ever arose of the quality of Balaam ben Beor and Abdymos of Gadara. The nations of the world came to Abnymos of Gadara. They said to him, 'Do you maintain that we can make war against this nation?'
	B.	"He said to them, 'Go and make the rounds of their synagogues and their study houses. So long as there are there children chirping out loud in their voices [and studying the Torah], then you cannot overcome them. If not, then you can conquer them, for so did their father promise them: *The voice is Jacob's voice* (Gen. 27:22), meaning that when Jacob's voice chirps in synagogues and study houses, *The hands are not the hands of Esau* [so Esau has no power].
	C.	"'So long as there are no children chirping out loud in their voices [and studying the Torah] in synagogues and study houses, *The hands are the hands of Esau* [so Esau has power].'"

The reference to Esau, that is, Rome, of course links the whole to the contemporary context and alleges that if the Israelites will support those who study the Torah and teach it, then their cities will be safe, and, still more, the rule of Esau/Rome will come to an end; then the Messiah will come, so the stakes are not trivial.

The disenlandisement of economics, the transvaluation of value so that Torah replaced land as the supreme measure of value and also, as a matter of fact, of social worth – these form (an) economics. It is, moreover, one that is fully the counterpart of the philosophical economics based upon real estate as true value that Aristotle and the framers of the Mishnah constructed, each party for its own systemic purpose. If we have not reviewed the components of the economics of the Torah – the theory of means of production and who controls the operative unit of production of value, the consideration of whether we deal with a market- or a distributive economics, the reason is that we have not had to. It is perfectly obvious that the sage controlled the means of production and fully mastered the power to govern them; the sage distributed valued resources – supernatural or material, as the case required – and the conception of a market was as alien to that economics as it was to the priestly economics revised and replicated by the Mishnah's system. Enough has been said, therefore, to establish beyond reasonable doubt the claim that in the Torah we deal with the system's counterpart category, its economics.

And yet that very fact calls into question my insistence that what we have is not (merely) another economics, with a different value, but a counterpart economics. For I claim that what we have is a systemic counterpart, not the same thing in another form: an anti-economics and the transvaluation of value, not merely the redefinition of what is to be valued. Obviously, I have reservations that have led me to insist that the systemic economics forms a counterpart to, but not a parallel and a mere replication of, another economics. A shift from valuing land to valuing liquid capital, or from valuing beads to valuing conches, for that matter, would not require the invention of the category, counterpart-economics, or the rather protracted argument offered earlier concerning the movement from the subject to the predicate of the operative language of definition. Why, then, my rather odd claim that we have an economics that is transvalued, not merely redefined?

It is because economics deals with scarce resources, and the disenlandisement of economics in the successor-Judaism has turned upon its head the very focus of economics: scarcity and the rational confrontation with scarcity. To land rigid limits are set by nature, to the Holy Land, still more narrow ones apply. But to knowledge of the Torah no limits pertain. So we find ourselves dealing with an economics that concern not the rational utilization of scarce resources, but the very opposite: the rational utilization of what can and ought to be the opposite of scarce. In identifying knowledge and teaching of the Torah as the ultimate value, the successor-system has not simply constructed a new economics in place of an old one, finding of value something other than had earlier been valued; it has redefined economics altogether. It has done so, as a matter of fact, in a manner that is entirely familiar, by setting forth in place of an economics of scarcity an economics of abundant productivity.

Disenlandising value thus transvalues value by insisting upon its (potential) increase as the definition of what is rational economic action. The task is not preservation of power over land but increase of power over the Torah, because one can only preserve land, but one can increase one's knowledge of the Torah. So, to revert to the theoretical point that in context seemed so excessive, the economics of the initial system concerns the rational disposition of the scarce resource comprised by particular real property; the rational increase of the potentially-abundant resource comprised by Torah-learning is – serves and functions as – the economics of the successor-system.

3

Empowerment and the Category, "The People Israel"

Philosophical politics stated roughly tells who may legitimately do what to whom. When a politics wants to know who ought *not* to be doing what to whom, we find in hand the counterpart-category to the received politics.[1] The received category set forth politics as the theory of legitimate violence, the counterpart-category, politics as the theory of *illegitimate* violence. The received politics had been one of isolation and interiority, portraying Israel as sui generis and autocephalic in all ways. The portrait in the successor-documents is a politics of integration among the nations; a perspective of exteriority replaces the inner-facing one of the Mishnah, which recognized no government of Israel but God's – and then essentially ab initio. The issues of power had found definition in questions concerning who legitimately inflicts sanctions upon whom within Israel. They now shift to give an account of who illegitimately inflicts sanctions upon ("persecutes") Israel. So the points of systemic differentiation are radically revised, and the politics of the successor-system becomes not a revision of the received category but a formation that in many ways mirrors the received one: once more a counterpart-category. Just as, in the definition of scarce resources, Torah-study has replaced land, so now weakness forms the focus in place of strength, illegitimacy in place of legitimacy. Once more the mirror-image of the received category presents the perspective of the counterpart-category.

---

[1] That is, of course, as much as, in the contrast of real wealth and true value, that is to say, land and Torah-learning, we identify not a revised economics but a counterpart-category to the familiar economics.

The politics of the successor-system turns outward, its attention focused upon the world in which Israel finds itself. Israel differentiated by its castes, Israel as taxic indicator – these categories no longer formed the center of exegetical attention.[2] Instead, with Israel viewed whole, the opposite of "Israel" is now not "Levite, then Priest," or (in the opposite direction) "gentile," but "the nations." Israel then is one and whole vis à vis outsiders, who are seen as many and distinct. Israel as the victim of illegitimate violence and the nations as illegitimately empowered now defined the main-beams of the categorical structure of the successor-system's politics. That fact justifies the classification of the system's politics as not a mere revision but an utter inversion, hence, as is now clear, a counterpart category. The received components – way of life, world view, social entity – all are recast in category, not merely content, and that explains why, in regard to the definition of the social entity, the realm of empowerment, in particular, to be "Israel" now meant to be the victim of the illegitimate exercise of power. The new system then classified Israel in context and transitively, as a nation among nations, subject to the will of outsiders, not out of context and intransitively, as an autonomous and free-standing social entity.

The data given to us in the successor-documents, when they speak on their own account and not in clarification of the Mishnah and related writings, shift in character. Now we find the answers to these questions: to whom is violence illegitimately done, and also, who may not legitimately inflict violence? With the move from the politics of legitimate to that of illegitimate power, the systemic interest now lies in defining not the who legitimately does what, but rather, the to whom, against whom, is power illegitimately exercised. And this movement represents not the revision of the received category, but its inversion. For thought on legitimate violence is turned on its head. A new category of empowerment is worked out alongside the old. The entity that is victim of power is at the center, rather than the entity that legitimately exercises power. That entity is now Israel *en masse*, rather than the institutions and agencies of Israel on earth, Heaven above – a very considerable shift in thought on the systemic social entity. Israel as

---

[2]The entire argument of this chapter forms an amplification of Jonathan Z. Smith's statement, "The history of religion is the exegesis of exegesis," in William Scott Green, ed., *Approaches to Ancient Judaism* (Chico, 19??: Scholars Press for Brown Judaic Studies).

disempowered, rather than king, high priest, and sage as Israel's media of empowerment, defines the new system's politics.

In laying claim to the status of empowerment, thought on legitimate violence now asks about the illegitimacy of violence inflicted upon social entities – which nonetheless also are conceived as political entities, rather than the legitimacy of violence inflicted by them.[3] This is as much a new mode of classification, an utterly fresh category as the odd and unpredictable economics reconsidered in the transvaluation of value But as that remained an economics, so in hand is still a politics. The reason is that the question we now seek to answer remains the same as before: who inflicts sanctions on whom and why? On what entities do discussions of violence focus?

It follows that we address a political question to an empowered entity. But the answer – the focus of attention within political thought – now centers upon the violence inflicted upon Israel, the nation, and differentiation now is among those who illegitimately act violently. True, when they speak of who legitimately exercises violence (in addition to Heaven, of course), sages refer to the sage. That happens to constitute a mere extension of the received system, which had assigned sages mastery of the courts, alongside the monarchy and the high priesthood. But when the successor-writings tell us upon whom violence is legitimately exercised and by whom, there is a wholly new realm of thinking going on.

We recall that the Mishnah's government for Israel had comprised, on earth, a tripartite structure of high priest and a king, with administrative courts of sages alongside, ascending upward to the authority of the Temple mount. Above, and corresponding, is the court in Heaven. That court bears its jurisdiction for some actions, the earthly political institutions each exercised its jurisdiction for others, and the point of differentiation set forth the urgent and compelling systemic issue in the political component of the system, just as it did in the other components. The Talmud of the Land of Israel and its companion-compilations of scriptural exegeses for their part do not even pretend that such an ordered, self-governing world existed in their time, or, for that matter, ever. They present the portrait of administration by an unstructured set of small-claims courts standing outside an appellate structure of authority, petty bureaus of administration of trivial things, over which rabbis, defined as judges, lawyers, and masters of disciples in the law,

---

[3]Israel in the successor-system is not only a social entity. It also is represented as empowered to make choices and set norms and impose sanctions, hence must be deemed also a political entity.

presided. At the head of it all is a patriarch, not a king, on the one side or a priest anointed for the purpose, on the other. And the patriarch is variously represented as honorable and not. So many well-composed institutions of politics now give way to a single kind of institution, and a vertical structure is set aside by a horizontal one. These institutional differences as to fact signal a deeper difference as to system.

The Mishnah's account of practical politics and that of the Yerushalmi prove discontinuous not only in structure but also in system, for the discontinuity reveals itself in the theory of empowerment. Now gentiles are deemed not only empowered but also subject to differentiation. The earlier system had concerned itself with the internal politics of (an) Israel, with politics seen as principal taxic indicator of the social order. The later politics, by contrast, turned toward the external relationships of (an) Israel located in the disorderly world of nations. So the new politics has not only inverted the issue of violence and turned its illegitimate side upward. It also has revised the systemic vision so that attention faced outward, differentiation among the outsider vis à vis (an) undifferentiated Israel being the result. So the successor-system's definition of what is at stake in the theory of legitimate violence that forms the centerpiece of politics therefore proves wholly other.

The burden of the systemic message assigned to the component of politics remained equally heavy in the successor-system. But the contents proved quite dissimilar. The Mishnah's political theory had focused upon the inner structure and composition of Israel's social order; politics served the systemic purpose of setting forth the hierarchical taxonomy of power, just as each of the other principal parts of the Mishnah's statement of the social order represented the classification and ordering of all classes of things. When, for the Mishnah's politics, we know who within Israel legitimately inflicts sanctions upon whom within Israel, the principle of differentiation yields a clear picture of the organization of Israelite society. So the role of politics in the philosophical statement of Judaism is to represent the theoretical standing of the empowered institutions, the ones that bear the political role and responsibility. As we shall now see, the task of politics in the successor-system accomplished a different sort of differentiation altogether.

The systemic message now concerned an Israel lacking all capacity to effect violence, requiring an explanation of its illegitimacy. No longer an empowered nation, Israel – within the systemic writings of the late fourth and fifth century – speculates on who is the worst among the nations, what will come of Israel, when Israel will once more take charge of its own affairs. That explains why, to deliver the systemic message, it was not only the *illegitimate* exercise of power, but differentiation among the entities, institutions and persons, that illegitimately inflict violence would require attention.[4] Formerly sorting out who properly inflicts which sanction upon whom, now the system's political analysis concerns both the actor, now the illegitimate one, and the victim, equally illegitimate. And that inversion brings us back to our interest in not the reformation of received categories but the formation of the counterpart ones: to what systemic purpose? The answer, for the economics of never-scarce Torah of the successor-system, lies right at the surface. What about the politics of weakness?

At stake is always the social entity, for a politics – commonplace and conventional or counterpart and odd – bears the burden of definition of the social entity of the encompassing system. And here we locate the systemic message delivered by the anti-politics. The counterpart-category is one that in fact rejects as beside the point what makes a politics political: the legitimate use of violence. The data that will be sought attest to the very opposite facts. For now, as a matter of fact, all violence, but God's and the sages', is illegitimate. The political entity that Israel is to form is an anti-political one, in that it defines itself not by appeal to its legitimate exercise of sanctions, but rather by its exercising no power at all. The social entity in the politics at hand is made, therefore, to affirm the status of the victim, once again a social entity for an anti-politics indeed.

This political ideal reaches its simplest formulation in the bald statement that all God – after all, the All-Powerful – wants is the victim, done to but never doing:[5]

---

[4]The explanation for the shift deriving from the change in Israel's historical political condition begs the question. When the Mishnah was written, Israel did not govern itself through a king, high priest, and sages' court, and such a system was a complete fabrication. There never was a point in the history of Israel in the land of Israel in which such a fabrication approximated political facts. So if the initial system presented a political fantasy, we have no reason to explain its revision, or complete rejection in favor of a different system, by reason of a discovery of a change in the facts of the matter. On the contrary, the sages of the successor-documents had no more keen interest in empirical observation and verification than did the ones of the Mishnah and its companions.

[5]Here is, by the way, another splendid example of Listenwissenschaft as practiced in the Midrash-compilations, evidence that the framers of those

Leviticus Rabbah XXVII:V

1. A. "God seeks what has been driven away" (Qoh. 3:15).
   B. R. Huna in the name of R. Joseph said, "It is always the case that 'God seeks what has been driven away' [favoring the victim].
   C. "You find when a righteous man pursues a righteous man, 'God seeks what has been driven away.'
   D. "When a wicked man pursues a wicked man, 'God seeks what has been driven away.'
   E. "All the more so when a wicked man pursues a righteous man, 'God seeks what has been driven away.'
   F. "[The same principle applies] even when you come around to a case in which a righteous man pursues a wicked man, 'God seeks what has been driven away.'"
2. A. R. Yosé b. R. Yudan in the name of R. Yosé b. R. Nehorai says, "It is always the case that the Holy One, blessed be He, demands an accounting for the blood of those who have been pursued from the hand of the pursuer.
   B. "Abel was pursued by Cain, and God sought [an accounting for] the pursued: 'And the Lord looked [favorably] upon Abel and his meal offering' [Gen. 4:4].
   C. "Noah was pursued by his generation, and God sought [an accounting for] the pursued: 'You and all your household shall come into the ark' [Gen. 7:1]. And it says, 'For this is like the days of Noah to me, as I swore [that the waters of Noah should no more go over the earth]' [Isa. 54:9].
   D. "Abraham was pursued by Nimrod, 'and God seeks what has been driven away': 'You are the Lord, the God who chose Abram and brought him out of Ur' [Neh. 9:7].
   E. "Isaac was pursued by Ishmael, 'and God seeks what has been driven away': 'For through Isaac will seed be called for you' [Gen. 21:12].
   F. "Jacob was pursued by Esau, 'and God seeks what has been driven away': 'For the Lord has chosen Jacob, Israel for his prized possession' [Ps. 135:4].
   G. "Moses was pursued by Pharaoh, 'and God seeks what has been driven away': 'Had not Moses His chosen stood in the breach before Him' [Ps. 106:23].
   H. "David was pursued by Saul, 'and God seeks what has been driven away': 'And he chose David, his servant' [Ps. 78:70].
   I. "Israel was pursued by the nations, 'and God seeks what has been driven away': 'And you has the Lord chosen to be a people to him' [Deut. 14:2].
   J. "And the rule applies also to the matter of offerings. A bull is pursued by a lion, a sheep is pursued by a wolf, a goat is pursued by a leopard.

---

compilations did not differ in fundamental mode of thought and argument from the authorship of the Mishnah.

K. "Therefore the Holy One, blessed be He, has said, 'Do not make offerings before me from those animals that pursue, but from those that are pursued: 'When a bull, a sheep, or a goat is born'" (Lev. 22:27).

I can offer no better evidence that a new sense altogether has been imputed to the consideration of the legitimacy of power. No longer does politics explain the uses of power: within what sort of institutions and upon the basis of what kind of rationale, for example. The issue is now exactly the opposite: the legitimacy of powerlessness, the illegitimacy of (nearly all) power. That at stake are issues we should regard as political, not (merely) theological is underlines when Israel as such enters: it is Israel contrasted with the nations, and as the latter form political entities, so does the former. That then shows what I mean when I speak of an anti-politics, an inversion of the category to focus upon not the legitimate but the illegitimate exercise of power, upon not the actor but the victim.

This new thinking draws attention to new foci of differentiation as well. Formerly, it was the social entity, Israel, that was differentiated by its taxic components. When we wished to know who legitimately inflicts sanctions upon whom, we turned to the diverse components of the social entity, Israel, analyzed and differentiated within the interiorities of its order and structure. Now the undifferentiation of Israel – no longer ordered by its castes, for instance – finds its mirror, opposite, and counterpart in the differentiation of the nations (and, of course, Israel among them). These are ordered, in the manner in which the Israelite castes had been ordered;[6] so now hierarchical taxonomy tells us how we are to sort out the affairs of nations in relationship to Israel. But what can this possibly mean? It is that the violence inflicted upon Israel by one nation may be more illegitimate than that inflicted upon Israel by another.

Then Israel's history entered systemic discourse, with the facts of what one gentile ruler had done compared to those of what some other had inflicted now enjoying importance as a medium for differentiation among outsiders. So "Israel" became a historical entity, subject to historical narratives. The Mishnah and related writings had not presented and, systemically, did not find necessary the provision of historical narratives. Now, by contrast, Israel became a hero of a story with a crisis and denouement. The story

---

[6]But, as we shall see, the ordering focused upon Israel and anti-Israel, Rome, and the point of ordering was to reckon with the temporal sequence of rule: Rome, then Israel.

bearing the systemic message of the social entity in a political form, in an infinity of ways always told a tale about what it meant to be empowered but also subjected to the empowerment of others.

Stories about illegitimacy violence then told what it meant to form a social entity with traits that were intrinsic and concrete and material, and not merely indicative aspects of abstract relationships of comparison and contrast.[7] The successors' systemic "Israel" now became transitive and contextual, not merely occupying a given, transitive position within a hierarchical order of being or exhibiting certain taxic indicators of hierarchical meaning. And, as a corollary, other important systemic categories, such as the "gentile," also acquired material definition and concrete nuance, as the systemic exercise in differentiation affected diverse components of the whole. In the successor-system, specifically, Israel bears three meanings: [1] family, that is, a social entity different from the nations because it is formed by a common genealogy; [2] nation among nations; and [3] Israel as *sui generis*, different not in indicative traits but categorically, that is to say, in its very category from all other nations.

To begin with, when sages in the successor-documents wished to know what (an) "Israel" was, they reread the story of Scripture's "Israel's" origins for the answer. Scripture told them the story of "Israel" a man, Jacob. His children therefore are "the children of Jacob." That man's name was also "Israel," and, it followed, "the children of Israel" comprised the extended family of that man. By extension upward, "Israel" formed the family of Abraham and Sarah, Isaac and Rebecca, Jacob and Leah and Rachel. "Israel" therefore invoked the metaphor of genealogy to explain the bonds that linked persons unseen into a single social entity; the shared traits were imputed, not empirical. That social metaphor of "Israel" – a simple one, really, and easily grasped – bore consequences in two ways. First, children in general are admonished to follow the good example of their parents. The deeds of the patriarchs and matriarchs therefore taught lessons on how the children were to act.

---

[7]"Israel" on its own terms therefore yielded not merely allusions or references to a given taxonomic classifier but accounts, including narratives or "histories," of "Israel" viewed as a social entity, a group, fully defined concretely and autonomously and not only as an abstraction. The appearance in this stratum of the canon of narratives is not accidental but entirely indicative, and that means we must ask systemic questions of narrative and its uses. I have explored this question in a very different context in my *Judaism and Story: The Evidence of The Fathers According to Rabbi Nathan* (Chicago, 1991: The University of Chicago Press).

Of greater interest in an account of "Israel" as a social metaphor, "Israel" lived twice, once in the patriarchs and matriarchs, a second time in the life of the heirs as the descendants relived those earlier lives. The stories of the family were carefully reread to provide a picture of the meaning of the latter-day events of the descendants of that same family. Accordingly, the lives of the patriarchs signaled the history of Israel.[8]

The metaphor of Israel as family supplied an encompassing theory of society, accounting for that sense of constituting a corporate social entity that clearly infused the documents of the Judaism of the Dual Torah from the very outset. Such a theory explained not only who "Israel" as a whole was. It also set forth the responsibilities of Israel's social entity, its society; it defined the character of that entity; it explained who owes what to whom at why, therefore, of course, the politics of empowerment as well; and it accounted for the inner structure and interplay of relationship within the community, here and now, constituted by Jews in their villages and neighborhoods of towns. Accordingly, "Israel" as family bridged the gap between an account of the entirety of the social group, "Israel," and a picture of the components of that social group as they lived out their lives in their households and villages. An encompassing theory of society, covering all components from least to greatest, holding the whole together in correct order and proportion, derived from "Israel" viewed as extended family.

A single example of the consequence of representing Israel as a family emerges from Genesis Rabbah. Here "Israel" as family also understood itself to form a nation or people. That nation-people held a land, a rather peculiar, enchanted or holy, Land at that, one that, in its imputed traits, was as *sui generis* as (presently we shall see) in the metaphorical thought of the system at hand, Israel also was. Competing for the same territory, Israel's claim to what it called the

---

[8]The polemical purpose of the claim that that abstraction, "Israel," was to be compared to the family of the mythic ancestor lies right at the surface. With another "Israel," the Christian Church, now claiming to constitute the true one, Jews found it possible to confront that claim and to turn it against the other side. "You claim to form 'Israel after the spirit.' Fine, and *we* are Israel after the flesh – and genealogy forms the link, that alone." (Converts did not present an anomaly, of course, since they were held to be children of Abraham and Sarah, who had "made souls," that is, converts, in Haran, a point repeated in the documents of the period.) That fleshly continuity formed of all of "us" a single family, rendering spurious the notion that "Israel" could be other than genealogically defined. But that polemic seems to me adventitious and not primary. At the same time the metaphor provided a quite separate component to sages' larger system.

Land of Israel – thus, *of Israel* in particular – now rested on right of inheritance such as a family enjoyed, and this was made explicit. The passage shows how high the stakes were in the claim to constitute the genealogical descendant of the ancestors.

Genesis Rabbah LXI:VII

1. A. "But to the sons of his concubines, Abraham gave gifts, and while he was still living, he sent them away from his son Isaac, eastward to the east country" (Gen. 25:6):
   B. In the time of Alexander of Macedonia the sons of Ishmael came to dispute with Israel about the birthright, and with them came two wicked families, the Canaanites and the Egyptians.
   C. They said, "Who will go and engage in a disputation with them."
   D. Gebiah b. Qosem [the enchanter] said, "I shall go and engage in a disputation with them."
   E. They said to him, "Be careful not to let the Land of Israel fall into their possession."
   F. He said to them, "I shall go and engage in a disputation with them. If I win over them, well and good. And if not, you may say, 'Who is this hunchback to represent us?'"
   G. He went and engaged in a disputation with them. Said to them Alexander of Macedonia, "Who lays claim against whom?"
   H. The Ishmaelites said, "We lay claim, and we bring our evidence from their own Torah: 'But he shall acknowledge the firstborn, the son of the hated' (Deut. 21;17). Now Ishmael was the firstborn. [We therefore claim the land as heirs of the first-born of Abraham.]"
   I. Said to him Gebiah b. Qosem, "My royal lord, does a man not do whatever he likes with his sons?"
   J. He said to him, "Indeed so."
   K. "And lo, it is written, 'Abraham gave all that he had to Isaac' (Gen. 25:2)."
   L. [Alexander asked,] "Then where is the deed of gift to the other sons?"
   M. He said to him, "'But to the sons of his concubines, Abraham gave gifts, [and while he was still living, he sent them away from his son Isaac, eastward to the east country]' (Gen. 25:6)."
   N. [The Ishmaelites had no claim on the land.] They abandoned the field in shame.

The metaphor now shifts, with the notion of Israel today as the family of Abraham, as against the Ishmaelites, also of the same family, gives way. But the theme of family records persists. Canaan has no claim, for Canaan was also a family, comparable to Israel – but descended from a slave. The power of the metaphor of family is that it can explain not only the social entity formed by Jews, but the social entities confronted by them. All fell into the same genus, making up diverse species. The theory of society before

Empowerment and the Category "The People Israel"

us – that is, the theory of "Israel" – thus accounts for the existence, also, of all societies, and when we deal with Rome, the theory of "Israel" does so with extraordinary force.

O. The Canaanites said, "We lay claim, and we bring our evidence from their own Torah. Throughout their Torah it is written, 'the land of Canaan.' So let them give us back our land."

P. Said to him Gebiah b. Qosem, "My royal lord, does a man not do whatever he likes with his slave?"

Q. He said to him, "Indeed so."

R. He said to him, "And lo, it is written, 'A slave of slaves shall Canaan be to his brothers' (Gen. 9:25). So they are really our slaves."

S. [The Cannanites had no claim to the land and in fact should be serving Israel.] They abandoned the field in shame.

The same metaphor serves both "Israel" and "Canaan." Each formed the latter-day heir of the earliest family, and both lived out the original paradigm. The mode of thought at hand assigns to the same genus both social entities, then makes it possible to distinguish among the two species at hand. The final claim in the passage before us moves away from the metaphor of family. But the notion of a continuous, physical descent is implicit here as well. "Israel" has inherited the wealth of Egypt. Since the notion of inheritance forms a component of the metaphor of family (a conception critical in the supernatural patrimony of the "children of Israel" in the merit of the ancestors), we survey the conclusion of the passage.

T. The Egyptians said, "We lay claim, and we bring our evidence from their own Torah. Six hundred thousand of them left us, taking away our silver and gold utensils: 'They despoiled the Egyptians' (Ex. 12:36). Let them give them back to us."

U. Gebiah b. Qosem said, "My royal lord, six hundred thousand men worked for them for two hundred and ten years, some as silversmiths and some as goldsmiths. Let them pay us our salary at the rate of a *denar* a day."

V. The mathematicians went and added up what was owing, and they had not reached the sum covering a century before the Egyptians had to forfeit what they had claimed. They abandoned the field in shame.

V. [Alexander] wanted to go up to Jerusalem. The Samaritans said to him, "Be careful. They will not permit you to enter their most holy sanctuary."

W. When Gebiah b. Qosem found out about this, he went and made for himself two felt shoes, with two precious stones worth twenty-thousand pieces of silver set in them. When he got to the mountain of the house [of the Temple], he said to him, "My royal lord, take off your shoes and put on these two felt slippers, for the floor is slippery, and you should not slip and fall."

	X.	When they came to the most holy sanctuary, he said to him, "Up to this point, we have the right to enter. From this point onward, we do not have the right to enter."
	Y.	He said to him, "When we get out of here, I'm going to even out your hump."
	Z.	He said to him, "You will be called a great surgeon and get a big fee."

The Ishmaelites, Abraham's children, deprived as they were of their inheritance, fall into the same genus as does Israel. So, too, did Canaan. As to the Egyptians, that is a different matter. Now "Israel" is that same "Israel" of which Scripture spoke. The social metaphor shifts within the story, though, of course, the story is not affected.

How about Israel as victim of illegitimate power, such as formed the centerpiece of the counterpart category of politics? Illegitimate power was exercised by a member of the same family, and the illegitimacy of his power derived from his genealogical illegitimacy. Indeed, the metaphor of family made possible the differentiation in material and concrete terms between the legitimate and the illegitimate, since, after all, to begin with these formed genealogical classifications, and only by analogy and metaphor, classifications of other sorts of data altogether. So the consequence of the appeal to the genealogical metaphor for the categorization of Israel emerges when we turn from the legitimate to the illegitimate political entity.

It is, of course, Rome. The comparison of one line of a family to another line of the same family, the legitimate and the illegitimate, prepares the way for the system's project of the comprehensive interpretation of world-politics. Here is how the comparison and contrast of political entities within the genealogical metaphor takes place.

Genesis Rabbah LXX:XV

1.	A.	"Now Laban had two daughters, the name of the older was Leah, and the name of the younger was Rachel" (Gen. 29:16):
	B.	They were like two beams running from one end of the world to the other.
	C.	This one produced captains and that one produced captains, this one produced kings and that one produced kings, this one produced lion-tamers and that one produced lion-tamers, this one produced conquerors of nations and that one produced conquerors of nations, this one produced those who divided countries and that one produced dividers of countries.

- D. The offering brought by the son of this one overrode the prohibitions of the Sabbath, and the offering brought by the son of that one overrode the prohibitions of the Sabbath.
- E. The war fought by this one overrode the prohibitions of the Sabbath, and the war fought by this one overrode the prohibitions of the Sabbath.
- F. To this one were given two nights, and to that one were given two nights.
- G. The night of Pharaoh and the night of Sennacherib were for Leah, and the night of Gideon for Rachel, and the night of Mordecai was for Rachel, as it is said, "On that night the king could not sleep" (Est 6:1).

The genealogical metaphor therefore encompasses not only "Israel" but also "Rome." It makes sense of all the important social entities, for in this metaphor, "Israel" is consubstantial with other social entities, which relate to "Israel" just as "Israel" as a society relates to itself, present and past.

What is important in the metaphor of Israel as family is how that metaphor governs the conceptualization of the other political components of sages' world. We recognize the result for the treatment of Rome: Rome is Edom, or Ishmael, or Esau – always the rejected line of the authentic ancestor. History works out the tale of siblings, of whom only one is legitimate, and history is written in the tale of the relationship of Israel and Rome. Rome as Israel's brother, counterpart, and nemesis. Rome is now is what stands in the way of Israel's, and the world's, ultimate salvation. It is, of course, not a (merely) political Rome but a political and messianic Rome, participating in the sacred, that is, the familial, history of Israel, that is at issue. At stake is Rome as surrogate for Israel, Rome as obstacle to Israel. But "Rome" as family shades over into "Rome" as empire and state, comparable to "Israel" as a nation or state – and as the coming empire too. For while "Rome" stands for "Esau," the metaphorization of Rome moves into fresh ground, since Rome is differentiated from other nations, and hence the exegetical task of the new politics shifts from the differentiation of entities within Israel to the comparison and contrast of entities outside.

Accordingly, "Rome" is a family just as is "Israel," and, more to the point, "Rome" enters into "Israel's" life in an intelligible way precisely because "Rome," too, is a part of that same family that is constituted by "Israel." The comparison of "Israel" and "Rome" to states, nations, peoples, empires, rests on, comes to expression in, and is generated by the genealogical metaphor. And that singles out Rome alongside Israel; now "Rome" is like "Israel" in a way in which no other state or nation is like "Israel." Rome emerges as both like and also not-like "Israel," in ways in which no other nation is ever represented as "like-Israel;" and, it follows, "Israel" is like "Rome" in ways in which "Israel is not like any other people or nation.

So the counterpart-category introduces illegitimate power and explains it. That initiative, within its own logic, then requires the differentiation of outsiders, who, being different from the outsider, Rome, by definition are – can be – no longer all the same. But the genealogical account takes no systemic risks[9] in simply turning the outsider into an illegitimate insider. The metaphor that joins past to present, household to household – the whole, then, to "all Israel," in fact encompasses the other noteworthy social entity and takes it into full account – a powerful, successful field-theory indeed. That the theory is a distinctively political one hardly requires extended argument; Rome imposes sanctions illegitimately, Israel, legitimately. The one forms the opposite of the other; the politics of the one is the mirror of that of the other.

But the systemic focus – the exegetical task imposed by the requirement of differentiation – has shifted, and so there is a new work of differentiation. Specifically, identifying Rome as different from other outsiders of political consequence now required differentiation among the rest of those same outsiders. And that led directly to an account of the history of the empires, all of them viewed within the same frame and perspective, and of Israel's place among them. Once introduced, Rome took up a place in the unfolding of the empires – Babylonia, Media, Greece, then Rome. "Israel" takes its place in that unfolding pattern, and hence is consubstantial with Babylonia, Media, Greece, and Rome. In that context, "Rome" and "Israel" do form counterparts and opposites. Still more important Rome is the penultimate empire on earth. Israel will constitute the ultimate one. The illegitimacy of the one politics will be replaced in due course by the legitimacy of power exercised by Israel through its anointed king. Politics now enters history: change, movement, direction, purpose. The initial system bore no teleology made explicit; the successor-system is all teleology, wholly historical in medium, entirely historical in message. That systemic message pointed to the shifts in world history to elicit a pattern and place at the apex Israel itself.

Metaphorical thinking moves beyond in context moves beyond the metaphor of genealogy. All of this required the invention of a new

---

[9]Within their context, systems never take risks, since always at stake is self-evidence.

metaphor, and the one that was chosen, borrowed of course from Daniel, bears a not-very-subtle polemic, comparing as it did, various nations with various animals. Only Israel is spared an assignment in the political bestiary. The main point, of course, is Esau. Esau is compared not only to Israel – unambiguous Israel – but also to a pig – the most ambiguous of beasts within the levitical taxonomy. The analogy is apt, for the pig exhibits public traits expected of a suitable beast, in that it shows a cloven hoof, such as the levitical laws of acceptable beasts require. But the pig does not exhibit the inner traits of a suitable beast, in that it does not chew the cud. Accordingly, the pig confuses and deceives.[10] Here is how the matter is expressed, in a passage that rings the changes on all of the themes before us: legitimate as against illegitimate power, the complex genealogy of Israel and Rome, the victim and the victor now and in the end of history:

Leviticus Rabbah XIII:V

9. A. Moses foresaw what the evil kingdoms would do [to Israel].
   B. "The camel, rock badger, and hare" (Deut. 14:7). [Compare: "Nevertheless, among those that chew the cud or part the hoof, you shall not eat these: the camel, because it chews the cud but does not part the hoof, is unclean to you. The rock badger, because it chews the cud but does not part the hoof, is unclean to you. And the hare, because it chews the cud but does not part the hoof, is unclean to you, and the pig, because it parts the hoof and is cloven-footed, but does not chew the cud, is unclean to you" (Lev. 11:4-8).]
   C. The camel (GML) refers to Babylonia, [in line with the following verse of Scripture: "O daughter of Babylonia, you who are to be devastated!] Happy will be he who requites (GML) you, with what you have done to us" (Ps. 147:8).
   D. "The rock badger" (Deut. 14:7) – this refers to Media.
   E. Rabbis and R. Judah b. R. Simon.
   F. Rabbis say, "Just as the rock badger exhibits traits of uncleanness and traits of cleanness, so the kingdom of Media produced both a righteous man and a wicked one."
   G. Said R. Judah b. R. Simon, "The last Darius was Esther's son. He was clean on his mother's side and unclean on his father's side."

---

[10]The polemic against Esau=Rome is simple. Rome claims to be Israel in that it adheres to the Old Testament, that is, the written Torah of Sinai. Specifically, Rome is represented as only Christian Rome can have been represented: it superficially *looks* kosher but it is unkosher. Pagan Rome cannot ever have looked kosher, but Christian Rome, with its appeal to continuity with ancient Israel, could and did and moreover claimed to. It bore some traits that validate, but lacked others that validate.

H.	"The hare" (Deut 14:7) – this refers to Greece. The mother of King Ptolemy was named "Hare" [in Greek: lagos].
I.	"The pig" (Deut. 14:7) – this refers to Edom [Rome].
J.	Moses made mention of the first three in a single verse and the final one in a verse by itself [(Deut. 14:7, 8)]. Why so?
K.	R. Yohanan and R. Simeon b. Laqish.
L.	R. Yohanan said, "It is because [the pig] is equivalent to the other three."
M.	And R. Simeon b. Laqish said, "It is because it outweighs them."
N.	R. Yohanan objected to R. Simeon b. Laqish, "'Prophesy, therefore, son of man, clap your hands [and let the sword come down twice, yea thrice]' (Ezek. 21:14)."
O.	And how does R. Simeon b. Laqish interpret the same passage? He notes that [the threefold sword] is doubled (Ezek. 21:14).

In the apocalypticizing of the animals of Lev. 11:4-8/Deut. 14:7, the camel, rock badger, hare, and pig, the pig, standing for Rome, again emerges as different from the others and more threatening than the rest. Just as the pig pretends to be a clean beast by showing the cloven hoof, but in fact is an unclean one, so Rome pretends to be just but in fact governs by thuggery. Edom does not pretend to praise God but only blasphemes. It does not exalt the righteous but kills them. I cannot imagine a more expressive anti-politics than the composition before us.[11] Of greatest importance, while all the other beasts bring further ones in their wake, the pig does not: "It does not bring another kingdom after it." It will restore the crown to the one who will truly deserve it, Israel. Esau will be judged by Zion, so Obadiah 1:21. Beyond Rome, standing in a straight line with the others, lies the true shift in politics, which is a caesura in history, the rule of Israel and the cessation of the dominion of the nations.

Metaphor hardly limited the modes of systemic thought. Israel also found representation as beyond all metaphor. Seeing "Israel" as *sui generis* yielded a sustained interest in the natural laws governing "Israel" in particular, statements of the rules of the group's history viewed as a unique entity within time. The historical-eschatological formulation of a political teleology in that way moved from an account of illegitimate power to a formulation of the theory of the inappropriate victim, that is to say, of Israel itself. Sentences out of

---

[11]That these symbols concede nothing to Christian monotheism and veneration of the Torah of Moses (in its written medium) is obvious, but not the point of analysis here. Rome in the fourth century became Christian. Sages responded by facing that fact quite squarely and saying, "Indeed, it is as you say, a kind of Israel, an heir of Abraham as your texts explicitly claim. But we remain the sole legitimate Israel, the bearer of the birthright – we and not you. So you are our brother: Esau, Ishmael, Edom." And the rest follows.

the factual record of the past formed into a cogent statement of the laws of "Israel's" destiny, laws unique to the social entity at hand. Second, the teleology of those laws for an Israel that was *sui generis* focused upon salvation at the end of history, that is, an eschatological teleology formed for a social entity embarked on its own lonely journey through time. The conception of "Israel" as *sui generis*, third, reaches expression in an implicit statement that Israel is subject to its own laws, which are distinct from the laws governing all other social entities. These laws may be discerned in the factual, scriptural record of "Israel's" past, and that past, by definition, belonged to "Israel" alone. It followed, therefore, that by discerning the regularities in "Israel's" history, implicitly understood as unique to "Israel," sages recorded the view that "Israel" like God was not subject to analogy or comparison. Accordingly, while not labeled a genus unto itself, Israel is treated in that way.

The theory of Israel as *sui generis* produced a political theory in which Israel's sole legitimate ruler is God, and whoever legitimately governs does so as God's surrogate. The theory of legitimate sanctions then is recast into a religious statement of God's place in Israel's existence, but retains its political valence when we recall that the sage, the man most fully "in our image, after our likeness," governs in accord with the law of the Torah. Here is a brief statement, framed out of the materials of Leviticus Rabbah, of the successor-documents' political theory that forms also a theological creed. In it we see the definition of legitimate violence: God's alone. The theory, stated in my own words by way of summary of the doctrine of Leviticus Rabbah, is as follows: God loves Israel, so gave them the Torah, which defines their life and governs their welfare. Israel is alone in its category (*sui generis*), proved by the fact that what is a virtue to Israel is a vice to the nation, life-giving to Israel, poison to the gentiles.

True, Israel sins, but God forgives that sin, having punished the nation on account of it. Such a process has yet to come to an end, but it will culminate in Israel's complete regeneration. Meanwhile, Israel's assurance of God's love lies in the many expressions of special concern, for even the humblest and most ordinary aspects of the national life: the food the nation eats, the sexual practices by which it procreates. These life-sustaining, life-transmitting activities draw God's special interest, as a mark of his general love for Israel. Israel then is supposed to achieve its life in conformity with the marks of God's love. These indications moreover signify also the character of Israel's difficulty, namely, subordination to the nations in general, but to the fourth kingdom, Rome, in particular.

Both food laws and skin diseases stand for the nations. There is yet another category of sin, also collective and generative of collective punishment, and that is social. The moral character of Israel's life, the treatment of people by one another, the practice of gossip and small-scale thuggery – these, too, draw down divine penalty. The nation's fate therefore corresponds to its moral condition. The moral condition, however, emerges not only from the current generation. Israel's richest hope lies in the merit of the ancestors, thus in the Scriptural record of the merits attained by the founders of the nation, those who originally brought it into being and gave it life.

This static tableau tells us the structure of the politics. What of its system: its account of how things actually work from day to day? Leviticus Rabbah also presents recurrent lists of events in Israel's (unique) history, meaning Israel's history solely in scriptural times, down through the return to Zion. The lists, all of them concerning the exercise of power, sometimes legitimately, sometimes not, again and again ring the changes on the one-time events of the generation of the flood, Sodom and Gomorrah, the patriarchs and the sojourn in Egypt, the exodus, the revelation of the Torah at Sinai, the golden calf, the Davidic monarchy and the building of the Temple, Sennacherib, Hezekiah, and the destruction of northern Israel, Nebuchadnezzar and the destruction of the Temple in 586, the life of Israel in Babylonian captivity, Daniel and his associates, Mordecai and Haman. These events occur over and over again. They turn out to serve as paradigms.

We find, in fact, a fairly standard repertoire of scriptural heroes or villains, on the one side, and conventional lists of Israel's enemies and their actions and downfall, on the other. The boastful, for instance, include the generation of the flood, Sodom and Gomorrah, Pharaoh, Sisera, Sennacherib, Nebuchadnezzar, the wicked empire (Rome) – contrasted to Israel, "despised and humble in this world." The four kingdoms recur again and again, always ending, of course, with Rome, with the repeated message that after Rome will come Israel. But Israel has to make this happen through its faith and submission to God's will. Cain, the Sodomites, Pharaoh, Sennacherib, Nebuchadnezzar, Haman – all exemplify the illegitimate uses of power, which expresses arrogance. So the political virtue is its opposite: to be politically correct, one must eschew power; to be politically illegitimate, one exercises power. I cannot think of a finer example of what it means to compose a counterpart-category, an anti-politics in place of a politics.

Then who rules legitimately? It can only be the sage, who defines the political class and the political institution of Israel, rightly construed. Israel is *sui generis* in that it exhibits the traits of the sages, and sages' group's traits, for their part, have no counterpart, in sages' view, in this world, but only in heaven. In God's image, after God's likeness, Moses "our rabbi" forms the model for sages, and sages, for "Israel." Conformity to sages' rule, which is the sole legitimate power within Israel, defines the condition for the Messiah's coming, that is, the establishment, in place of the illegitimate government, of a legitimate politics. That conviction comes to expression in repeated calls for "repentance," meaning, of course, conformity to the Torah as sages represented it. Here is a rather general statement of matters, speaking not of the sage in the model of Moses, our rabbi, in the likeness of God at Sinai, but only of conformity to sages' norms:

Y. Taanit 1:1:IX.

J. "'The oracle concerning Dumah. One is calling to me from Seir, "Watchman, what of the night? Watchman, what of the night?" (Isa. 21:11).'"

K. The Israelites said to Isaiah, "O our Rabbi, Isaiah, What will come for us out of this night?"

L. He said to them, "Wait for me, until I can present the question."

M. Once he had asked the question, he came back to them.

N. They said to him, "Watchman, what of the night? What did the Guardian of the ages tell you?"

O. He said to them, "The watchman says: 'Morning comes; and also the night. If you will inquire, inquire; come back again' (Isa. 21:12)."

P. They said to him, "Also the night?"

Q. He said to them, "It is not what you are thinking. But there will be morning for the righteous, and night for the wicked, morning for Israel, and night for idolaters."

R. They said to him, "When?"

S. He said to them, "Whenever you want, He, too, wants [it to be] – if you want it, He wants it."

T. They said to him, "What is standing in the way?"

U. He said to them, "Repentance: 'Come back again' (Isa. 21:12)."

V. R. Aha in the name of R. Tanhum b. R. Hiyya, "If Israel repents for one day, forthwith the son of David will come.

W. "What is the Scriptural basis? 'If today you would hearken to his voice'" (Ps. 95:7).

The realization of true, legitimate government for Israel depended upon adherence to the sage and acceptance of his discipline. Here once more we find the successor-system's anti-politics: Israel, God's nation, conformed to a different law from the nations, worked out a history that was subject to its own rules, and constituted a social and political entity with no counterpart, not merely as to species, but especially, as to genus. Then only sages should rule unique Israel, and when that happens, then Israel assumes that power that its submission and humility yield, legitimate power coming from one's abnegation of power, legitimate sanctions being imposed, in the end, by oneself upon oneself.

For a more concrete portrait of legitimate power we turn to David, ideal king in the past, model of the coming messiah in the future. What mattered of course is that David then adhered to the model of the sage now. If David, King of Israel, was like a rabbi today, then a rabbi today would be the figure of the son of David who was to come as King of Israel. He was the sage of the Torah, the avatar and model for the sages of their own time. David and Moses are represented as students of Torah, just like the disciples and sages of the current time. An important presentation shows us how David is represented as a rabbi, and how, specifically, what made David exemplary was his devotion to study of the Torah:

Y. Berakhot 1:1.XII

O. "I will awake the dawn" (Ps. 5:7, 8) – I will awaken the dawn; the dawn will not awaken me.

P. David's [evil] impulse tried to seduce him [to sin]. And it would say to him, "David. It is the custom of kings that awakens them. And you say, I will awake the dawn. It is the custom of kings that they sleep until the third hour [of the day]. And you say, At midnight I rise." And [David] used to say [in reply], "[I rise early] because of thy righteous ordinances (Ps. 119:62)."

Q. And what would David do? R. Phineas in the name of R. Eleazar b. R. Menahem [said], "[He used to take a harp and lyre and set them at his bedside. And he would rise at midnight and play them so that the associates of Torah should hear. And what would the associates of Torah say? 'If David involves himself with Torah, how much more so should we.' We find that all of Israel was involved in Torah [study] on account of David."[12]

This long extract has shown us how the Talmud's authorities readily saw their concerns in biblical statements attributed to David. "Water" meant "a teaching of Torah." "Three mighty men" were of course judges. At issue was whether or not the decision was to be stated in David's own name – and so removed from the authoritative consensus of sages.

Since systems set forth their messages through their selection of opposites, we turn to ask how legitimate power finds its exact match

---

[12](Trans. by T. Zahavy, *The Talmud of the Land of Israel*. I. *Tractate Berakhot* [Chicago, 1990: The University of Chicago Press]).

Empowerment and the Category "The People Israel" 113

in the illegitimate kind. Sages, in the model of David, educated in the Torah of our rabbi, Moses, weigh in the balance against pagan kings, in the model of every malefactor in scriptural times. At stake in the outcome is God's rule and presence upon earth: once more, the sole legitimate power. That the stakes in politics have been revised upward – infinitely upward – is shown in the following statement that illegitimate power aims at destroying knowledge of God in the world, and legitimate power, nurturing that knowledge and consequence submission to God's will:

Genesis Rabbah XLII:III

2. A. "And it came to pass in the days of Ahaz" (Isa. 7:1):
    B. "The Aramaeans on the east and the Philistines on the west devour Israel with open mouth" (Isa. 9:12):
    C. The matter [of Israel's position] may be compared to the case of a king who handed over his son to a tutor, who hated the son. The tutor thought, "If I kill him now, I shall turn out to be liable to the death penalty before the king. So what I'll do is take away his wet-nurse, and he will die on his own."
    D. So thought Ahaz, "If there are no kids, there will be no he-goats. If there are no he-goats, there will be no flock. If there is no flock, there will be no Shepherd, if there is no Shepherd, there will be no world."
    E. So did Ahaz plan, "If there are no children, there will be no adults. If there are no adults, there will be no disciples. If there are no disciples, there will be no sages. If there are no sages, there will be no prophets. If there are no prophets, the Holy One, blessed be He, will not allow his presence to come to rest in the world." [Lev. R.: ...Torah. If there is no Torah, there will be no synagogues and schools. If there are no synagogues and schools, then the Holy One, blessed be He, will not allow his presence to come to rest in the world.]
    F. That is in line with the following verse of Scripture: "Bind up the testimony, seal the Torah among my disciples" (Isa. 8:16).
    G. R. Huna in the name of R. Eleazar: "Why was he called Ahaz? Because he seized (*ahaz*) synagogues and schools."

The vision of an "Israel" as a political entity defined by the absence of power and the presence of humility and submission, an entity that takes shape around synagogues and schools, which none can possibly (then or now) have identified with a political structure and system.

That judgment requires qualification, however, since the master in the setting of the school also served as clerk in the context of the administration and court. Not only so, but the sage as clerk exercised power that was not that of abnegation or denial, but of material sanctions. So the political theory of humility and powerlessness contrasted with the representation of a political reality of sages' forceful intervention into the social order. Sages' political authority was practical and involved empowerment; sages formed a political class in the this-worldly sense indeed. The first and most important sort of power a rabbi under some circumstances and in some cases maintained he could exercise was to sort out and adjudicate rights to property and personal status affecting property. The rabbi is described as able to take chattels or real estate from one party and to give them into the rightful ownership of some other.

The second sort of power rabbis are supposed to have wielded was to tell people what to do, or not to do, in matters not involving property rights. Sages moreover are represented as defining the status of persons in such ways as to affect property and marital rights and standing. Rabbis declare a woman married or free to marry; permitted as wife of a priest to eat food in the status of leave-offering or prohibited from doing so; enjoying the support of a husband's estate or left without that support; having the right to collect a previously contracted marriage settlement or lacking that right. In all of these ways, as much as in their control of real estate, commercial, and other material and property transactions among Jews, the rabbis held they governed the Jewish community as effective political authorities.[13]

The sage, moreover, is represented as mediating between Jews and the outside world. The legitimacy of that mediation derived solely from his mastery of the law. That is, he could permit actions normally prohibited in the law. He is represented not as negotiating, but only as accommodating. The unstated supposition is that Israel stands in a subordinated relationship, able to resist only with difficulty, and then at a very high cost. The alternative to submission is assumed to be death. The rabbi's authority as representative of the Jewish nation and mediator between that nation and the gentile world in general, and the government in particular, bore heavy symbolic weight. The rabbi as a public official was expected to perform certain supernatural deeds, power in its legitimate form. He stood at the border between heaven and earth, as much as he stood at the frontier between Israel and the nations: wholly liminal, entirely exemplary, at one and the same time.

What is important here is the representation of the rabbi as public authority deemed to exercise supernatural power. His task

---

[13]In these paragraphs I summarize the results of my *Judaism in Society: The Evidence of the Yerushalmi. Toward the Natural History of a Religion*. Chicago, 1983: The University of Chicago Press.

was to use his supernatural power in pretty much the same context and for the same purpose as he used his political-judicial and legal power and learning, on the one side, and his local influence and moral authority, on the other. What is striking is that sages exercised their responsibility equally through this-worldly and other-worldly means. One example of legitimate power suffices to make the point:

Y. Taanit 3:4.I.

A. There was a pestilence in Sepphoris, but it did not come into the neighborhood in which R. Haninah was living. And the Sepphoreans said, "How is it possible that that elder lives among you, he and his entire neighborhood, in peace, while the town goes to ruin?"

B. [Haninah] went in and said before them, "There was only a single Zimri in his generation, but on his account, twenty-four thousand people died. And in our time, how many Zimris are there in our generation? And yet you are raising a clamor!"

C. One time they had to call a fast, but it did not rain. R. Joshua carried out a fast in the South, and it rained. The Sepphoreans said, "R. Joshua b. Levi brings down rain for the people in the South, but R. Haninah holds back rain for us in Sepphoris."

D. They found it necessary to declare a second time of fasting, and sent and summoned R. Joshua b. Levi. [Haninah] said to him, "Let my lord go forth with us to fast." The two of them went out to fast, but it did not rain.

E. He went in and preached to them as follows: "It was not R. Joshua b. Levi who brought down rain for the people of the South, nor was it R. Haninah who held back rain from the people of Sepphoris. But as to the Southerners, their hearts are open, and when they listen to a teaching of Light [Torah] they submit [to accept it], while as to the Sepphoreans, their hearts are hard, and when they hear a teaching of Light, they do not submit [or accept it]."

F. When he went in, he looked up and saw that the [cloudless] air was pure. He said, "Is this how it still is? [Is there no change in the weather?]" Forthwith, it rained. He took a vow for himself that he would never do the same thing again. He said, "How shall I say to the creditor [God] not to collect what is owing to him."

True, God could do miracles. But if the people caused their own disasters by not listening to rabbis' Torah teachings, they could hardly expect God always to forgo imposing the sanction for disobedience, which was holding back rain. Accordingly, there were reliable laws by which one could deal with the supernatural world which kept those laws too. The particular power of the rabbi was in knowing the law. The storyteller took for granted, to be sure, that in the end the clerk could bring rain in a pinch.

If the sage stood for the legitimate exercise of power, who represented, even within Israel, illegitimate power? It was not only the patriarch, but – much more to the point – the illegitimate Messiah. And what makes a Messiah a false Messiah is not his claim to save Israel, but his claim to save Israel without the help of God. The meaning of the true Messiah is Israel's total submission, through the Messiah's gentle rule, to God's yoke and service. Israel does not save itself. The anti-politics before us never permits to control its own destiny, either on earth or in Heaven. The only choice is whether to cast one's fate into the hands of cruel, deceitful men, or to trust in the living God of mercy and love. We shall now see how this critical position is spelled out in the setting of discourse about the Messiah in the Talmud of the Land of Israel.

Bar Kokhba, above all, exemplifies arrogance against God. He lost the war because of that arrogance. In particular, he ignored the authority of sages:

Y. Taanit 4:5.X

J. Said R. Yohanan, "Upon orders of Caesar Hadrian, in Betar they killed eight hundred thousand."

K. Said R. Yohanan, "There were eighty thousand pairs of trumpeteers surrounding Betar. Each one was in charge of a number of troops. Ben Kozeba was there, and he had two hundred thousand troops who, as a sign of loyalty, had cut off their little fingers.

L. "Sages sent word to him, 'How long are you going to turn Israel into a maimed people?'

M. "He said to them, 'How otherwise is it possible to test them?'

N. "They replied to him, 'Whoever cannot uproot a cedar of Lebanon while riding on his horse will not be inscribed on your military rolls.'

O. "So there were two hundred thousand who qualified in one way, and another two hundred thousand who qualified in another way."

P. When he would go forth to battle, he would say, "Lord of the world! Do not help and do not hinder us! *'Hast thou not rejected us, O God? Thou dost not go forth, O God, with our armies'*" (Ps. 60:10).

Q. Three and a half years did Hadrian besiege Betar.

R. R. Eleazar of Modiin would sit on sackcloth and ashes and pray every day, saying "Lord of the ages! Do not judge in accord with strict judgment this day!"

S. Hadrian wanted to go to him. A Samaritan said to him, "Do not go to him, until I see what he is doing, and so hand over the city [of Betar] to you. ['Make peace... for you.']"

Empowerment and the Category "The People Israel"

T. He got into the city through a drain pipe. He went and found R. Eleazar of Modiin standing and praying. He pretended to whisper something into his ear.

U. The townspeople saw [the Samaritan] do this and brought him to Ben Kozeba. They told him, "We saw this man having dealings with your friend."

V. [Bar Kokhba] said to him, "What did you say to him, and what did he say to you?"

W. He said to [the Samaritan], "If I tell you, then the king will kill me, and if I do not tell you, then you will kill me. It is better that the king kill me, and not you.

X. "[Eleazar] said to me, 'I should hand over my city.' ['I shall make peace...']."

Y. He turned to R. Eleazar of Modiin. He said to him, "What did this Samaritan say to you?"

Z. He replied, "Nothing."

AA. He said to him, "What did you say to him?"

BB. He said to him, "Nothing."

CC. [Ben Kozeba] gave [Eleazar] one good kick and killed him.

DD. Forthwith an echo came forth and proclaimed the following verse:

EE. *"Woe to my worthless shepherd, who deserts the flock! May the sword smite his arm and his right eye! Let his arm be wholly withered, his right eye utterly blinded! (Zech. 11:17).*

FF. "You have murdered R. Eleazar of Modiin, the right arm of all Israel, and their right eye. Therefore may the right arm of that man wither, may his right eye be utterly blinded!"

GG. Forthwith Betar was taken, and Ben Kozeba was killed.

We notice two complementary themes. First, Bar Kokhba treats Heaven with arrogance, asking God merely to keep out of the way. Second, he treats an especially revered sage with a parallel arrogance. The sage had the power to preserve Israel. Bar Kokhba destroyed Israel's one protection. The result was inevitable.

Bar Kokhba, an Israelite, stands for illegitimate power; the sage, in the form of Eleazar of Modin, legitimate and also true power (both).[14] The one shows us how the reality of power is misunderstood, the other, the transvaluation of values that, in politics, serves as the counterpart to the same rereading of real value accomplished in the formation of the counterpart-category to economics. The upshot is that the successor-system has reconsidered not merely the contents of the received structure, but the composition of the structure itself. In place of its philosophy, we have now a new medium for the formulation of a world-view; in place of a way of life formulated as

---

[14]That both are Israelites proves that the differentiating criterion is not gentile versus Israelite, but virtue within Israel. Gentile power is a fact of life, not a systemically consequential consideration.

an economics, a new valuation of value, in place of an account of the social entity framed as a politics, a new conception of legitimate violence. So much for the formation of counterpart categories. Our task is now to portray the results of this categorical reformation in the new structure, seen whole and on its own.

4

The New Learning: The Gnostic Torah

In the successor-system, knowledge more than merely informs, it saves. And knowledge that saves is gnostic. What happens to me in Torah-study in the theory of the religious successor-system that does not happen to me in Torah-study in the theory of the initial, philosophical system is that I am changed in my very being. This transformation of the one who knows is not alone as to knowledge and understanding (let alone mere information), nor even as to virtue and taxic status, but as to what the knower is. I become something different from, better and more holy than, what I was before I knew, and whether the complement is "the mysteries" or "the Torah [as taught by sages]" makes no material difference.

But, as a matter of fact, that conception of the Torah as transformative contains another important trait we call gnostic, which is, the power to do things I could not do before I had attained knowledge in the correct way. The marks of the transformation emerge in the supernatural power that I have by reason of my (new) knowledge, learning in the Torah. That is what I mean by the new learning and what justifies the classification of Torah-learning as gnostic. For when (mere) knowledge so transforms the knower that he or she is deemed "saved," or otherwise transformed into something utterly different from the condition characteristic of the prior one marked by ignorance and by unredemption, then that knowledge may be called gnostic. For in general, by "gnostic," people mean salvific knowledge, transitive, transformative learning, joining the two quite distinct categories of intellect and personal salvation or regeneration.[1]

That jarring juxtaposition, identifying ignorance (not knowing a given fact) with the personal condition of unregeneracy, knowledge with supernatural standing and, hence, also power – that juxtaposition relates what need not, and commonly is not, correlated: the moral or existential condition of the person and the level of intellectual enlightenment of that same person. Certainly the framers of the Mishnah did not imagine that such a correlation could be made, nor did their heirs for quite some time. But in the successor-system, a principal point of integration of what philosophy had deemed distinct was between knowledge and one's condition or classification as to supernatural things. Knowledge of the Torah, quite specifically, changed a person and made him (never her) simply different from what he had been before or without that same knowledge: physically weaker, but also strengthened by power that we might call magical, but that they called supernatural. Before proceeding, let me give a good example of what I mean by knowledge of Torah represented as transformative and salvific.

The salvific consequence of knowing the Torah may seem implicit in the passage of Genesis Rabbah cited above. Here, moreover, I can point to a story that explicitly states the proposition that the obeying the Torah, with obedience founded on one's own knowledge thereof, constitutes a source of salvation. In this story we shall see that because people observed the rules of the Torah, they expected to be saved. And if they did not observe, they accepted their punishment. So the Torah now stands for something more than revelation and life of study, and (it goes without saying) the sage now appears as a holy, not merely a learned, man. This is because his knowledge of the Torah has transformed him. Accordingly, we deal with a category of stories and sayings about the Torah entirely different from what has gone before. We find at Y. Taanit 3:8 one among numerous examples in which the symbol of the Torah and knowledge of the Torah bear salvific consequence, a claim never set forth in behalf of knowledge, let alone knowledge of the Torah, in the Mishnah:[2]

---

[1] I of course bypass the word, Gnostic, with a capital G, bearing quite specific meanings in the study of late antiquity. A variety of meanings circulate, attached to various writings. What the common adjective, gnostic, with the denotative adjective, Gnostic, have in common is that the latter falls into the class of the former: saving knowledge.

[2] Not even at M. Hag. 2:2!

The New Learning: The Gnostic Torah

[II A]   As to Levi ben Sisi: troops came to his town. He took a scroll of the Torah and went up to the roof and said, "Lord of the ages! If a single word of this scroll of the Torah has been nullified [in our town], let them come up against us, and if not, let them go their way."

[B]   Forthwith people went looking for the troops but did not find them [because they had gone their way].

[C]   A disciple of his did the same thing, and his hand withered, but the troops went their way.

[D]   A disciple of his disciple did the same thing. His hand did not wither, but they also did not go their way.

[E]   This illustrates the following apophthegm: You can't insult an idiot, and dead skin does not feel the scalpel.

What is interesting here is how taxa into which the word Torah previously fell have been absorbed and superseded in a new taxon. The Torah is an object: "He took a scroll...." It also constitutes God's revelation to Israel: "If a single word...." The outcome of the revelation is to form an ongoing way of life, embodied in the sage himself: "A disciple of his did the same thing...." The sage plays an intimate part in the supernatural event: "His hand withered...." Here the Torah is a source of salvation. How so? The Torah stands for, or constitutes, the way in which the people Israel saves itself from marauders. This straightforward sense of salvation will not have surprised the author of Deuteronomy. But in our documents, there is more to the relationship of the Torah to salvation than mere obedience to its rules.

For now we discern an approach to the mere learning of the Torah – as distinct from obedience to its rules – that promises not merely intellectual enlightenment but personal renewal or transfiguration or some other far-reaching change. And since that view presents a gnostic[3] reading of learning, in the successor-system we confront a Torah, knowledge of which not merely informs or presents right rules of conduct, but which transforms, regenerates, saves.[4] In that context and by these definitions, the theory of the

---

[3] Resorting to the adjective "Faustian" while defensible seems to me less exact.

[4] Obviously, this "gnostic" is with a small g; I in no way mean to identify the Torah of the successor-Judaism with the Gnostic systems, Christian, Judaic, and pagan, of which we have knowledge in the same time and place, as well as earlier and later. My supposition is that, in any religious system, the intellectual component by the nature of the systemic setting is going to bear the same transformative and salvific valence as I show here pertained to the Torah. The counterparts in other religions, which impute to knowledge of the correct sort in the proper manner salvific power, are numerous. That seems to me to justify treating "gnostic" as a generic classification for

Torah and of Torah-study set forth in the successor-documents promises a fully-realized transformation to those who study and therefore know the Torah. They gained not merely intellectual enlightenment but supernatural power and standing. In this context, that encompassed such salvation as would take place prior to the end of time. The new learning defined as the consequence of Torah-study imputed by the Talmud of the Land of Israel, Genesis Rabbah, Leviticus Rabbah, and Pesiqta deRab Kahana – but not by the Mishnah and its companions, tractate Abot and the Tosefta – changes not merely the mind but the moral and salvific condition of the one who engages in that learning.

That conception would have surprised the philosophers represented by the Mishnah.[5] For if we ask ourselves, where in the Mishnah do we find promises of transformation of the person effected through study of the Torah? these, we recall full well,[6] concern only the issue of one's status in the hierarchical order of being, but not one's very character and essence. Quite to the contrary, as to the Mishnah's generative concerns on taxonomy, knowledge of the Torah changed nothing; the *mamzer* who mastered the Torah remained in the caste of the *mamzer*, so that, while if he lost his ass along with others, his would be returned first, still, he could not marry the daughter of a priest or even an Israelite. That means the

---

religious knowledge. But is there religious knowledge that is not gnostic, but merely (for one example) validating or qualifying? Indeed, there is a great deal of such knowledge, and the Mishnah's conception of knowing, as set forth in the apologetic of tractate Avot, is exactly of that kind. There, as we shall see, studying the Torah brings God's presence to join those who repeat Torah-words, whether one or many. But there is no consequent claim that the Torah-words' repetition has changed those who have said them, only that God has joined their study-circle. And that claim is of a considerably different kind from the one we shall see in numerous stories of the correlation between knowing the Torah and supernatural power.

[5] And hardly them alone. For the prevailing philosophical traditions the consequence of enlightenment in intellect cannot be said to have encompassed personal salvation (let alone national salvation, such as, in the Yerushalmi, was covered as well). Virtue depended upon right thinking, e.g., knowing what is the good, the true, and the beautiful. But the consequence of that knowledge did not commonly yield supernatural power in the philosophical systems of Greco-Roman antiquity. And, along these same lines, knowledge of the Torah served, e.g., the Israelite priesthood as a medium of validation, in that through knowledge they knew how to do their job, but it was a job that they got by reason of genealogy, not knowledge, as Mishnah-tractate Yoma 1:3 has already reminded us. So too, the Israelite scribal profession identified knowledge of the Torah as the foundation of their professional qualification.

[6] E.g., Mishnah-tractate Horayot 3:3-6, given above.

transformation in no way affected the being of the man, but only his virtue. True, we find at M. Hagigah 2:1 statements that have suggested to some[7] knowledge possessed traits of an other-than-wholly secular character, in that correct knowledge required attention to status (sage) and also the source and character of learning ("understands of his own knowledge," whatever that means):

Mishnah-tractate Hagigah 2:1

A. They do not expound upon the laws of prohibited relationships [Lev. 18] before three persons, the works of creation [Gen. 1] before two, or the Chariot [Ezek. 1] before one,

B. unless he was a sage and understands of his own knowledge.

C. Whoever reflects upon four things would have been better off had he not been born:

D. what is above, what is below, what is before, and what is beyond.

E. And whoever has no concern for the glory of his Maker would have been better off had he not been born.

These sentences have been quite plausibly interpreted to refer to personal, not merely intellectual, change effected by knowledge, hence to a gnostic reading of learning.

But they then do not impute to Torah-study as a general classification of intellectual activity the potentiality of (dangerous) change in one's own being. They speak of only specific topics and texts. The statements before us identify a very few specific passages and do not contain the conception that studying the Torah in general constitutes a transformative and salvific action. Their specificity may justify spelling the adjective Gnostic, but not gnostic.[8] At best, therefore, we may say that, within the compilation of the authorship of the Mishnah, we find *in nuce* the possibility of a

---

[7]It is conventional to read the following as "Gnostic," for instance, note Gershom G. Scholem, *Jewish Gnosticism, Merkabah Mysticism, and Talmudic Tradition* (N.Y., 1960: Jewish Theological Seminary of America). Taking the attributions at face value, moreover, various scholars, typified by Scholem, have forthwith assigned to "Judaism," or to "the rabbis" a fully-realized Gnostic experience. But if they had not decided in advance that these sayings had to mean what they suppose they mean, the proponents of such views about the condition of "Judaism" in the first century will have had to consider a variety of meanings and alternatives, including the one that we simply do not know what is going on in these statements.

[8]And here, in the received scholarly tradition in all languages Gnostic with a capital G is routinely given. But that seems to me to read into the passage much that is not explicit and need not be present at all; still, I admit, I do not claim to understand the passage at all, nor those in proximity in the Tosefta.

gnostic approach to knowledge; but that very representation, unrealized in context, hardly extends to the entirety of learning in the Torah and indeed by its formulation precludes such a general approach to the act of intellect performed upon the Torah.

A somewhat protracted survey of the Mishnah's and tractate Abot's theory of what happens to me because I study the Torah that will not happen to me if I do not readies us to see what is fresh and unprecedented in the representation of the same matter in the successor-documents.[9] When we come to tractate Abot, a generation beyond the Mishnah, we find heavy emphasis upon the importance of correlating one's actions with one's knowledge. A variety of sayings insist that if one knows the Torah but does not act in accord with its teachings, one gains nothing. One must change one's life to conform with one's knowledge of the Torah. That point of insistence, of course, invites as its next, small step, the doctrine that knowing the Torah changes one in being and essence, not only intellectually, by reason of illumination, but taxically, by reason of transformation. But the gnostic Torah, which would treat knowing the Torah on its own as a medium for one's transformation from merely natural to supernatural character,[10] would be some time in coming and would make its appearance only in the successor-system. A survey of tractate-Abot yields no such conception, but only the point that

---

[9]Without a full review of the sayings on the relationship of learning to one's personal condition as to salvation, what is fully new in the later documents will not be discerned. The nuances of language here do matter, especially since the received reading of the sayings surveyed in the following paragraphs imposes upon them the supernatural valence accorded only in the later writings to Torah-knowledge or Torah-study. Here the master of Torah-learning is saved only by what he does in consequence of what he knows, or by matching what he knows with what he does. Knowing by itself does not save, though it can effect attitudes that will affect one's actions in one way rather than in some other, and right action will then yield salvation. Not only so, but Torah-study will draw God's presence among those who study, but that does not yield the claim either that the sages are changed or that they thereby gain supernatural power. None of the indicators of the gnostic Torah occur, but only by the following survey will readers appreciate how much has been read into the sayings adduced in behalf of the contrary view.

[10]Indeed, the emphasis on the importance of correlating learning and deed and on the priority of deed seems to me to deny that very correlation of learning with transformation. Merely knowing is insufficient. But to a gnostic theory of knowledge, merely knowing itself saves. So I suppose proponents of the theory of a Gnostic Judaism of the first and second centuries will adduce these statements as evidence of not Gnostic Judaism but a reaction against Gnostic Judaism. But the evidence once more would then be asked to bear too heavy a burden of interpretation.

The New Learning: The Gnostic Torah 125

knowledge must be confirmed in deeds, a conception of moral but not existential weight, as in the following saying in Abot:

Tractate Abot 1:17

A. Simeon his son says, "Not the learning is the main thing but the doing. And whoever talks too much causes sin."

True, the statement that if one keeps his eye on three things, he will not sin, can yield the conception that knowledge bears salvific consequence. But that does not speak of a personal transformation in one's status and condition. The knowledge that saves me from sin is instrumental, not transformative:

> "Know what is above you: (1) An eye which sees, and (2) an ear which hears, and (3) all your actions are written down in a book."

The same conception, that knowledge is essential to attitudes that bring salvation, is stated in the following:

Tractate Abot 3:1

A. Aqabiah b. Mehallalel says, "Reflect upon three things and you will not fall into the clutches of transgression:
B. "Know (1) from whence you come, (2) whither you are going, and (3) before whom you are going to have to give a full account [of yourself].
C. "From whence do you come? From a putrid drop.
D. "Whither are you going? To a place of dust, worms, and maggots.
E. "And before whom are you going to give a fluff account of Yourself? Before the King of kings of kings, the Holy One, blessed be He."

We have not strayed far from the notion that knowledge of the Torah promises a good reward here and after death because it keeps me from sin, that is to say, the position, vis à vis studying a trade, of Nehorai. Here again, what I get for knowing treats knowledge as necessary in an instrumental sense; it yields a given goal, it does not effect a desired transformation. A promise that in context is quite consistent is that, if I study the Torah, I encounter God:

Tractate Abot 3:2

C. R. Hananiah b. Teradion says, "[If] two sit together and between them do not pass teachings of Torah, lo, this is a seat of the scornful....
E. "Two who are sitting, and words of Torah do pass between them – the Presence is with them, as it is said, 'Then they that feared the Lord spoke with one another, and the Lord hearkened and heard, and a book of remembrance was written

	before him, for them that feared the Lord and gave thought to His name' (Mal. 3:16)."
G.	I know that this applies to two.
H.	How do I know that even if a single person sits and works on Torah, the Holy One, blessed be He, sets aside a reward for him? As it is said, 'Let him sit alone and keep silent, because he has laid it upon him' (Lam. 3:28)."

Tractate Abot 3:6

A.	R. Halafta of Kefar Hananiah says, "Among ten who sit and work hard on Torah the Presence comes to rest,
B.	"as it is said, 'God stands in the congregation of God' (Ps. 82:1).
C.	"And how do we know that the same is so even of five? For it is said, And he has founded his group upon the earth (Am. 9:6).
D.	"And how do we know that this is so even of three? Since it is said, 'And he judges among the judges' (Ps. 82:1).
E.	"And how do we know that this is so even of two? Because it is said, Then they that feared the Lord spoke with one another, and the Lord hearkened and heard (Mal. 3:16).
F.	"And how do we know that this is so even of one? 'Since it is said, In every place where I record my name I will come to you and I will bless you' (Ex. 20:24)."

"Knowing God" or bringing God into one's study circle certainly represent desirable goals of illumination. But these do not encompass the transformative experience promised the one who knows by the gnostic theory of the Torah. Why not? Because even though God has joined my study-circle and brought the divine presence to rest among the disciples, we still do not then claim supernatural powers as the consequence; in neither the Mishnah nor the Tosefta nor Abot do we find the claim that the disciple of the sage by reason of his learning does miracles.[11]

The contrast between getting a good name for oneself and getting the world to come, in the following saying, also is not quite to the point:

---

[11] The contrary view, that the one who does miracles is not necessarily a disciple of a sage, though he may be a holy man, is presented at Mishna-tractate Taanit 3:8 with reference to Honi, for one instance. What is important to my argument is simply that no one correlates Torah-learning with wonder-working. Whether or not the component of the canon represented by the Mishnah and its associated writings favors wonder-working or opposes it, fears it or admires it, is not at stake here. What concerns me is the working of the categories, and the process of category-formation adumbrated by the correlation of distinct categories simply has not taken place by the end of the formation of the Mishnah's component of the canon of the Dual Torah.

The New Learning: The Gnostic Torah

"[If] one has gotten a good name, he has gotten it for himself. [If] he has gotten teachings of Torah, he has gotten himself life eternal."

Here we speak of repute, a form of virtue, but not wonder-working. The same point as Simeon's, above, moreover comes to the fore in the following:

Tractate Abot 3:9

A. R. Haninah b. Dosa says, "For anyone whose fear of sin takes precedence over his wisdom, his wisdom will endure,

B. "And for anyone whose wisdom takes precedence over his fear of sin, his wisdom will not endure."

C. He would say, "Anyone whose deeds are more than his wisdom – his wisdom will endure.

D. "And anyone whose wisdom is more than his deeds–his wisdom will not endure."

Tractate Abot 3:17

I. He would say, "Anyone whose wisdom is greater than his deeds – to what is he to be likened? To a tree with abundant foliage, but few roots.

J. "When the winds come, they will uproot it and blow it down,

K. "as it is said, 'He shall be like a tamarisk in the desert and shall not see when good comes but shall inhabit the parched places in the wilderness' (Jer. 17:6).

L. "But anyone whose deeds are greater than his wisdom – to what is he to be likened? To a tree with little foliage but abundant roots.

M. "For even if all the winds in the world were to come and blast at it, they will not move it from its place,

N. "as it is said, He shall be as a tree planted by the waters, and that spreads out its roots by the river, and shall not fear when heat comes, and his leaf shall be green, and shall not be careful in the year of drought, neither shall cease from yielding fruit (Jer. 17:8)."

Tractate Abot 4:5

A. R. Ishmael, his son, says, "He who learns so as to teach – they give him a chance to learn and to teach.

B. "He who learns so as to carry out his teachings – they give him a chance to learn, to teach, to keep, and to do."

A variety of sayings, indeed, explicitly identify not Torah-learning but other virtues as primary, and furthermore scarcely concede to Torah-learning transformative, let alone salvific, power:

Tractate Abot 4:13

C. R. Simeon says, "There are three crowns: the crown of Torah, the crown of priesthood, and the crown of sovereignty.

D. "But the crown of a good name is best of them all."

Tractate Abot 4:17

A. He would say, "Better is a single moment spent in penitence and good deeds in this world than the whole of the world to come.

B. "And better is a single moment of inner peace in the world to come than the whole of a lifetime spent in this world."

These and similar sayings attest to a variety of modes of human regeneration, none of them connected with Torah-learning in particular.

Now, as a matter of fact, in the successor-documents, a quite different theory of Torah-learning predominates. It is the simple fact that knowledge of the Torah changes the one who knows. He becomes physically weaker,[12] but gains, in compensation, supernatural powers. The legitimating power of the Torah and study thereof imputed in the pages of the Talmud of the Land of Israel is explicit: knowledge of the Torah changes a man into a sage and also saves Israel. The Torah then involves not mere knowledge, for example, correct information, valid generalization, but gnosis: saving knowledge.[13]

To the rabbis the principal salvific deed was to "study Torah," by which they meant memorizing Torah sayings by constant repetition, and, as the Talmud itself amply testifies, (for some sages) profound analytic inquiry into the meaning of those sayings. This act of "study of Torah" imparted supernatural power. For example, by repeating words of Torah, the sage could ward off the angel of death and accomplish other kinds of miracles as well. So Torah formulas served as incantations. Mastery of Torah transformed the man who engaged in Torah learning into a supernatural figure, able to do things ordinary folk could not do. In the nature of things, the category of "Torah" was vastly expanded so that the symbol of Torah, a Torah scroll, could be compared to a man of Torah, namely, a rabbi. Since what made a man into a sage or a disciple of a sage or a rabbi was studying the Torah through discipleship, what is at stake in the symbolic transfer is quite obvious.

The Torah is then identified with and personified by the sage; so he is changed because of what he knows. That is a material and

---

[12]As we noted in Chapter Two.

[13]One important qualification is required. Knowledge is not the only medium of salvation. Salvation, as before, derives from keeping the law of the Torah. Keeping the law in the right way is the way to bring the Messiah, the son of David. This is stated by Levi, as follows. "If Israel would keep a single Sabbath in the proper way, forthwith the son of David would come" (Y. Taanit 1:1.IX.X, cited above). But the issue of not doing but (mere) knowing, of salvation through study of the Torah, is distinct.

palpable claim, not a mere mode of ascription of great sanctity, lacking any concrete consequence. the vastly expanded definition of the symbol of "Torah." The claim that a sage (or, disciple of a sage) himself was equivalent to a scroll of the Torah forms a material, legal comparison, not merely a symbolic metaphor.

Y. Moed Qatan 3:7.X

A. He who sees a disciple of a sage who has died is as if he sees a scroll of the Torah that has been burned.

Y. Moed Qatan 3:1.XI.

I. R. Jacob bar Abayye in the name of R. Aha: "An elder who forgot his learning because of some accident which happened to him – they treat him with the sanctity owed to an ark [of the Torah]."

In both instances actual behavior was affected. That view is expressed in stories indicating the belief that while a sage is repeating Torah sayings, the angel of death cannot approach him.

Y. Moed Qatan 3:5.XXI

F. [Proving that while one is studying Torah, the angel of death cannot touch a person, the following is told:] A disciple of R. Hisda fell sick. He sent two disciples to him, so that they would repeat Mishnah-traditions with him. [The angel of death] turned himself before them into the figure of a snake, and they stopped repeating traditions, and [the sick man] died.

G. A disciple of Bar Pedaiah fell ill. He sent to him two disciples to repeat Mishnah-traditions with him. [The angel of death] turned himself before them into a kind of star, and they stopped repeating Mishnah-traditions, and he died.

Repeating Mishnah traditions thus warded off death. It is hardly surprising that stories were told about wonders associated with the deaths of various rabbis. These validated the claim of supernatural power imputed to the rabbis. A repertoire of such stories includes two sorts.

First, there is a list of supernatural occurrences accompanying sages' deaths, and, second, we have a claim of specific miracles that were done by Heaven when a great sage died. The former are as in the following.

Y. Abodah Zarah 3:1.II

A. When R. Aha died, a star appeared at noon.
B. When R. Hanah died, the statues bowed down.
C. When R. Yohanan died, the icons bowed down.
D. They said that [this was to indicate] there were no icons like him [so beautiful as Yohanan himself].

E.	When R. Hanina of Bet Hauran died, the Sea of Tiberias split open.
F.	They said that [this was to commemorate the miracle that took place] when he went up to intercalate the year, and the sea split open before him.
G.	When R. Hoshaiah died, the palm of Tiberias fell down.
H.	When R. Isaac b. Elisheb died, seventy [infirm] thresholds of houses in Galilee were shaken down.
I.	They said that [this was to commemorate the fact that] they [were shaky and] had depended on his merit [for the miracle that permitted them to continue to stand].
J.	When R. Samuel bar R. Isaac died, cedars of the land of Israel were uprooted.
K.	They said that [this was to take note of the fact that] he would take branch [of a cedar] and [dance, so] praising a bride [at her wedding, and thereby giving her happiness].
L.	The rabbis would ridicule them [for lowering himself by doing so]. Said to them R. Zeira, "Leave him be. Does the old man not know what he is doing?"
M.	When he died, a flame came forth from heaven and intervened between his bier and the congregation. For three hours there were voices and thunderings in the world: "Come and see what a sprig of cedar has done for this old man!"
N.	[Further] an echo came forth and said, "Woe that Samuel b. R. R. Isaac has died, the doer of merciful deeds."
O.	When R. Yosa bar Halputa died, the gutters ran with blood in Laodicea.
P.	They said [that the reason was] that he had given his life for the rite of circumcision.
Q.	When R. Abbahu died, the pillars of Caesarea wept.
R.	The [gentiles] said [that the reason was] that [the pillars] were celebrating. The Israelites said to them, "And do those who are distant [such as yourselves] know why those who are near [we ourselves] are raising a cry?"

Y. Abodah Zarah 3:1.II

BB.	One of the members of the patriarchate died, and the [burial] cave folded over [and received the bier], so endangering the lives [of those who had come to bury him]. R. Yose went up and took leave [of the deceased], saying "Happy is a man who has left this world in peace."
CC.	When R. Yosa died, the castle of Tiberias collapsed, and members of the patriarchate were rejoicing. R. Zeira said to them, "There is no similarity [between this case and the miracle described at BB]. The peoples' lives were endangered, here no one's life was endangered. In that case, no pagan worship was removed, while here, an idol was uprooted [so, consequently, the event described in BB was not a miracle, while the event described here was a miracle and a sign of divine favor].

The New Learning: The Gnostic Torah

What is important in the foregoing anthology is the linkage between the holy deeds of the sage and the miracles done at their demise. The sages' merit, attained through study of Torah or through acts of saintliness and humility was demonstrated for all to see. So the sage was not merely a master of Torah. But his mastery of Torah laid the foundations for all the other things he was: he was changed into something other than what he had been before he studied the Torah, and all else follows.

Second, specific miracles, as distinct from natural wonders, were related with regard to the death of the Patriarch.

Y. Ketubot 12:3.IV

E. R. Nathan in the name of R. Mana: "There were miracles done that day. It was the eve of the Sabbath, and all the villagers assembled to make a lamentation for him. They put down the bier eighteen times en route to burial to mourn him, and they accompanied him down to Bet Shearim. The daylight was protracted until each one of them had reached his home [in time for the Sabbath] and had time to fill up a jug of water and light the Sabbath lamp. When the sun set, the cock crowed, and the people began to be troubled, saying, 'Perhaps we have violated the Sabbath.'

F. "But an echo came to them, 'Whoever did not refrain from participation in the lamentations for Rabbi may be given the good news that he is going to enjoy a portion in the world to come

G. "'except for the launderer [who used to come to Rabbi day by day, but did not bother to participate in his funeral].' When he heard this, he went up to the roof and threw himself down and died. Then an echo went forth and said, 'Even the laundryman [will enjoy the life of the world to come].'"

Y. Ketubot 12:3.VII

J. When R. Huna, the exilarch, died, they brought his bones up here. They said, "If we are going to bury him properly, let us place him near R. Hiyya, because he comes from there."

K. They said, "Who is worthy of placing him there?"

L. Said to them R. Haggai, "I shall go up and place him there."

M. They said to him, "You are looking for an excuse, for you are an old man, so you want to go up there and die and be buried there next to Hiyya."

N. He said to them, "Tie a rope to my feet, and if I delay there too long you can drag me out."

O. He went in and found three biers.

P. [He heard,] "Judah, my son, is after you, and no one else. Hezekiah, my son, is after you, and no one else. Joseph, son of Israel, and no one else."

Q. He raised his eyes and looked. One said to him, "Lower your face."

R.	Said R. Hiyya the Elder, "Judah, my son, make room for R. Huna."
S.	He made a place for him, but [Huna] did not accept being buried [next to Hiyya the Elder, out of modesty].
T.	[Haggai] said, "Just as [out of modesty] he did not accept being buried next to him, so may his seed never die out."
U.	R. Haggai left that place at the age of eighty years, and they doubled the number of his years, [so that he lived another eighty years].

That the sage was different from ordinary men seems to me well established. But in context that claim was not surprising; holy men in general were deemed supernatural. What makes this claim distinctive in the present system is not only that it is unprecedented in its canonical context, but also that it is a claim of supernatural power gained specifically through the autocephalous act of undertaking to study the Torah.

The Torah, of course, in context was deemed true, and that explained why rabbis were shown more effective than other magicians, specifically in those very same settings in which, all parties conceded, other wonder-workers, as much as rabbis, were able to perform magical deeds. What is important in the following is the fact that in a direct contest between a rabbi and another sort of magician, an Israelite heretic, the rabbi was shown to enjoy superior magical power.

Y. Sanhedrin 7:12.III

A.	When R. Eleazar, R. Joshua, and R. Aqiba went in to bathe in the baths of Tiberias, a *min* [in context: Israelite heretic] saw them. He said what he said, and the arched chamber in the bath [where idolatrous statues were put up] held them fast, [so that they could not move].
B.	Said R. Eleazar to R. Joshua, "Now Joshua b. Haninah, see what you can do."
C.	When that *min* tried to leave, R. Joshua said what he said, and the doorway of the bath seized and held the min firm, so that whoever went in had to give him a knock [to push by], and whoever went out had to give him a knock [to push by].
D.	He said to them, "Undo whatever you have done [to let me go]."
E.	They said to him, "Release us, and we shall release you."
F.	They released one another.
G.	Once they got outside, said R. Joshua to that *min*, "Lo, you have learned [from us whatever you are going to learn]."
H.	He said, "Let's go down to the sea."
I.	When they got down to the sea, that *min* said whatever it was that he said, and the sea split open.
J.	He said to them, "Now is this not what Moses, your rabbi, did at the sea?"

The New Learning: The Gnostic Torah

	K.	They said to him, "Do you not concede to us that Moses, our rabbi, walked through it?"
	L.	He said to them, "Yes."
	M.	They said to him, "Then walk through it."
	N.	He walked through it.
	O.	R. Joshua instructed the ruler of the sea, who swallowed him up.
IV.	A.	When R. Eliezer, R. Joshua, and Rabban Gamaliel went up to Rome, they came to a certain place and found children making little piles [of dirt]. They said, "Children of the Land of Israel make this sort of thing, and they say, 'This is heave offering,' and 'That is tithe.' It's likely that there are Jews here."
	B.	They came into one place and were received there.
	C.	When they sat down to eat, [they noticed] that each dish which they brought into them would first be brought into a small room, and then would be brought to them, and they wondered whether they might be eating sacrifices offered to the dead. [That is, before the food was brought to them, it was brought into a small chamber, in which, they suspected, sacrifices were taken from each dish and offered to an idol.]
	D.	They said to [the host], "What is your purpose, in the fact that, as to every dish which you bring before us, if you do not bring it first into a small room, you do not bring it in to us?"
	E.	He said to them, "I have a very old father, and he has made a decree for himself that he will never go out of that small room until he will see the sages of Israel."
	F.	They said to him, "Go and tell him, 'Come out here to them, for they are here.'"
	G.	He came out to them.
	H.	They said to him, "Why do you do this?"
	I.	He said to them, "Pray for my son, for he has not produced a child."
	J.	Said R. Eliezer to R. Joshua, "Now, Joshua b. Hananiah, let us see what you will do."
	K.	He said to them, "Bring me flax seeds," and they brought him flax seeds.
	L.	He appeared to sow the seed on the table; he appeared to scatter the seed; he appeared to bring the seed up; he appeared to take hold of it, until he drew up a woman, holding on to her tresses.
	M.	He said to her, "Release whatever [magic] you have done [to this man]."
	N.	She said to him, "I am not going to release [my spell]."
	O.	He said to her, "If you don't do it, I shall publicize your [magical secrets]."
	P.	She said to him, "I cannot do it, for [the magical materials] have been cast into the sea."
	Q.	R. Joshua made a decree that the sea release [the magical materials] and they came up.

R.	They prayed for [the host], and he had the merit of begetting a son, R. Judah b. Bathera.
S.	They said, "If we came up here only for the purpose of begetting that righteous man, it would have been enough for us."
T.	Said R. Joshua b. Haniniah, "I can take cucumbers and pumpkins and turn them into rams and hosts of rams, and they will produce still more."

These long extracts leave no doubt that the Talmud imputed to Israel's sages precisely the powers generally assigned to magicians. The sage did precisely what the magician did, only he did it better. When the magician then pretended to do what Moses had done, it was his end. The story about Joshua's magic in Rome is similar, in its explicit reference to sympathetic magic, K-L. The result was the discovery that the childless man had been subject to a spell.

There can be no doubt that distinctions between magic and supernatural power meant nothing to the Talmud's storytellers. The clerks were not merely holy men; they were a particular kind of holy men. In consequence of the belief that rabbis had magical powers, it was quite natural to impute to rabbis the ability both to bless those who favored them and to curse those who did not.

Thus far I have shown only that sages studied the Torah and also that sages through study of the Torah gained supernatural standing (for example, when they were buried) and power, which they imputed to their knowledge of the Torah. What I have yet to demonstrate is that knowledge of the Torah itself changed the sage in such a way that he not only could manipulate the supernatural power inhering in the Torah but also could himself join in the processes of forming the Torah. For I have alleged that the man himself was transformed through Torah-study. And what I have already offered in evidence demands an explanation of how that transformation took place. For the allegation that knowledge in particular changes the person can itself refer to a merely instrumental power: if I know thus and so, I can do such and such. At stake in the gnostic Torah was much, much more.

Specifically, if I know the Torah, I can join in the making of the Torah, and that claim in my behalf as a sage forms solid evidence of the allegation that studying the Torah not only endows one with power but actually changes the man from what he had been into something else. He had been ordinary, now he is not merely powerful but holy. And his holiness is shown by the fact that, just as we study the Torah in its written and oral forms, so we may study the Torah in its quotidian form: the sage himself, his gestures, his actions then forming precedents valid within the practice of the

Torah itself. And when I allege that because I have studied the Torah, I am changed so that I can now join in the process of revealing the Torah, studying the Torah provides a gnostic experience of transformation, regeneration, and salvation. Accordingly, I have now to demonstrate that the supernatural status accorded to the person of the sage endowed his deeds with normative, therefore revelatory power.

What the sage did had the status of law; the sage was the model of the law, thus having been changed, transformed, regenerated, saved, turned by studying the Torah into the human embodiment of the Torah. That gnostic view of Torah-study as transformative and salvific – now without explicit appeal to deeds in conformity to the law, though surely that is taken for granted – accounts for the position that the sage was a holy man. For what made the sage distinctive was his combination of this-worldly authority and power and otherworldly influence. The clerk in the court and the holy man on the rooftop praying for rain or calling Heaven to defend the city against marauders, in the Yerushalmi's view were one and the same. The tight union between salvation and law, the magical power of the sage and his law-giving authority, was effected through the integrative act of studying the Torah. And that power of integration accounts for the successor-system's insistence that if the sage exercised supernatural power as a kind of living Torah, his very deeds served to reveal law, as much as his word expressed revelation.

The capacity of the sage himself to participate in the process of revelation is illustrated in two types of materials. First of all, tales told about rabbis' behavior on specific occasions immediately are translated into rules for the entire community to keep. Accordingly, he was a source not merely of good example but of prescriptive law. Here is a humble and mundane case of how that view came to expression.

Y. Abodah Zarah 5:4:III

X.	R. Aha went to Emmaus, and he ate dumpling [prepared by Samaritans].
Y.	R. Jeremiah ate leavened bread prepared by them.
Z.	R. Hezekiah ate their locusts prepared by them.
AA.	R. Abbahu prohibited Israelite use of wine prepared by them.

These reports of what rabbis had done enjoyed the same authority, as statements of the law on eating what Samaritans cooked, as did citations of traditions in the names of the great authorities of old or of the day. What someone did served as a norm, if the person was a sage of sufficient standing.

Far more common in the Talmud are instances in which the deed of a rabbi is adduced as an authoritative precedent for the law under discussion. It was everywhere taken for granted that what a rabbi did, he did because of his mastery of the law. Even though a formulation of the law was not in hand, a tale about what a rabbi actually did constituted adequate evidence on how to formulate the law itself. So from the practice of an authority, a law might be framed quite independent of the person of the sage. The sage then functioned as a lawgiver, like Moses. Among a great many instances of that mode of generating law are the following.

Y. Abodah Zarah 3:11.II

A. Gamaliel Zuga was walking along, leaning on the shoulder of R. Simeon b. Laqish. They came across an image.
B. He said to him, "What is the law as to passing before it?"
C. He said to him, "Pass before it, but close [your] eyes."
D. R. Isaac was walking along, leaning on the shoulder of R. Yohanan. They came across an idol before the council building.
E. He said to him, "What is the law as to passing before it?"
F. He said to him, "Pass before it, but close [your] eyes."
G. R. Jacob bar Idi was walking along, leaning upon R. Joshua b. Levi. They came across a procession in which an idol was carried. He said to him, "Nahum, the most holy man, passed before this idol, and will you not pass by it? Pass before it but close your eyes."

Y. Abodah Zarah 2:2.III

FF. R. Aha had chills and fever. [They brought him] a medicinal drink prepared from the phallus of Dionysian revelers. But he would not drink it. They brought it to R. Jonah, and he did drink it. Said R. Mana, "Now if R. Jonah, the patriarch, had known what it was, he would never have drunk it."
GG. Said R. Huna, "That is to say, 'They do not accept healing from something that derives from an act of fornication.'"

What is important is GG, the restatement of the story in the form of a fixed rule, hence as a law. The example of a rabbi served to teach how one should live a truly holy life. The requirements went far beyond the measure of the law, extending to refraining from deeds of a most commonplace sort. The example of rabbinical virtue, moreover, was adduced explicitly to account for the supernatural or magical power of a rabbi. There was no doubt, in people's imagination, therefore, that the reason rabbis could do the amazing things people said they did was that they embodied the law and exercised its supernatural or magical power. The correlation between learning and teaching, on the one side, and supernatural power or recognition, on the other, is explicit in the following.

Y. Ketubot 12:3.VII

A. R. Yosa fasted eighty fasts in order to see R. Hiyya the Elder [in a dream]. He finally saw him, and his hands trembled and his eyes grew dim.

B. Now if you say that R. Yosa was an unimportant man, [and so was unworthy of such a vision, that is not the case]. For a weaver came before R. Yohanan. He said to him, "I saw in my dream that the heaven fell, and one of your disciples was holding it up."

C. He said to him, "Will you know him [when you see him]?"

D. He said to him, "When I see him, I shall know him." Than all of his disciples passed before him, and he recognized R. Yosa.

E. R. Simeon b. Laqish fasted three hundred fasts in order to have a vision of R. Hiyya the Elder, but he did not see him.

F. Finally he began to be distressed about the matter. He said, "Did he labor in learning of Torah more than I?"

G. They said to him, "He brought Torah to the people of Israel to a greater extent than you have, and not only so, but he even went into exile [to teach on a wider front]."

H. He said to them, "And did I not go into exile too?"

I. They said to him, "You went into exile only to learn, but he went into exile to teach others."

This story shows that the storyteller regarded as a fact of life the correlation between mastery of Torah sayings and supernatural power – visions of the deceased, in this case. That is why Simeon b. Laqish complained, E-F, that he had learned as much Torah as the other, and so had every right to be able to conjure the dead. The greater supernatural power of the other then was explained in terms of the latter's superior service to "Torah." The upshot is that the sage was changed by Torah learning and could save Israel through Torah.

Precisely how did sages explain the transformation effected by study of the Torah? It was by appeal to the character of the saints of Scripture. Seeing Scripture in their own model, they took the position that the Torah of old, its supernatural power and salvific promise, in their own day continued to endure among themselves. By studying the Torah, they turned themselves into the model of those sages whose holy deeds the Torah recorded: Moses, David and Isaiah being called rabbis, for instance. In consequence, the promise of salvation contained in every line of Scripture was to be kept in every deed of learning and obedience to the law effected under their auspices. Learning in the Torah was salvific because it turned ordinary men into saints in the model of the saints of the Torah.

That fact helps us to understand the constant citation of Scripture in the context of sages' rulings and doings. It was not to establish authority alone. Rather, it was to identify what was happening just then with what had happened long ago. The purpose was not merely to demonstrate and authenticate the *bona fide* character of a new figure of salvation, but to show the continuity of the salvific process, a process then that relied for its persistence upon learning in particular. The act of study of the Torah, in the system before us, had to be endowed with gnostic status, supernatural power to save, because the act of learning formed the medium for the transmission of not merely the lessons, but the supernatural power, of old. The Torah presented not merely rules but examples of holiness, and salvation lay in sanctification: "Today, if you repent," that is, conform now, as not before: accept transformation, regeneration, salvation.

It followed that the pattern and promise of salvation contained therein lay within their way of life: studying the Torah in discipleship. That is the meaning of the explicit reading of the present into the past – the implicit arrogation of the hope of the past to the salvific heroes of the present: themselves. To state matters simply, if David, King of Israel, was like a rabbi today, then a rabbi today would be the figure of the son of David who was to come as King of Israel. It is not surprising, therefore, that among the many biblical heroes whom the Talmudic rabbis treated as sages, principal and foremost was David himself, now made into a messianic rabbi or a rabbinical Messiah. He was the sage of the Torah, the avatar and model for the sages of their own time. That view was made explicit, both specifically and in general terms. If a rabbi was jealous to have his traditions cited in his own name, it was because that was David's explicit view as well. In more general terms, both David and Moses are represented as students of Torah, just like the disciples and sages of the current time. We recall how David is represented as a devoted student of the Torah. Here is one re-presentation of a biblical story in the mode of an academic tale:

Y. Sanhedrin 2:6.IV

A. It is written, "And David said longingly, 'O that someone would give me water to drink from the well of Bethlehem [which is by the gate]'" (I Chron. 11:17).

B. R. Hiyya bar Ba said, "He required a teaching of law."

C. "Then the three mighty men broke through [the camp of the Philistines]" (I Chron. 11:18).

D. Why three? Because the law is not decisively laid down by fewer than three.

E. "But David would not drink of it; [he poured it out to the Lord, and said, 'Far be it from me before my God that I should do

The New Learning: The Gnostic Torah

this. Shall I drink the lifeblood of these men? For at the risk of their lives they brought it']" (I Chron. 11:1819).

F. David did not want the law to be laid down in his own name.

G. "He poured it out to the Lord" – establishing [the decision] as [an unattributed] teaching for the generations, [so that the law should be authoritative and so be cited anonymously].

Y. Sheqalim 2:4.V.

O. David himself prayed for mercy for himself, as it is said, "Let me dwell in thy tent for ever! Oh to be safe under the shelter of thy wings, selah" (Ps. 61:4).

P. And did it enter David's mind that he would live for ever?

Q. But this is what David said before the Holy One, blessed be He, "Lord of the world, may I have the merit that my words will be stated in synagogues and schoolhouses."

R. Simeon b. Nazira in the name of R. Isaac said, "Every disciple in whose name people cite a teaching of law in this world – his lips murmur with him in the grave, as it is said, 'Your kisses are like the best wine that goes down smoothly, gliding over lips of those that sleep' (Song 7:9).

S. "Just as in the case of a mass of grapes, once a person puts his finger in it, forthwith even his lips begin to smack, so the lips of the righteous, when someone cites a teaching of law in their names – their lips murmur with them in the grave."

David as a model of the disciple of the sage is represented in the following for the virtue of conscious and zealous Torah-study:

Y. Berakhot 1:1 (trans. by Tzvee Zahavy).XII.

O. "I will awake the dawn" (Ps. 5:7, 8) – I will awaken the dawn; the dawn will not awaken me.

P. David's [evil] impulse tried to seduce him [to sin]. And it would say to him, "David. It is the custom of kings that awakens them. And you say, I will awake the dawn. It is the custom of kings that they sleep until the third hour [of the day]. And you say, At midnight I rise." And [David] used to say [in reply], "[I rise early] because of thy righteous ordinances (Ps. 119:62)."

Q. And what would David do? R. Phineas in the name of R. Eleazar b. R. Menahem [said], "[He used to take a harp and lyre and set them at his bedside. And he would rise at midnight and play them so that the associates of Torah should hear. And what would the associates of Torah say? 'If David involves himself with Torah, how much more so should we.' We find that all of Israel was involved in Torah [study] on account of David."

This long extract has shown us how the Talmud's authorities readily saw their concerns in biblical statements attributed to David. "Water" meant "a teaching of Torah." "Three mighty men" were of course judges. At issue was whether or not the decision was to be stated in David's own name – and so removed from the authoritative consensus of sages. David exhibits precisely those concerns for the preservation of his views in his name that, in earlier sections, we saw attributed to rabbis. All of this fully reveals the rabbis' deeper convictions when we remember that David, the rabbi, also was in everyone's mind David, the Messiah.

Enough has been set forth to suggest that I mean to represent the gnostic Torah as the centerpiece of the successor-system. But our evidence suggests precisely the opposite, for, as a matter of fact, even the stories contained in the Talmud of the Land of Israel in which the priority and sanctity of the sage's knowledge of the Torah form the focus of discourse prevent me from doing so. Time and again, knowledge of the Torah forms a way-station on a path to a more distant, more central goal: attaining *zekhut,* which, readers recall, I have translated as "the heritage of virtue and its consequent entitlements." Torah-study is one means of attaining access to that heritage, of gaining zekhut. There are other equally suitable means, and, not only so, but the merit gained by Torah-study is no different from the merit gained by acts of supererogatory grace. Since, in the successor-system, it is points of integration, not of differentiation, that guide us to the systemic problematic, we must take seriously the contingent status, the standing of a dependent variable, accorded to Torah-study in such stories as the following:

Y. Taanit 3:11.IV

C. There was a house that was about to collapse over there [in Babylonia], and Rab set one of his disciples in the house, until they had cleared out everything from the house. When the disciple left the house, the house collapsed.

D. And there are those who say that it was R. Adda bar Ahwah.

E. Sages sent and said to him, "What sort of good deeds are to your credit [that you have that much merit]?"

F. He said to them, "In my whole life no man ever got to the synagogue in the morning before I did. I never left anybody there when I went out. I never walked four cubits without speaking words of Torah. Nor did I ever mention teachings of Torah in an inappropriate setting. I never laid out a bed and slept for a regular period of time. I never took great strides among the associates. I never called my fellow by a nickname. I never rejoiced in the embarrassment of my fellow. I never cursed my fellow when I was lying by myself in bed. I never walked over in the marketplace to someone who owed me money.

G. "In my entire life I never lost my temper in my household."

H. This was meant to carry out that which is stated as follows: "I will give heed to the way that is blameless. Oh when wilt thou come to me? I will walk with integrity of heart within my house" (Ps. 101:2).

What I find striking in this story is that mastery of the Torah is only one means of attaining the *zekhut* that had enabled the sage to keep the house from collapsing. And Torah-study is not the primary means of attaining *zekhut*. The question at E provides the key, together with its answer at F. For what the sage did to gain such remarkable *zekhut* is not to master such-and-so many tractates of the Mishnah. It was rather acts of courtesy, consideration, gentility, restraint. These produced *zekhut*, all of them acts of self-abnegation or the avoidance of power over others and the submission to the will and the requirement of self-esteem of others. Torah-study is simply an item on a list of actions or attitudes that generate *zekhut*.

Here, in a moral setting, we find the politics replicated: the form of power that the system promises derives from the rejection of power that the world recognizes – legitimate violence replaced by legitimation of the absence of the power to commit violence or of the failure to commit violence. And, when we ask, whence that sort of power? the answer lies in the gaining of *zekhut* in a variety of ways, not in the acquisition of *zekhut* through the study of the Torah solely or even primarily. But, we note, the story at hand speaks of a sage in particular. He has gained *zekhut* by not acting the way sages are commonly assumed to behave but in a humble way.

In context of this story, *zekhut* then may prove a virtue dependent upon the situation of the Torah and its study, in consequence of which we should have to impute to the gnostic Torah systemic priority, indeed centrality, finding in the new learning the key to the successor-system as a whole. But that is, in fact, not so. At hand is not a religious system in which the transformation of the individual through salvific knowledge provides the compelling answer to the question of personal salvation. A different question stands at center-stage, and a different answer altogether defines the dramatic tension of the theatrical globe. At stake, as we shall now see, is a public and a national question, one concerning Israel's history and destiny, to which the individual and his salvation, while important, are distinctly subordinated. Not Torah-study, which may generate *zekhut*, but *zekhut* itself defines what is at issue, the generative problematic of the system, and only when we grasp the answer provided by *zekhut* shall we reach a definition of the question that precipitated the systemic construction and the formation of its categories, principal and contingent alike.[14]

---

[14]But Torah is contingent and instrumental, *zekhut* is uncontingent and the system's sole (so it appears at this moment) independent variable. And yet, it seems to me clear, the symbol of Torah does remain the center and heart of

The importance of the gnostic Torah in no way diminishes when we recognize the subordinate position of the Torah in the successor-system. For the upshot remains systemically indicative. In unifying the distinct categories of learning and not deeds or virtue but one's personal condition in the supernatural world, the recasting of the category of the world-view from an intellectual and even a moral to a salvific and a supernatural indicator, encompassing data not formerly noted or even assembled at all, shows the successor-system's novel power of integration. If Torah-study changes me not only in my knowledge or even virtue but my relationship to Heaven, endowing me with the supernatural power, then the system as a whole signals a union of Heaven and earth that was formerly unimagined. What I know concerns not only earth but Heaven, the power that knowledge brings governs in both realms.

Study of the Torah changed the one who studied because through it he entered into the mind of God, learning how God's mind worked when God formed the Torah, written and oral alike and (in the explicit view of Genesis Rabbah 1:1) consulted the Torah in created the world. And there, in the intellect of God, in their judgment humanity gained access to the only means of uniting intellect with existential condition as to salvation. The Mishnah had set forth the rules that governed the natural world in relationship to Heaven. But knowledge of the Torah now joined the one world, known through nature, with the other world, the world of supernature, where, in the end, intellect merely served in the quest for salvation. Through Torah-study sages claimed for themselves a place in that very process of thought that had given birth to nature; but it was a supernatural process, and knowledge of that process on its own terms would transform and, in the nature of things, save. That explains the integrative power of imputing supernatural power to learning. And, now that we realize what was at stake in the gnostic Torah, we understand the full gravity of the simple statement that the system's orbit encircled not the Torah but *zekhut*.

---

the Judaism that emerged from late antiquity. What this impression suggests to me is that in the third stage in the formation of the Judaism of the Dual Torah, attested by the Bavli and associated Midrash-compilations, I should find *zekhut* a not-central, but now-contingent variable, replaced by Torah as the independent variable and court of final appeal. Whether that will be the case I cannot now predict.

5

The New Order: The Political Economy of *Zekhut*

Zekhut, special grace from Heaven, scarce or common as our capacity for uncoerced action dictated, puissant or supine as our strength to refrain from deeds of worldly power decided, accomplished the systemic integration of the successor-documents. That protean conception formed into a cogent political economy for the social order of Israel the economics and the politics that made powerlessness into power, disinheritance into wealth. Acts of will consisting of submission, on one's own, to the will of Heaven endowed Israel with a lien and entitlement upon Heaven. What we cannot by will impose, we can by will evoke. What we cannot accomplish through coercion, we can achieve through submission. God will do for us what we cannot do for ourselves, when we do for God what God cannot make us do. In a wholly concrete and tangible sense, love God with all the heart, the soul, the might, we have. That systemic statement justifies classifying the successor-system as religious in as profound and complete a way as the initial system had been wholly and restrictedly philosophical.

Zekhut stands for the empowerment, of a supernatural character, that derives from the virtue of one's ancestry or from one's own virtuous deeds of a very particular order. No single word in English bears the same meaning, nor can I identify a synonym for *zekhut* in the canonical writings in the original either. The difficulty of translating a word of systemic consequence with a single word in some other language (or in the language of the system's documents themselves) tells us we deal with what is unique, beyond comparison and therefore contrast and comprehension. What is most particular to, distinctive of, the systemic structure and its functioning requires definition through circumlocution: "the heritage of virtue and its consequent entitlements."[1] The word *zekhut* for the successor-system forms the systemic counterpart to the mythologoumenon of the resurrection of Jesus Christ, unique son of God, for important Christianities.

It must follow that *zekhut*, not Torah, in a single word defines the generative myth, the critical symbol of the successor-Judaism. The signal that the gnostic Torah formed a mere component in a system that transcended Torah-study and defined its structure in some way other than by appeal to the symbol and activity of the Torah comes from a simple fact. Ordinary folk, not disciples of sages, have access to *zekhut* entirely outside of study of the Torah. In stories not told about rabbis, a single remarkable deed, exemplary for its deep humanity, sufficed to win for an ordinary person the *zekhut* – "the heritage of virtue and its consequent entitlements" – that elicits the same marks of supernatural favor enjoyed by some rabbis on account of their Torah-study.

Accordingly, the systemic centrality of *zekhut* in the structure, the critical importance of the heritage of virtue together with its supernatural entitlements – these emerge in a striking claim. It is framed in extreme form – another mark of the unique place of *zekhut* within the system. Even though a man was degraded, one action sufficed to win for him that heavenly glory to which rabbis in lives of Torah-study aspired. The mark of the system's integration around *zekhut* lies in its insistence that all Israelites, not only sages, could gain *zekhut* for themselves (and their descendants). A single remarkable deed, exemplary for its deep humanity, sufficed to win for an ordinary person the *zekhut* that elicits supernatural favor enjoyed by some rabbis on account of their Torah-study. The centrality of *zekhut* in the systemic structure, the critical importance of the heritage of virtue together with its supernatural entitlements

---

[1] The commonly-used single word, "merit," does not apply, but "merit" bears the sense of reward for carrying out an obligation, for example, by doing such and such, he merited so and so. *Zekhut*, by contrast, commonly refers to acts of supererogatory free will, and therefore while such acts are meritorious in the sense of being virtuous (by definition), they are not acts that one owes but that one gives. And the rewards that accumulate in response to such actions are always miraculous or supernatural or signs of divine grace, for example, an unusually long life, the power to prevent a dilapidated building from collapsing. I return to this matter below, note 4, when I take up the amplification of the meaning of *zekhut* in response to concrete usages of the word in the earliest document in which it plays a significant role, tractate Avot and also appears in a context sufficiently broad to allow for philological exegesis to take place.

The New Order: The Political Economy of Zekhut

therefore emerge in a striking claim. Even though a man was degraded, one action sufficed to win for him that heavenly glory to which rabbis in general aspired. The rabbinical storyteller whose writing we shall consider assuredly identifies with this lesson, since it is the point of his story and its climax.

In all three instances that follow, defining what the individual must do to gain *zekhut*, the point is that the deeds of the heroes of the story make them worthy of having their prayers answered, which is a mark of the working of *zekhut*. It is deeds beyond the strict requirements of the Torah, and even the limits of the law altogether, that transform the hero into a holy man, whose holiness served just like that of a sage marked as such by knowledge of the Torah The following stories should not be understood as expressions of the mere sentimentality of the clerks concerning the lower orders, for they deny in favor of a single action of surpassing power sages' lifelong devotion to what the sages held to be the highest value, knowledge of the Torah:

Y. Taanit 1:4.I.

F. A certain man came before one of the relatives of R. Yannai. He said to him, "Rabbi, attain *zekhut* through me [by giving me charity]."

G. He said to him, "And didn't your father leave you money?"

H. He said to him, "No."

I. He said to him, "Go and collect what your father left in deposit with others."

J. He said to him, "I have heard concerning property my father deposited with others that it was gained by violence [so I don't want it]."

K. He said to him, "You are worthy of praying and having your prayers answered."

The point of K, of course, is self-evidently a reference to the possession of entitlement to supernatural favor, and it is gained, we see, through deeds that the law of the Torah cannot require but must favor: what one does on one's own volition, beyond the measure of the law. Here I see the opposite of sin. A sin is what one has done by one's own volition beyond all limits of the law. So an act that generates *zekhut* for the individual is the counterpart and opposite: what one does by one's own volition that also is beyond all requirements of the law.

L. A certain ass driver appeared before the rabbis [the context requires: in a dream] and prayed, and rain came. The rabbis sent and brought him and said to him, "What is your trade?"

M. He said to them, "I am an ass driver."

N. They said to him, "And how do you conduct your business?"

O. He said to them, "One time I rented my ass to a certain woman, and she was weeping on the way, and I said to her, 'What's with you?' and she said to me, 'The husband of that woman [me] is in prison [for debt], and I wanted to see what I can do to free him.' So I sold my ass and I gave her the proceeds, and I said to her, 'Here is your money, free your husband, but do not sin [by becoming a prostitute to raise the necessary funds].'"

P. They said to him, "You are worthy of praying and having your prayers answered."

The ass-driver clearly has a powerful lien on Heaven, so that his prayers are answered, even while those of others are not. What he did to get that entitlement? He did what no law could demand: impoverished himself to save the woman from a "fate worse than death."

Q. In a dream of R. Abbahu, Mr. Pentakaka ["Five sins"] appeared, who prayed that rain would come, and it rained. R. Abbahu sent and summoned him. He said to him, "What is your trade?"

R. He said to him, "Five sins does that man [I] do every day, [for I am a pimp:] hiring whores, cleaning up the theater, bringing home their garments for washing, dancing, and performing before them."

S. He said to him, "And what sort of decent thing have you ever done?"

T. He said to him, "One day that man [I] was cleaning the theater, and a woman came and stood behind a pillar and cried. I said to her, 'What's with you?' And she said to me, 'That woman's [my] husband is in prison, and I wanted to see what I can do to free him,' so I sold my bed and cover, and I gave the proceeds to her. I said to her, 'Here is your money, free your husband, but do not sin.'"

U. He said to him, "You are worthy of praying and having your prayers answered."

Q moves us still further, since the named man has done everything sinful that one can do, and, more to the point, he does it every day. So the singularity of the act of *zekhut*, which suffices if done only one time, encompasses its power to outweigh a life of sin – again, an act of *zekhut* as the mirror-image and opposite of sin. Here again, the single act of saving a woman from a "fate worse than death" has sufficed.

V. A pious man from Kefar Imi appeared [in a dream] to the rabbis. He prayed for rain and it rained. The rabbis went up to him. His householders told them that he was sitting on a hill. They went out to him, saying to him, "Greetings," but he did not answer them.

W. He was sitting and eating, and he did not say to them, "You break bread too."

X.	When he went back home, he made a bundle of faggots and put his cloak on top of the bundle [instead of on his shoulder].
Y.	When he came home, he said to his household [wife], "These rabbis are here [because] they want me to pray for rain. If I pray and it rains, it is a disgrace for them, and if not, it is a profanation of the Name of Heaven. But come, you and I will go up [to the roof] and pray. If it rains, we shall tell them, 'We are not worthy to pray and have our prayers answered.'"
Z.	They went up and prayed and it rained.
AA.	They came down to them [and asked], "Why have the rabbis troubled themselves to come here today?"
BB.	They said to him, "We wanted you to pray so that it would rain."
CC.	He said to them, "Now do you really need my prayers? Heaven already has done its miracle."
DD.	They said to him, "Why, when you were on the hill, did we say hello to you, and you did not reply?"
EE.	He said to them, "I was then doing my job. Should I then interrupt my concentration [on my work]?"
FF.	They said to him, "And why, when you sat down to eat, did you not say to us 'You break bread too'?"
GG.	He said to them, "Because I had only my small ration of bread. Why would I have invited you to eat by way of mere flattery [when I knew I could not give you anything at all]?"
HH.	They said to him, "And why when you came to go down, did you put your cloak on top of the bundle?"
II.	He said to them, "Because the cloak was not mine. It was borrowed for use at prayer. I did not want to tear it."
JJ.	They said to him, "And why, when you were on the hill, did your wife wear dirty clothes, but when you came down from the mountain, did she put on clean clothes?"
KK.	He said to them, "When I was on the hill, she put on dirty clothes, so that no one would gaze at her. But when I came home from the hill, she put on clean clothes, so that I would not gaze on any other woman."
LL.	They said to him, "It is well that you pray and have your prayers answered."

The pious man of V, finally, enjoys the recognition of the sages by reason of his lien upon Heaven, able as he is to pray and bring rain. What has so endowed him with *zekhut*? Acts of punctiliousness of a moral order: concentrating on his work, avoiding an act of dissimulation, integrity in the disposition of a borrowed object, his wife's concern not to attract other men and her equal concern to make herself attractive to her husband. None of these stories refers explicitly to *zekhut*; all of them tell us about what it means to enjoy not an entitlement by inheritance but a lien accomplished by one's own supererogatory acts of restraint.

Zekhut integrates what has been differentiated. Holding together learning, virtue, and supernatural standing, by explaining how Torah-study transforms the learning man, *zekhut* further makes implausible those points of distinction between economics, and politics that bore the systemic message of the initial philosophy. Hierarchical classification, with its demonstration of the upward-reaching unity of all being, gives way to a different, and more compelling proposition: the unity of all being within the heritage of *zekhut*, to be attained equally and without differentiation in all the principal parts of the social order. The definition of *zekhut* therefore carries us to the heart of the integrating and integrated religious system of Judaism.

My claim to describe the transformation of one system by a connected but autonomous successor-system, therefore stands or falls not upon the unprecedented character of the concept, but upon the capacity of the category at hand to hold the whole together. What we shall now see is that *zekhut*, an entirely available idea, had been systemically tangential to the philosophical Judaism, and only now proved itself systemically critical in the successor-structure. That fact will accomplish the twin-tasks facing anyone who claims to describe the connections between two historically related systems, represented by a single canon. Specifically, showing that *zekhut* was both available and systemically inert will both prove the connectedness of the two systems, and also show also how the successor-system transformed the first. That is to say, the system-builders represented by the Talmud of the Land of Israel, Genesis Rabbah, Leviticus Rabbah, and Pesiqta deRab Kahana made their own choices within their inheritance. Their system consequently defined its own categories and accomplished through its own medium the integration of its systemic components, the counterpart-categories.[2] But before we explore the place and integrating power of *zekhut* within the systemic structure and system, we had best reconsider the definition of the word that seems to me so critical to the statement of this Judaism.

---

[2]In my *Judaism: The Evidence of the Mishnah*, pp. 230-286, I have asked and answered in terms of the power of intentionality as the medium of classification the question of what holds the system together, and in the counterpart study of the philosophical system of Judaism attested by the Mishnah, *Judaism as Philosophy. The Method and Message of the Mishnah*. Columbia, 1991: University of South Carolina Press, I have identified the integrating and generative problematic, that of hierarchical classification. These two answers seem to me cogent with one another, even though the one appeals to psychological, the other to philosophical considerations.

The New Order: The Political Economy of Zekhut

The word *zekhut* bears a variety of meanings, as Jastrow summarizes the data,[3] and the pertinence of each possible meaning is to be determined in context: [1] acquittal, plea in favor of the defendant; [2] doing good, blessing; [3] protecting influence of good conduct, merit; [4] advantage, privilege, benefit. The first meaning pertains solely in juridical (or metaphorically-juridical) contexts; the second represents a very general and imprecise use of the word, since a variety of other words bear the same meaning. Only the third and the fourth meanings pertain, since they are particular to this word, on the one side, and also religious, on the other. That is to say, only through using the word *zekhut* do authors of compositions and authorships of composites express the sense given at No. 3. Moreover, it will rapidly become clear, in context that No. 4 is not to be distinguished from No. 3, since "protecting influence of good conduct" when the word *zekhut* appears always yields "advantage, privilege, benefit." It follows that, for the purposes of systemic analysis, passages in which the word *zekhut* bears the sense, in Jastrow's words, of "the protecting influence of good conduct" which yields "advantage, privilege, or benefit" will tell us how the word *zekhut* functions.

My simple definition emphasizes "heritage," because the advantages or privileges conferred by *zekhut* may be inherited and also passed on; it stresses "entitlements" because advantages or privileges always, invariably result from receiving *zekhut* from ancestors or acquiring it on one's own; and I use the word "virtue" to refer to those supererogatory acts that demand a reward because they form matters of choice, the gift of the individual and his or her act of free will, an act that is at the same time [1] uncompelled, for example, by the obligations imposed by the Torah, but [2] also valued by the Torah. The systemic importance of the conception of *zekhut* derives from its capacity to unite the generations in a heritage of entitlements; *zekhut* is fundamentally a historical category and concept, in that, like all historical systems of thought, it explains the present in terms of the past, and the future in terms of the present.

Because *zekhut* is something one may receive as an inheritance, out of the distant past, *zekhut* imposes upon the definition of the social entity, "Israel," a genealogical meaning. It furthermore imparts a distinctive character to the definitions of way of life. So

---

[3]Marcus Jastrow, *A Dictionary of the Targumim, The Talmud Babli and Yerushalmi, and the Midrashic Literature* (repr. N. Y., 1950: Pardes Publishing House, Inc.), p. 398.

the task of the political component of a theory of the social order, which is to define the social entity by appeal to empowerment, and of the economic component, which is to identify scarce resources by specification of the rationality of right management, is accomplished in a single word, which stands for a conception, a symbol, and a myth. All three components of this religious theory of the social order turn out to present specific applications, in context, for the general conception of *zekhut*. For the first source of *zekhut* derives from the definition of Israel as family; the entitlements of supernatural power deriving from virtue then care inherited from Abraham, Isaac, and Jacob. The second source is personal: the power one can gain for one's own heirs, moreover, by virtuous deeds. *Zekhut* deriving from either source is to be defined in context: what can you do if you have *zekhut*., that you cannot do if you do not have *zekhut*. and to whom can you do it. The answer to that question tells you the empowerment of *zekhut*.

Now in the nature of things, a theory of power or violence that is legitimately exercised falls into the category of a politics, and a conception of the scarce resource, defined as supernatural power that is to be rationally managed, falls into the category of an economics. That is why in the concept of *zekhut*, we find the union of economics and politics into a political economy: a theory of the whole society in its material and social relationships as expressed in institutions that permanently are given the right to impose order through real or threatened violence and in the assignment of goods and benefits, as systemically defined to be sure, through a shared rationality.

Since I have identified as systemically active not the conception but the word and its usages, we shall focus not upon general situations, for example, in which one receives some sort of benefit by reason of in inheritance from some other person, but upon specific usages of the word at hand.[4] That focus is required not only by the logic of this study, but also by the difficulty of knowing what belongs and what does not belong when *zekhut* bears the confusing translation of "merit," and when "merit" promiscuously refers to pretty much anything that one gets *not* by one's own merit or just desserts at all, but despite what one has done. Scripture for example knows that God loves Israel because he loved the patriarchs (Deut. 4:37); the memory or deeds of the righteous patriarchs and matriarchs appear in a broad range of contexts, for example, "Remember your servants, Abraham, Isaac, and Jacob" (Ex. 32:13), for Moses, and "Remember the good deeds of David, your servant" (II Chr. 6:42), for David. At

---

[4]In this context, the concordance is the key. In others, of course, it is not.

The New Order: The Political Economy of Zekhut

stake throughout is giving people what they do not merit, to be sure. But in these contexts, "remembering" what X did as an argument in behalf of favor for Y does not invoke the word *zekhut*, and the context does not require use of that word either.[5] Accordingly, our problem of definition requires limitation to precise usages of a given word. Were we to propose to work our way back from situations that seem to exhibit conceptual affinities to the concept represented by the word under consideration, cases, for instance, in which someone appeals to what is owing the fathers in behalf of the children, we shall not accomplish the goal at hand, which is one of definition of a word that in this system, meaning, in these documents in particular, bears a very particular meaning, and, more to the point, carries out a highly critical role.

At M. San. 4:1, 5:4, 5:5, and 6:1 we find *zekhut* in the sense of "acquittal," as against conviction; at M Ket 13:6 the sense is, "right," as in "right of ownership;" at M Git 8:8 the sense is not "right of ownership" in a narrow sense, but "advantage," in a broader one of prerogative: "It is not within the power of the first husband to render void the right of the second." These usages of course bear no point in common with the sense of the word later on. But the evidence of the Mishnah seems to me to demonstrate that the sense of *zekhut* paramount in the successor-documents is not original to them. The following usage at M. Qid. 4:14 seems to me to invite something very like the sense that I have proposed here. So states M. Qid. 4:14E-I:

> R. Meir says, "A man should always teach his son a clean and easy trade. And let him pray to him to whom belong riches and possessions. For there is no trade which does not involve poverty or wealth. For poverty does not come from one's trade, nor does wealth come from one's trade. But all is in accord with a man's *zekhut*."

Quite how to translate our key-word in this passage is not self-evident. The context permits a variety of possibilities. The same usage seems to me to be located at M. Sot. 3:4, 3:5, and here there is clear indication of the presence of a conception of an entitlement deriving from some source other than one's own deed of the moment:

---

[5]God's "remembering" is the principal point in the scriptural situations adduced as evidence for the ancient origins of the concept of *zekhut*. Then the other part of the same concept, that there are deeds I may do that gain *zekhut* for myself, is excluded, and hence *zekhut* as it is revealed in the systemic sources is not represented in the scriptural ones.

Mishnah-tractate Sotah 3:4-5

3:4. E. There is the possibility that *zekhut* suspends the curse for one year, and there is the possibility that *zekhut* suspends the curse for two years, and there is the possibility that *zekhut* suspends the curse for three years.

F. On this basis Ben Azzai says, "A man is required to teach Torah to his daughter.

G. "For if she should drink the water, she should know that [if nothing happens to her], *zekhut* is what suspends [the curse from taking effect]."

3:5 A. R. Simeon says, "*Zekhut* does not suspend the effects of the bitter water.

B. "And if you say, '*Zekhut* does suspend the effects of the bitter water,' you will weaken the effect of the water for all the women who have to drink it.

C. "And you give a bad name to all the women who drink it who turned out to be pure.

D. "For people will say, 'They are unclean, but *zekhut* suspended the effects of the water for them.'"

E. Rabbi says, "*Zekhut* does suspend the effects of the bitter water. But she will not bear children or continue to be pretty. And she will waste away, and in the end she will have the same [unpleasant] death."

Now if we insert for *zekhut* at each point, "the heritage of virtue and its consequent entitlements," (thus: "For people will say, 'They are unclean, but *zekhut* suspended the effects of the water for them, then, "For people will say, 'They are unclean, but the heritage of virtue and its consequent entitlements suspended the effects of the water for them)."we have good sense. That is to say, the woman may not suffer the penalty to which she is presumably condemnable, not because her act or condition (for example, her innocence) has secured her acquittal or nullified the effects of the ordeal, but because she enjoys some advantage extrinsic to her own act or condition. She may be guilty, but she may also possess a benefice deriving by inheritance, hence, heritage of virtue, and so be entitled to a protection not because of her own, but because of someone else's action or condition.

That meaning may be sustained by the passage at hand, even though it is not required by it; still, it seems to me plausible that the word *zekhut* in the Mishnah bears not only a juridical but a religious sense. But, if it does, that usage is not systemically critical, or even very important. If we search the pages of the Mishnah for places in which, absent the word *zekhut*, the conception in hand is present, we find none – not one. For example, there simply is no reference to gaining *zekhut* through doing one's duty, for example, in reciting the *Shema* or studying the Torah, and references to studying the Torah, for example, at M. Peah 1:1, do not encompass the conception that, in

The New Order: The Political Economy of Zekhut 153

doing so, one gains an advantage or entitlement for either one's own descendants or for all Israel. On that basis we are on firm ground in holding the twin-positions [1] that the word bore, among its meanings, the one important later on, and also [2] that the word played no systemic role, in the philosophical system adumbrated by the Mishnah, commensurate with the importance accorded to the word and its sense in the religious system that took shape and came to expression in the successor-writings.[6]

The evidence of tractate Abot is consistent with that of the Mishnah. The juridical sense of *zekhut* occurs at 1:6, "Judge everybody as though to be acquitted," more comprehensibly translated, "And give everybody the benefit of the doubt," forming a reasonably coherent with the usages important in Mishnah-tractate Sanhedrin. In Abot, however, we have clear evidence for the sense of the word that seems to me demanded later on. At M. Abot 2:2 we find the following:

Tractate Abot 2:2

C. "And all who work with the community- – let them work with them for the sake of Heaven.
D. "For the [1] *zekhut* of their fathers strengthens them, and their [fathers'] [2] righteousness stands forever.
E. "And as for you, I credit you with a great reward, as if you had done [all of the work required by the community on your own merit alone]."

Here there is no meaning possible other than that I have given above: "the heritage of virtue and its consequent entitlements." The reference to an advantage that one gains by reason of inheritance out of one's fathers' righteousness is demanded by the parallel between *zekhut* of clause [1] and *righteousness* of clause [2]. Whatever the conceivable ambiguity of the Mishnah, none is sustained by the

---

[6]A rapid review of the Tosefta's usages of the word *zekhut* suffices, since there are no surprises. Juridical usages are at these passages: T. Git. 1:5 (zekhut in the sense of an advantage or a benefit); Sanhedrin 1:8, 3:3, 9:1, 2, 3, 4, 10:11; T. Qid. 1:13. An indeterminate sense of zekhut in the sense of "advantage" or "entitlement," without a clear definition of what one must do or why one gains a benefit therefrom, is at T. Pe. 1:2, T. Yoma 5:12=T. Ta. 4:9 (*zekhut* in contrast to disadvantage or liability, conceivably a juridical usage). The sense, "by reason of the claim..." or "the entitlement of..." seems to me justified in context at T. M.S. 5:27, 29, T. Sot. 11:10, and T. B.B> 7:9. Overall, I do not find here anything as decisive as what we see in tractate-Avot, though the case may be made that some of the Tosefta's passages use the word in the same sense as is revealed in that tractate. In the balance, nonetheless, I judge that a full-scale review of Tosefta's usages would not greatly change the results just now given for the Mishnah.

context at hand, which is explicit in language and pellucid in message. That the sense is exactly the same as the one I have proposed is shown at the following passages, which seem to me to exhibit none of the possible ambiguity that characterized the usage of *zekhut* in the Mishnah:

Tractate Abot 5:18

A. He who causes *zekhut* to the community never causes sin.
B. And he who causes the community to sin – they never give him a sufficient chance to attain penitence.

Here the contrast is between causing *zekhut* and causing sin, so *zekhut* is the opposite of sin. The continuation is equally clear that a person attained *zekhut* and endowed the community with *zekhut*, or sinned and made the community sin:

C. Moses attained *zekhut* and bestowed *zekhut* on the community.
D. So the *zekhut* of the community is assigned to his [credit],
E. as it is said, "He executed the justice of the Lord and his judgments with Israel" (Deut. 33:21).
F. Jeroboam sinned and caused the community to sin.
G. So the sin of the community is assigned to his [debit],
H. as it is said, "For the sins of Jeroboam which he committed and wherewith he made Israel to sin" (I Kings 15:30).

The appropriateness of interpreting the passage in the way I have proposed will now be shown to be self-evident. All that is required is to substitute for *zekhut* the proposed translation:

C. Moses attained the heritage of virtue and bestowed its consequent entitlements on the community.
D. So the heritage of virtue end its entitlements enjoyed by the community are assigned to his [credit],

The sense then is simple. Moses through actions of his own (of an unspecified sort) acquired *zekhut*, which is the credit for such actions that accrued to him and bestowed upon him certain supernatural entitlements; and he for his part passed on as an inheritance that credit, a lien on Heaven for the performance of these same supernatural entitlements: *zekhut*, pure and simple.

If we may now define *zekhut* as the initial system explicated in tractate Abot has used the word, we must pay close attention to the antonymic structure before us. The juridical opposites are guilty as against innocent, the religious ones, sin as against the opposite of sin. That seems to me to require our interpreting *zekhut* as [1] an action, as distinct from a (mere) attitude; that [2] is precisely the opposite of a sinful one; it is, moreover, an action that [3] may be done by an individual or by the community at large, and one that [4] a leader

The New Order: The Political Economy of Zekhut

may provoke the community to do (or not do). The contrast of sin to *zekhut* requires further attention. Since, in general, two classes that are compared to begin with, if different, must constitute opposites, the ultimate definition of *zekhut* requires us to ask how *zekhut* is precisely the opposite of sin. For one thing, as we recall, Scripture is explicit that the burden of sins cannot be passively inherited, willy-nilly, but, to form a heritage of guilt, must be actively accepted and renewed; the children cannot be made to suffer for the sins of the parents, unless they repeat them. Then *zekhut*, being a mirror-image, can be passively inherited, not by one's own merit[7] but by one's good fortune alone. But what constitute these *actions* that form mirror-images of sins? Answers to that critical question must emerge from the systemic documents before us, since they do not occur in those of the initial system.

That simple fact, too, attests to the systemic centrality of *zekhut*: it defines a principal point of exegesis.[8] For the question left open by the Mishnah's merely episodic, and somewhat opaque, reference to the matter and the incomplete evidence provided by its principal apologetic's representation as well, alas, is the critical issue. Precisely what actions generate *zekhut,* and which ones do not? To find answers to those questions, we have to turn to the successor-documents, since not a single passage in the Mishnah or in tractate-Abot provides me with information on the matter of what I must do to secure for myself or my descendants a lien upon Heaven, that is, an entitlement to supernatural favor and even action of a miraculous order.

We turn first to the conception of the *zekhut* that has been accumulated by the patriarchs and been passed on to Israel, their

---

[7] Indeed, the conception of merit is so alien to the concept of *zekhut*, which one enjoys whether or not one personally has done something to merit it, that I am puzzled on how "merit" ever seemed to anyone to serve as a translation of the word *zekhut*. If I can inherit the entitlements accrued by my ancestors, then these entitlements not only cannot be classed as merit(ed by me), they must be classed as a heritage bestowed by others and not merited by me at all. And, along these same lines, the *zekhut* that I gain for myself may entitle me to certain benefits, but it may also accrue to the advantage of the community in which I live (as is made explicit by Avot for Moses's *zekhut*) and also of my descendants. The transitive character of zekhut, the power we have of receiving it from others and handing it on to others, serves as the distinctive trait of this particular entitlement, and, it must follow from that definitive characteristic, zekhut is the opposite of merit, as I said, and its character is obscured by the confusion created through that long-standing and conventional, but wrong translation of the word.

[8] Here again, the exegesis of exegesis defines the history of religion.

children. The reason is that the single distinctive trait of *zekhut* is its transitive quality: one need not earn or merit the supernatural power and resource represented by the things you can do if you have *zekhut* but cannot do if you do not have it. One can inherit that entitlement from others, dead or living. Moses not only attains *zekhut* but he also imparts *zekhut* to the community of which he is leader, and the same is so for any Israelite. That conception is broadened in the successor-documents into the deeply historical notion of *zekhut abot*, empowerment of a supernatural character to which Israel is entitled by reason of what the patriarchs and matriarchs in particular did long ago. That conception forms the foundation for the paramount sense of *zekhut* in the successor-system: the Israelite possesses a lien upon Heaven by reason of God's love for the patriarchs and matriarchs, his appreciation for certain things they did, and his response to those actions not only in favoring them but also in entitling their descendants to do or benefit from otherwise unattainable miracles. *Zekhut* explains the present – particularly what is odd and unpredictable in the presence – by appeal to the past, hence forms a distinctively historical conception.

Within the historically-grounded metaphor of Israel as a family expressed by the conception of *zekhut abot*, Israel was a family, the children of Abraham, Isaac, and Jacob, or children of Israel, in as concrete and genealogical sense. Israel hence fell into the genus, family, as the particular species of family generated by Abraham and Sarah. The distinguishing trait of that species was that it possessed the inheritance, or heritage, of the patriarchs and matriarchs, and that inheritance, consisting of *zekhut*, served the descendants and heirs as protection and support. It follows that the systemic position of the conception of *zekhut* to begin with lies in its power to define the social entity, and hence, *zekhut* (in the terms of the initial category-formation, the philosophical one) forms a fundamentally political conception[9] and only secondarily an economic and philosophical one.

---

[9]And that political definition of the systemic role and function of *zekhut* is strengthened by the polemical power of the concept vis à vis the Christian critique of Israel after the flesh. The doctrine of the *zekhut* of the ancestors served as a component of the powerful polemic concerning Israel. Specifically, that concrete, historical Israel, meaning for Christian theologians "Israel after the flesh," in the literature before us manifestly and explicitly claimed fleshly origin in Abraham and Sarah. The extended family indeed constituted precisely what the Christian theologians said: an Israel after the flesh, a family linked by genealogy. The heritage then became an inheritance, and what was inherited from the ancestors was a

But *zekhut* serves, in particular, that counterpart category that speaks of not legitimate but illegitimate violence, not power but weakness. In context, time and again, we observe that *zekhut* is the power of the weak. People who through their own merit and capacity can accomplish nothing, can accomplish miracles through what others do for them in leaving a heritage of *zekhut*.. And, not to miss the stunning message of the triplet of stories cited above, *zekhut* also is what the weak and excluded and despised can do that outweighs in power what the great masters of the Torah have accomplished. In the context of a system that represents Torah as supernatural, that claim of priority for *zekhut* represents a considerable transvaluation of power, as much as of value. And, by the way, *zekhut* also forms the inheritance of the disinherited: what you receive as a heritage when you have nothing in the present and have gotten nothing in the past, that scarce resource that is free and unearned but much valued. So let us dwell upon the definitive character of the transferability of *zekhut* in its formulation, *zekhut abot*, the *zekhut* handed on by the ancestors, the transitive character of the concept and its standing as a heritage of entitlements.

It is in the successor-documents that the concept of *zekhut* is joined with *abot*, that is, the *zekhut* that has been left as Israel's family inheritance by the patriarchs or ancestors, yielding the very specific notion, defining the systemic politics, its theory of the social entity, of Israel not as a (mere) community (for example, as in tractate Abot's reference to Moses's bestowing *zekhut* upon the community) but as a family, with a history that takes the form of a genealogy, precisely as Genesis has represented that history.[10] Now *zekhut* was joined to the metaphor of the genealogy of patriarchs and matriarchs and served to form the missing link, explaining how the inheritance and heritage were transmitted from them to their heirs. Consequently, the family, called "Israel," could draw upon the

---

heavenly store, a treasure of *zekhut*, which protected the descendants when their own *zekhut* proved insufficient. The conflict is a political one, involving the legitimacy of the power of the now-Christian empire, denied by this "Israel," affirmed by the other one.

[10] And it is by no means an accident, therefore, that Genesis was one of the two pentateuchal books selected by the system-builders for their Midrash-exegesis. The systemic centrality of *zekhut* accounts for their selection. In my *Judaism and Scripture*, pp. 94-125, I have accounted for the selection of the book of Leviticus, an explanation that accords in a striking way with the one pertaining to Genesis. That means that any system-analysis must explain why one scriptural book, and not some other, has been chosen for the Midrash-compilation(s) that that system sets forth alongside its Mishnah-amplification.

family estate, consisting of the inherited *zekhut* of matriarchs and patriarchs in such a way as to benefit today from the heritage of yesterday. This notion involved very concrete problems. If "Israel, the family" sinned, it could call upon the "*zekhut*" accumulated by Abraham and Isaac at the binding of Isaac (Genesis 22) to win forgiveness for that sin. True, "fathers will not die on account of the sin of the sons," but the children may benefit from the *zekhut* of the forebears. That concrete expression of the larger metaphor imparted to the metaphor a practical consequence, moral and theological, that was not at all neglected.

A survey of Genesis Rabbah proves indicative of the character and use of the doctrine of *zekhut*, because that systematic reading of the book of Genesis dealt with the founders of the family and made explicit the definition of Israel as family. What we shall see is that *zekhut* draws in its wake the notion of the inheritance of an on-going (historical) family, that of Abraham and Sarah, and *zekhut* worked itself out in the moments of crisis of that family in its larger affairs. So the Israelites later on enjoy enormous *zekhut* through the deeds of the patriarchs and matriarchs. That conception comes to expression in what follows:

Genesis Rabbah LXXVI:V.

2. A. "...for with only my staff I crossed this Jordan, and now I have become two companies:"
   B. R. Judah bar Simon in the name of R. Yohanan: "In the Torah, in the Prophets, and in the Writings we find proof that the Israelites were able to cross the Jordan only on account of the *zekhut* achieved by Jacob:
   C. "In the Torah: '...for with only my staff I crossed this Jordan, and now I have become two companies.'
   D. "In the prophets: 'Then you shall let your children know, saying, "Israel came over this Jordan on dry land"' (Josh. 4:22), meaning our father, Israel.
   E. "In the Writings: 'What ails you, O you sea, that you flee? You Jordan, that you burn backward? At the presence of the God of Jacob' (Ps. 114:5ff.)."

Here is a perfect illustration of my definition of *zekhut* as an entitlement I enjoy by reason of what someone else – an ancestor – has done; and that entitlement involves supernatural power. Jacob did not only leave *zekhut* as an estate to his heirs. The process is reciprocal and on-going. *Zekhut* deriving from the ancestors had helped Jacob himself:

Genesis Rabbah LXXVII:III.3.

A. "When the man saw that he did not prevail against Jacob, [he touched the hollow of his thigh, and Jacob's thigh was put out of joint as he wrestled with him]" (Gen. 32:25):

B. Said R. Hinena bar Isaac, "[God said to the angel,] 'He is coming against you with five "amulets" hung on his neck, that is, his own *zekhut*, the *zekhut* of his father and of his mother and of his grandfather and of his grandmother.

C. "'Check yourself out, can you stand up against even his own *zekhut* [let alone the *zekhut* of his parents and grandparents].'

D. "The matter may be compared to a king who had a savage dog and a tame lion. The king would take his son and sick him against the lion, and if the dog came to have a fight with the son, he would say to the dog, 'The lion cannot have a fight with him, are you going to make out in a fight with him?'

E. "So if the nations come to have a fight with Israel, the Holy One, blessed be He, says to them,. 'Your angelic prince could not stand up to Israel, and as to you, how much the more so!'"

The collectivity of *zekhut*, not only its transferability, is illustrated here as well: what an individual does confers *zekhut* on the social entity. It is, moreover, a matter of the legitimate exercise of supernatural power. And the reciprocity of the process extended in all directions. Accordingly, what we have in hand is first and foremost a matter of the exercise of legitimate violence, hence a political power. *Zekhut* might project not only backward, deriving from an ancestor and serving a descendant, but forward as well. Thus Joseph accrued so much *zekhut* that the generations that came before him were credited with his *zekhut*:

Genesis Rabbah LXXXIV:V.2.

A. "These are the generations of the family of Jacob. Joseph [being seventeen years old, was shepherding the flock with his brothers]" (Gen. 37:2):

B. These generations came along only on account of the *zekhut* of Joseph.

C. Did Jacob go to Laban for any reason other than for Rachel?

D. These generations thus waited until Joseph was born, in line with this verse: "And when Rachel had borne Joseph, Jacob said to Laban, 'Send me away'" (Gen. 30:215).

E. Who brought them down to Egypt? It was Joseph.

F. Who supported them in Egypt? It was Joseph.

G. The sea split open only on account of the *zekhut* of Joseph: "The waters saw you, O God" (Ps. 77:17). "You have with your arm redeemed your people, the sons of Jacob and Joseph" (Ps. 77:16).

H. R. Yudan said, "Also the Jordan was divided only on account of the *zekhut* of Joseph."

The passage at hand asks why only Joseph is mentioned as the family of Jacob. The inner polemic is that the *zekhut* of Jacob and Joseph would more than suffice to overcome Esau. Not only so, but Joseph survived because of the *zekhut* of his ancestors:

Genesis Rabbah LXXXVII:VIII.1.

A. "She caught him by his garment....but he left his garment in her hand and fled and got out of the house. [And when she saw that he had left his garment in her hand and had fled out of the house, she called to the men of her household and said to them, 'See he has brought among us a Hebrew to insult us; he came in to me to lie with me, and I cried out with a loud voice, and when he heard that I lifted up my voice and cried, he left his garment with me and fled and got out of the house']" (Gen. 39:13-15):

B. He escaped through the *zekhut* of the fathers, in line with this verse: "And he brought him forth outside" (Gen. 15:5).

C. Simeon of Qitron said, "It was on account of bringing up the bones of Joseph that the sea was split: 'The sea saw it and fled' (Ps. 114:3), on the *zekhut* of this: '...and fled and got out.'"

Zekhut, we see, is both personal and national. B refers to Joseph's enjoying the *zekhut* he had inherited, C referring to Israel's enjoying the zekhut that they gained through their supererogatory loyalty to that same *zekhut*-rich personality. How do we know that the *zekhut* left as a heritage by ancestors is in play? Here is an explicit answer:

Genesis Rabbah LXXIV:XII.1

A. "If the God of my father, the God of Abraham and the Fear of Isaac, had not been on my side, surely now you would have sent me away empty-handed. God saw my affliction and the labor of my hand and rebuked you last night" (Gen. 31:41-42):

B. Zebedee b. Levi and R. Joshua b. Levi:

C. Zebedee said, "Every passage in which reference is made to 'if' tells of an appeal to the *zekhut* accrued by the patriarchs."[11]

D. Said to him R. Joshua, "But it is written, 'Except we had lingered' (Gen. 43:10) [a passage not related to the *zekhut* of the patriarchs]."

E. He said to him, "They themselves would not have come up except for the *zekhut* of the patriarchs, for it if it were not for the *zekhut* of the patriarchs, they never would have been able to go up from there in peace."

The issue of the *zekhut* of the patriarchs comes up in the reference to the God of the fathers. The conception of the *zekhut* of the patriarchs is explicit, not general. It specifies what later benefit to

---

[11] Freedman, *Genesis Rabbah* (London, 1948), p. 684, n. 2: It introduces a plea for or affirmation of protection received for the sake of the patriarchs.

The New Order: The Political Economy of Zekhut

the heir, Israel the family, derived from which particular action of a patriarch or matriarch.

Genesis Rabbah XLIII:VIII.2

A. "And Abram gave him a tenth of everything" (Gen. 14:20):

B. R. Judah in the name of R. Nehorai: "On the strength of that blessing the three great pegs on which the world depends, Abraham, Isaac, and Jacob, derived sustenance.

C. "Abraham: 'And the Lord blessed Abraham in *all* things' (Gen. 24:1) on account of the *zekhut* that 'he gave him a tenth of *all* things' (Gen. 14:20).

D. "Isaac: 'And I have eaten of *all*' (Gen. 27:33), on account of the *zekhut* that 'he gave him a tenth of *all* things' (Gen. 14:20).

E. "Jacob: 'Because God has dealt graciously with me and because I have all' (Gen. 33:11) on account of the *zekhut* that 'he gave him a tenth of *all* things' (Gen. 14:20).

Genesis Rabbah XLIII:VIII.3

A. Whence did Israel gain the *zekhut* of receiving the blessing of the priests?

B. R. Judah said, "It was from Abraham: 'So shall your seed be' (Gen. 15:5), while it is written in connection with the priestly blessing: 'So shall you bless the children of Israel' (Num. 6:23)."

C. R. Nehemiah said, "It was from Isaac: 'And I and the lad will go so far' (Gen. 22:5), therefore said the Holy One, blessed be He, 'So shall you bless the children of Israel' (Num. 6:23)."

D. And rabbis say, "It was from Jacob: 'So shall you say to the house of Jacob' (Ex. 19:3) (in line with the statement, 'So shall you bless the children of Israel' (Num. 6:23)."

No. 2 links the blessing at hand with the history of Israel. Now the reference is to the word "all," which joins the tithe of Abram to the blessing of his descendants. Since the blessing of the priest is at hand, No. 3 treats the origins of the blessing. The picture is clear. "Israel" constitutes a family as a genealogical and juridical fact. It inherits the estate of the ancestors. It hands on that estate. It lives by the example of the matriarchs and patriarchs, and its history exemplifies events in their lives. And *zekhut* forms that entitlement that one generation may transmit to the next, in a way in which the heritage of sin is not to be transmitted except by reason of the deeds of the successor-generation. The good that one does lives onward, the evil is interred with the bones.

To conclude this brief survey of *zekhut* as the medium of historical existence, that is, the *zekhut* deriving from the patriarchs or *zekhut abot*, let me present a statement of the legitimate power – sufficient to achieve salvation, which, in this context, always bears a political dimension – imparted by the *zekhut* of the ancestors. That *zekhut* will enable them to accomplish the political goals of

Israel: its attaining self-rule and avoiding government by gentiles. This statement appeals to the binding of Isaac as the source of the *zekhut*, deriving from the patriarchs and matriarchs, which will in the end lead to the salvation of Israel. What is important here is that the *zekhut* that is inherited joins together with the *zekhut* of one's own deeds; one inherits the *zekhut* of the past, and, moreover, if one does what the progenitors did, one not only receives an entitlement out of the past, one secures an entitlement on one's own account. So the difference between *zekhut* and sin lies in the sole issue of transmissibility:

Genesis Rabbah LVI:II.5

A. Said R. Isaac, "And all was on account of the *zekhut* attained by the act of prostration.

B. "Abraham returned in peace from Mount Moriah only on account of the *zekhut* owing to the act of prostration: '...and we will worship [through an act of prostration] and come [then, on that account] again to you' (Gen. 22:5).

C. "The Israelites were redeemed only on account of the *zekhut* owing to the act of prostration: And the people believed...then they bowed their heads and prostrated themselves' (Ex. 4:31).

D. "The Torah was given only on account of the *zekhut* owing to the act of prostration: 'And worship [prostrate themselves] you afar off' (Ex. 24:1).

E. "Hannah was remembered only on account of the *zekhut* owing to the act of prostration: 'And they worshipped before the Lord' (1 Sam. 1:19).

F. "The exiles will be brought back only on account of the *zekhut* owing to the act of prostration: 'And it shall come to pass in that day that a great horn shall be blown and they shall come that were lost...and that were dispersed...and they shall worship the Lord in the holy mountain at Jerusalem' (Isa. 27:13).

G. "The Temple was built only on account of the *zekhut* owing to the act of prostration: 'Exalt you the Lord our God and worship at his holy hill' (Ps. 99:9).

H. "The dead will live only on account of the *zekhut* owing to the act of prostration: 'Come let us worship and bend the knee, let us kneel before the Lord our maker' (Ps. 95:6)."

The entire history of Israel flows from its acts of worship ("prostration") beginning with that performed by Abraham at the binding of Isaac. Every sort of advantage Israel has ever gained came about through that act of worship done by Abraham and imitated thereafter. Israel constitutes a family and inherits the *zekhut* laid up as a treasure for the descendants by the ancestors. It draws upon that *zekhut* but, by doing the deeds they did, it also enhances its heritage of *zekhut* and leaves to the descendants greater entitlement than they would enjoy by reason of their own actions. But their own actions – here, prostration in worship – generate *zekhut* as well.

Accordingly, *zekhut* may be personal or inherited. The *zekhut* deriving from the prior generations is collective and affects all Israel. But one's own deeds can generate *zekhut* for oneself, with the simple result that *zekhut* is as much personal as it is collective. Specifically, Jacob reflects on the power that Esau's own *zekhut* had gained for Esau. He had gained that *zekhut* by living in the land of Israel and also by paying honor and respect to Isaac. Jacob then feared that, because of the *zekhut* gained by Esau, he, Jacob, would not be able to overcome him. So *zekhut* worked on its own; it was a credit gained by proper action, which went to the credit of the person who had done that action. What made the action worthy of evoking Heaven's response with an act of supernatural favor is that it was an action not to be required but if done to be rewarded, an act of will that cannot be coerced but must be honored. In Esau's case, it was the simple fact that he had remained in the holy land:

Genesis Rabbah LXXVI:II.

2. A. "Then Jacob was greatly afraid and distressed" (Gen. 32:7): [This is Jacob's soliloquy:] "Because of all those years that Esau was living in the Land of Israel, perhaps he may come against me with the power of the *zekhut* he has now attained by dwelling in the Land of Israel.
   B. "Because of all those years of paying honor to his father, perhaps he may come against me with the power of the *zekhut* he attained by honoring his father.
   C. "So he said: 'Let the days of mourning for my father be at hand, then I will slay my brother Jacob' (Gen. 27:41).
   D. "Now the old man is dead."

The important point, then, is that *zekhut* is not only inherited as part of a collective estate left by the patriarchs. It is also accomplished by an individual in his or her own behalf. By extension, we recognize, the successor-system opens a place for recognition of the individual, both man and woman as a matter of fact, within the system of *zekhut*. What a man or a woman does may win for that person an entitlement upon Heaven for supernatural favor of some sort. So there is space, in the system, for a private person, and the individual is linked to the social order through the shared possibilities of generating or inheriting an entitlement upon Heaven.[12]

---

[12]The philosophical system, by contrast, had regarded as important principally the issue of classifying persons, for example, by castes or by other

For if we now ask, what are the sorts of deeds that generate *zekhut*, we realize that those deeds produce a common result of gaining for their doer, as much as for the heirs of the actor, an entitlement for Heavenly favor and support when needed. And that fact concerning gaining and benefiting from *zekhut* brings us to the systemic message to the living generation, its account of what now is to be done. And that message proves acutely contemporary, for its stress is on the power of a single action to create sufficient *zekhut* to outweigh a life of sin. Then the contrast between sin and *zekhut* gains greater depth still. One sin of sufficient weight condemns, one act of *zekhut* of sufficient weight saves; the entire issue of entitlements out of the past gives way, then, when we realize what is actually at stake.

We recall that Torah-study is one – but only one – means for an individual to gain access to that heritage, to get *zekhut*. There are other equally suitable means, and, not only so, but the merit gained by Torah-study is no different from the merit gained by acts of a supererogatory character.[13] If one gets *zekhut* for studying the Torah, then we must suppose there is no holy deed that does not generate its share of *zekhut*. But when it comes to specifying the things one does to get *zekhut*, the documents before us speak of what the Torah does not require but does recommend: not what we are commanded to do in detail, but what the right attitude, formed within the Torah, leads us to do on our own volition:

Y. Taanit 3:11.IV.

C. There was a house that was about to collapse over there [in Babylonia], and Rab set one of his disciples in the house, until they had cleared out everything from the house. When the disciple left the house, the house collapsed.

D. And there are those who say that it was R. Adda bar Ahwah.

E. Sages sent and said to him, "What sort of good deeds are to your credit [that you have that much merit]?"

F. He said to them, "In my whole life no man ever got to the synagogue in the morning before I did. I never left anybody there when I went out. I never walked four cubits without speaking words of Torah. Nor did I ever mention teachings of Torah in an inappropriate setting. I never laid out a bed and slept for a regular period of time. I never took great strides among the associates. I never called my fellow by a nickname. I never

---

indicators; the Mishnah's paramount system of hierarchical classification had treated the individual in the way it treated all other matters, and so, we now see, does the system of *zekhut*: now to be broadened into the definition, accomplishing a lien upon Heaven.

[13] Note also the important cases given above, pp. 000-000.

The New Order: The Political Economy of Zekhut

rejoiced in the embarrassment of my fellow. I never cursed my fellow when I was lying by myself in bed. In the marketplace I never walked over to someone who owed me money.

G. "In my entire life I never lost my temper in my household."

H. This was meant to carry out that which is stated as follows: "I will give heed to the way that is blameless. Oh when wilt thou come to me? I will walk with integrity of heart within my house" (Ps. 101:2).

What I find striking in this story is that mastery of the Torah is only one means of attaining the merit that enabled the sage to keep the house from collapsing. For what the sage did to gain such remarkable merit is not to master such-and-so many tractates of the Mishnah. Nor does the story-teller refer to carrying out the commandments of the Torah as specified. It was rather acts of that expressed courtesy, consideration, restraint. These acts, which no specification can encompass in detail, produced the right attitude, one of gentility, that led to gaining merit. Acts rewarded with an entitlement to supernatural power are those self-abnegation or the avoidance of power over others – not taking great strides among the associates, not using a nickname, not rejoicing in the embarrassment of one's fellow, not singling out one's debtor – and the submission to the will and the requirement of self-esteem of others.

Here, in a moral setting, we find the politics replicated: the form of power that the system promises derives from the rejection of power that the world recognizes – legitimate violence replaced by legitimation of the absence of the power to commit violence or of the failure to commit violence. Not exercising power over others, that is, the counterpart politics, moreover, produced that scarcest of all resources, supernatural favor, by which the holy man could hold up a tottering building. Here then we find politics and economics united in the counterpart-category formed of *zekhut*: the absence of power yielding supernatural power, the valuation of the intangible, Torah, yielding supernatural power. It was, then, that entitlement to supernatural favor that formed the systemic center.

What about what we have to do to secure an inheritance of *zekhut* for our heirs? Here is a concrete example of how acts of worth or *zekhut* accrue to the benefit of the heirs of those that do them. What makes it especially indicative is that here gentiles have the power to acquire zekhut for their descendants, which is coherent with the system's larger interest in not only Israel (as against the faceless, undifferentiated outsider) but the gentiles as well. Here we see that the successor-system may hold within the orbit of its generative conception even the history of the gentiles:

Genesis Rabbah C:VI.1

A. "When they came to the threshing floor of Atad, which is beyond the Jordan, they lamented there with a very great and sorrowful lamentation, and he made a mourning for his father seven days" (Gen. 50:10):

B. Said R. Samuel bar Nahman, "We have reviewed the entire Scripture and found no other place called Atad. And can there be a threshing floor for thorns [the Hebrew word for thorn being *atad*]?

C. "But this refers to the Canaanites. It teaches that they were worthy of being threshed like thorns. And on account of what *zekhut* were they saved? It was on account of the acts of kindness that they performed for our father, Jacob [on the occasion of the mourning for his death]."

D. And what were the acts of kindness that they performed for our father, Jacob?

E. R. Eleazar said, "[When the bier was brought up there,] they unloosened the girdle of their loins."

F. R. Simeon b. Laqish said, "They untied the shoulder-knots."

G. R. Judah b. R. Shalom said, "They pointed with their fingers and said, 'This is a grievous mourning to the Egyptians' (Gen. 50:11).

H. Rabbis said, "They stood upright."

I. Now is it not an argument *a fortiori* : now if these, who did not do a thing with their hands or feet, but only because they pointed their fingers, were saved from punishment, Israel, which performs an act of kindness [for the dead] whether they are adults or children, whether with their hands or with their feet, how much the more so [will they enjoy the *zekhut* of being saved from punishment]!

J. Said R. Abbahu, "Those seventy days that lapsed between the first letter and the second match the seventy days that the Egyptians paid respect to Jacob. [Seventy days elapsed from Haman's letter of destruction until Mordecai's letter announcing the repeal of the decree (cf. Est. 3:12, 8:9). The latter letter, which permitted the Jews to take vengeance on their would-be destroyers, should have come earlier, but it was delayed seventy days as a reward for the honor shown by the Egyptians to Jacob."[14]

The Egyptians gained *zekhut* by honoring Jacob in his death, so Abbahu. This same point then registers for the Canaanites. The connection is somewhat farfetched, that is, through the reference to the threshing floor, but the point is a strong one. And the explanation of history extends not only to Israel's, but also the Canaanites', history.

---

[14] Freedman, *Genesis Rabbah* (London, 1948: Soncino), p. 992, n. 6.

If the Egyptians and the Canaanites, how much the more so Israelites! What is it that Israelites as a nation do to gain a lien upon Heaven for themselves or entitlements of supernatural favor for their descendants? Here is one representative answer to that question:

Genesis Rabbah LXXIV:XII.1.

A. "If the God of my father, the God of Abraham and the Fear of Isaac, had not been on my side, surely now you would have sent me away empty-handed. God saw my affliction and the labor of my hand and rebuked you last night" (Gen. 31:41-42):
B. Zebedee b. Levi and R. Joshua b. Levi:
C. Zebedee said, "Every passage in which reference is made to 'if' tells of an appeal to the *zekhut* accrued by the patriarchs."[15]
D. Said to him R. Joshua, "But it is written, 'Except we had lingered' (Gen. 43:10) [a passage not related to the *zekhut* of the patriarchs]."
E. He said to him, "They themselves would not have come up except for the *zekhut* of the patriarchs, for it if it were not for the *zekhut* of the patriarchs, they never would have been able to go up from there in peace."
F. Said R. Tanhuma, "There are those who produce the matter in a different version." [It is given as follows:]
G. R. Joshua and Zebedee b. Levi:
H. R. Joshua said, "Every passage in which reference is made to 'if' tells of an appeal to the *zekhut* accrued by the patriarchs except for the present case."
I. He said to him, "This case, too, falls under the category of an appeal to the *zekhut* of the patriarchs."

So much for *zekhut* that is inherited from the patriarchs, a now familiar notion. But what about the deeds of Israel in the here and now?

J. R. Yohanan said, "It was on account of the *zekhut* achieved through sanctification of the divine name."
K. R. Levi said, "It was on account of the *zekhut* achieved through faith and the *zekhut* achieved through Torah.

Faith despite the here and now, study of the Torah – these are what Israel does in the here and now with the result that they gain an entitlement for themselves or their heirs.

L. "The *zekhut* achieved through faith: 'If I had not believed...' (Ps. 27:13).
M. "The *zekhut* achieved through Torah: 'Unless your Torah had been my delight' (Ps. 119:92)."

---

[15]Freedman, *Genesis Rabbah*, p. 684, n. 2: It introduces a plea for or affirmation of protection received for the sake of the patriarchs.

2. A. "God saw my affliction and the labor of my hand and rebuked you last night" (Gen. 31:41-42):
   B. Said R. Jeremiah b. Eleazar, "More beloved is hard labor than the *zekhut* achieved by the patriarchs, for the *zekhut* achieved by the patriarchs served to afford protection for property only, while the *zekhut* achieved by hard labor served to afford protection for lives.
   C. "The *zekhut* achieved by the patriarchs served to afford protection for property only: 'If the God of my father, the God of Abraham and the Fear of Isaac, had not been on my side, surely now you would have sent me away empty-handed.'
   D. "The *zekhut* achieved by hard labor served to afford protection for lives: 'God saw my affliction and the labor of my hand and rebuked you last night.'"

Here is as good an account as any of the theology of *zekhut*. The issue of the *zekhut* of the patriarchs comes up in the reference to the God of the fathers. The conception of the *zekhut* of the patriarchs is explicit, not general. It specifies what later benefit to the heir, Israel the family, derived from which particular action of a patriarch or matriarch. But acts of faith and Torah-study form only one medium; hard labor, that is, devotion to one's calling, defines that source of *zekhut* that is going to be accessible to those many Israelites unlikely to distinguish themselves either by Torah-study and acts of faith, encompassing the sanctification of God's name, or by acts of amazing gentility and restraint.

The system here speaks to everybody, Jew and gentile, past and present and future; *zekhut* therefore defines the structure of the cosmic social order and explains how it is supposed to function. It is the encompassing quality of *zekhut*, its pertinence to past and future, high and low, rich and poor, gifted and ordinary, that marks as the systemic statement the message of *zekhut*, now fully revealed as the conception of reciprocal response between Heaven and Israel on earth, to acts of devotion beyond the requirements of the Torah but defined all the same by the Torah. As Scripture had said, God responds to the faith of the ancient generations by supernatural acts to which, on their own account, the moderns are not entitled, hence a heritage of entitlement. But those acts, now fully defined for us, can and ought to be done, also, by the living generation. And, as a matter of fact, no one today, at the time of the system-builders, is exempt from the systemic message and its demands: even steadfastness in accomplishing the humble work of the everyday and the here and now.

The systemic statement made by the usages of *zekhut* speaks of relationship, function, the interplay of humanity and God. One's store of *zekhut* derives from a relationship, that is, from one's forebears. That is one dimension of the relationships in which one stands. *Zekhut* also forms a measure of one's own relationship with Heaven, as the power of one person, but not another, to pray and so bring rain attests. What sort of relationship does *zekhut*, as the opposite of sin, then posit? It is not one of coercion, for Heaven cannot force us to do those types of deeds that yield *zekhut*, and that, story after story suggests, is the definition of a deed that generates *zekhut*: doing what we ought to do but do not have to do. But then, we cannot coerce Heaven to do what we want done either, for example, by carrying out the commandments. These are obligatory, but do not obligate Heaven.

Whence then our lien on Heaven?[16] It is through deeds of a supererogatory character – to which Heaven responds by deeds of a supererogatory character: supernatural favor to this one, who through deeds of ingratiation of the other or self-abnegation or restraint exhibits the attitude that in Heaven precipitates a counterpart attitude, hence generating *zekhut*, rather than to that one, who does not. The simple fact that rabbis cannot pray and bring rain, but a simple ass-driver can, tells the whole story. The relationship measured by *zekhut* – Heaven's response by an act of uncoerced favor to a person's uncoerced gift, for example, act of gentility, restraint, or self-abnegation – contains an element of unpredictability for which appeal to the *zekhut* inherited from ancestors accounts. So while I cannot coerce heaven, I can through *zekhut* gain acts of favor from Heaven, and that is by doing what Heaven cannot require of me. Heaven then responds to my attitude in carrying out my duties – and more than my duties. That act of pure disinterest – giving the woman my means of livelihood – is the one that gains for me Heaven's deepest interest.

So *zekhut* forms the political economy of the religious system of the social order put forward by the Talmud of the Land of Israel, Genesis Rabbah, Leviticus Rabbah, and related writings. Here we find the power that brought about the transvaluation of value, the reversal of the meaning of power and its legitimacy. *Zekhut* expresses and accounts for the economic valuation of the scarce resource of what we should call moral authority. *Zekhut* stands for

---

[16]The answer to that question forms the bridge to the interpretation, in context, of the system as a whole: the determination of the self-evidently valid answer that the system posits – and therefore the identification of the urgent question that precipitated the formation of the system as a whole. Chapter Nine leads to my proposal for the interpretation of the system as a whole, both on its own and in relationship with the antecedent one.

the political valorization of weakness, that which endows the weak with a power that is not only their own but their ancestors'. It enables the weak to accomplish goals through not their own power, but their very incapacity to accomplish acts of violence – a transvaluation as radical as that effected in economics. And *zekhut* holds together both the economics and the politics of this Judaism: it makes the same statement twice.

Zekhut as the power of the powerless, the riches of the disinherited, the valuation and valorization of the will of those who have no right to will. In the context of Christian Palestine, Jews found themselves on the defensive. Their ancestry called into question, their supernatural standing thrown into doubt, their future denied, they called themselves "Israel," and the land, "the Land of Israel." But what power did they possess, legitimately, if need be through violence, to assert their claim to form "Israel"? And, with the holy land passing into the hands of others, what scarce resource did they own and manage to take the place of that measure of value that now no longer was subjected to their rationality? Asserting a politics in which all violence was illegitimate, an economics in which nothing tangible, even real property in the Holy Land,[17] had value, the system through its counterpart-categories made a single, simple, and sufficient statement. But those whom Judaism knows as "our sages of blessed memory" were not the only system-builders, and theirs was not the only question about the social order framed in historical and theological, rather than analytical and philosophical terms. Their contemporary, the Bishop of Hippo whom Christianity knows as Saint Augustine, set forth an account of the social order framed in the same terms and addressed to the same urgent and critical question. It is in the context of comparison that, in the end, we interpret the system that has now been described and analyzed: the Judaism transformed from a philosophy to a religion.

---

[17] A test of this interpretation is whether or not in the provenance of Babylonia stories are told about the equivalence of owning land and studying the Torah. That is to say, if studying the Torah is represented as outweighing owning real estate in Babylonia as much as in the Land of Israel, then something is awry with my results in Chapter Seven and in this chapter. But if a survey, for example, of the Talmud of Babylonia, shows that, in the context of Babylonia and not the Land of Israel, stories of the superiority of Torah-study over land ownership do not occur, then that would form a fair confirmation of my point of insistence here. This test of falsification will be carried on in the context of the next phase of my ouevre, which will bring me deep into the Babylonian part of the canon of the Dual Torah.

6

Enchanted Judaism and *The City of God*

"Make his wishes yours, so that he will make your wishes his... Anyone from whom people take pleasure, God takes pleasure" (Abot 2:4). These two statements hold together the two principal elements of the conception of the relationship to God that in a single word *zekhut* conveys. Give up, please others, do not impose your will but give way to the will of the other, and Heaven will respond by giving a lien that is not coerced but evoked. By the rationality of discipline within, we have the power to form rational relationships beyond ourselves, with Heaven; and that is how the system expands the boundaries of the social order to encompass not only the natural but also the supernatural world.[1]

For it is the rationality of that relationship to God that governs the social order, defining the three components thereof: ethics, ethnos, ethos. For within that relationship we discern the model of not merely ethics but economics, not merely private morality in society but the public policy, the politics that delineates the limns of the ethnic community, and not alone the right attitude of the virtuous individual but the social philosophy of an entire nation – so the system proposes. And that is the this-worldly social order that joins with Heaven, the society that is a unique and holy family, so

---

[1] I use the word "rationality" in the sense in which it is used in the thought of Max Weber: the systemic sense of what is appropriate and proper. The comparison of the rationalities of the initial and the successor systems is undertaken in the closing paragraphs of this chapter. This is not, of course, an account of the concept of rationality in the thought of Weber. I believe my characterization, for the limited purpose of these remarks, is entirely accurate.

transformed by *zekhut* inherited and *zekhut* accomplished as to transcend the world-order. That ordering of humanity in society, empowered and enriched in an enchanted political economy, links private person to the public polity through the union of a common attitude: the one of renunciation that tells me how to behave at home and in the streets, and that instructs Israel how to conduct its affairs among the nations and throughout history.

Treating every deed, every gesture as capable of bringing about enchantment, the successor-system imparted to the givens of everyday life – at least in their potential – remarkable power. The conviction that, by dint of special effort, I may so conduct myself as to acquire an entitlement of supernatural power turns my commonplace circumstance into an arena encompassing Heaven and earth. God responds to my – and holy Israel's – virtue, filling the gap – so to speak – about myself and about my entire family that I and we leave when we forebear, withdraw, and give up what is mine and ours: our space, my self. When I do, then God responds; my sacrifice evokes memories of Abraham's readiness to sacrifice Isaac;[2] my devotion to the other calls up from Heaven what by demanding I cannot coerce. What imparts critical mass to the conception of *zekhut*, that gaining of supernatural entitlements through the surrender of what is mine, is the recasting, in the mold and model of that virtue of surrender, of the political economy of Israel in the Land of Israel. That accounts for the definition of legitimate power in politics as only weakness, economics as the rational increase of resources that are, but need not be, scarce, valued things that are capable of infinite increase.

That not only accounts for the inversion of the received categories and their reformation into mirror-images of what the philosophers had made of them. In my view it also explains why a quite fresh, deeply religious system has taken the place of a compelling and well-composed philosophical one. The Mishnah's God can scarcely compete with the God of the Yerushalmi and the Midrash-

---

[2] Note the fine perception of S. Levy, Original Virtue and Other Studies, pp. 2-3: "Some act of obedience, constituting the Ascent of man, is the origin of virtue and the cause of reward for virtue...What is the conspicuous act of obedience which, in Judaism, forms the striking contrast to Adam's act of disobedience, in Christianity? The submission of Isaac in being bound on the altar...is regarded in Jewish theology as the historic cause of the imputation of virtue to his descendants." It is not an accident, then, as we shall see, that Augustine selected as his paradigmatic historical exemplum the conflict of Cain and Abel, the city of God being inhabited by Abel and his descendants; he required a virtue pertinent to all of humanity, not to Israel alone, for his argument, so it seems to me as an outsider to the subject.

compilations.³ For the God of the philosophers, the apex of the hiarcharchy of all being as the framers of the Mishnah have positioned God, has made the rules and is shown by them to form the foundation of order. All things reach up to one thing, one thing contains within itself many things: these twin-propositions of monotheism, which the philosophical system demonstrates in theory and proposes to realize in the facts of the social order, define a God who in an orderly way governs all the palpable relationships of nature as of supernature – but who finds a place, who comes to puissant expression, in not a single one of them. The God of the philosophers assures, sustains, supports, nourishes, guarantees, governs. But the way that God responds to what we do is all according to the rule. That is, after all, what natural philosophy proposes to uncover and discern, and what more elevated task can God perform than the nomothetic one accomplished in the daily creation of the world.

But God in the successor-system gains what the philosophical God lacks, which is personality, active presence, pathos and empathy. The God of the religious system breaks the rules, accords an entitlement to this one, who has done some one remarkable deed, but not to that one, who has done nothing wrong and everything right. So a life in accord with the rules – even a life spent in the study of the Torah – in Heaven's view is outweighed by a single moment, a gesture that violates the norm, extending the outer limits of the rule, for instance, of virtue. And who but a God who, like us, feels, not only thinks, responds to impulse and sentiment, can be portrayed in such a way as this?

> So I sold my ass and I gave her the proceeds, and I said to her, 'Here is your money, free your husband, but do not sin [by becoming a prostitute to raise the necessary funds].'"
>
> They said to him, "You are worthy of praying and having your prayers answered."

No rule exhaustively describes a world such as this. If the God of the philosophers' Judaism makes the rules, the God of the religious Judaism breaks them. The systemic difference, of course, is readily extended outward from the personality of God: the philosophers' God thinks, the God of the religious responds, and we are in God's image, after God's likeness, not only because we through right thinking penetrate the principles of creation, but through right attitude

---

³My initial comments on that matter are in The Incarnation of God: The Character of Divinity in Formative Judaism (Philadelphia, 1988: Fortress Press).

replicate the heart of the Creator. Humanity on earth incarnates God on high, the Israelite family in particular, and, in consequence, earth and Heaven join – within.

Perhaps the first system contained within itself the flaw that, like a grain of sand in an oyster, so irritated the innards as to form a pearl. And perhaps even the philosophers, with their exquisitely ordered and balanced social world, can have made a place for God to act; but, knowing how they thought, we must imagine that like philosophers later on, they will have insisted that miracles, too, follow rules and demonstrate the presence of rules. But now, in the religious Judaism, the world now is no longer what it seems. At stake in what is remarkable is what falls beyond all power of rules either to describe or to prescribe.

What is asked of Israel and of the Israelite individual now is Godly restraint, supernatural generosity of soul that is "in our image, after our likeness:" that is what sets aside all rules. And, since as a matter of simple fact, that appeal to transcend the norm defined not personal virtue but the sainthood of all Israel, living all together in the here and in the now, we must conclude that, within Israel's society, within what the Greco-Roman world will have called its *polis*, its political and social order, the bounds of earth have now extended to Heaven. In terms of another great system composed in the same time and in response to a world-historical catastrophe of the same sort, Israel on earth dwells in the city of God. And, it must follow, God dwells with Israel, in Israel: "today, if you will it."

That insistence upon the systemic centrality of the conception of *zekhut*, with all its promise for the reshaping of value, draws our attention once more to the power of a single, essentially-theological, conception to impart shape and structure to the social order. The Judaism set forth in the successor-documents portrayed a social order in which, while taking full account of circumstance and historical context, individuals and nation alike controlled their own destiny. The circumstance of genealogy dictated whether or not the moral entity, whether the individual or the nation, would enjoy access to entitlements of supernatural favor without regard to the merit of either one. But, whether favored by a rich heritage of supernatural empowerment as was the nation, or deprived, by reason of one's immediate ancestors, of any lien upon Heaven, in the end both the nation and the individual had in hand the power to shape the future. How was this to be done? It was not alone by keeping the Torah, studying the Torah, dressing, eating, making a living, marrying, procreating, raising a family, burying and being buried, all in accord with those rules.

Enchanted Judaism and The City of God

That life in conformity with the rule, obligatory but merely conventional, did not evoke the special interest of Heaven. Why should it? The rules describe the ordinary. But (in language used only in a later document) "God wants the heart," and that is not an ordinary thing. Nor was the power to bring rain or hold up a tottering house gained through a life of merely ordinary sanctity. Special favor responded to extraordinary actions, in the analogy of special disfavor, misfortune deemed to punish sin. And just as culpable sin, as distinct from mere error, requires an act of will, specifically, arrogance, so an act of extraordinary character requires an act of will. But, as mirror image of sin, the act would reveal in a concrete way an attitude of restraint, forbearance, gentility, and self-abnegation. A sinful act, provoking Heaven, was on that one did deliberately to defy Heaven. Then an act that would evoke Heaven's favor, so imposing upon Heaven a lien that Heaven freely gave, was one that, equally deliberately and concretely, displayed humility.

But the systemic focus upon the power of a single act of remarkable generosity, the surrender to the other of what is most precious to the self, whether that constituted an opinion or a possession or a feeling, in no way will have surprised the framers of the philosophical Judaism. They had laid heavy emphasis upon the power of human intentionality to settle questions of the status of interstitial persons, objects, or actions, within the larger system of hierarchical classification. So in the philosophical Judaism attitude and intentionality classified what was of doubtful status, that is to say, forming the active and motivating component of the structure and transforming the structure, a tableau of fixed and motionless figures, into a system of action and reaction. Then, in the process of transformation, we should hardly find surprising the appeal to the critical power of attitude and intentionality. For what we find in the successor-system is a fundamental point of connection. What was specific before, intentionality, is now broadened and made general through extension to all aspects of one's attitude.

Now the powerful forces coalescing in intentionality gained very precise definition, and in their transformation from merely concrete cases of the taxonomic power of intentionality that worked one way here, another way there, into very broad-ranging but quite specific and prescribed attitudes, the successor-system took its leave from the initial one without a real farewell. Then what is the point of departure? It is marked by the intense interest, in the religious

Judaism, upon not the fixed given of normative intentionality,[4] but rather changing people, both individually and nationally, from what they were to something else. And, if the change is in a single direction, it is, nonetheless, also always personal and individual.

The change is signaled by the conception that study of the Torah not only illuminated and educated but transformed, and, moreover, so changed the disciple that he gained in supernatural standing and authority. This gnostic conception of knowledge, however, proved only a component of a larger conception of national transformation and personal regeneration, since Torah-study produced *zekhut*, and all things depended upon the *zekhut* that a person, or the nation as a whole, possessed. Mastery of what we classify as "the system's world-view" changed a person by generating *zekhut*, that is, by so affecting the person as to inculcate attitudes that would produce remarkable actions (often: acts of omission, restraint, and forbearance) to generate *zekhut*. The change was the end, the Torah-study, the medium.

But the system's world-view was not the sole, or even the principal, component that showed how the received system was transformed by the new one. The conception of *zekhut* came to the fore to integrate of the system's theory of the way of life of the social order, its economics, together with its account of the social entity of the social order, its politics. The remarkable actions – perhaps those of omission more than those of commission – that produced *zekhut* yielded an increase in the scarcest of all resources, supernatural favor, and at the same time endowed a person rich in entitlements to Heavenly intervention with that power to evoke that vastly outweighed the this-worldly power to coerce in the accomplishment of one's purpose.

This rapid account of the systemic structure and system, its inversion of the received categories and its formation of anti-categories of its own, draws our attention to the specificity of the definition of right attitude and puissant intentionality by contrast to the generality of those same matters when represented in the philosophical system of the Mishnah. We have, therefore, to ask ourselves whether the quite concrete and definition of those attitudes and correct will and proper intentionality that lead to acts that generate *zekhut* will have surprised framers of documents prior to

---

[4]That is, an assessment of what people will ordinarily think or propose or wish to have happen. The rule is set by that norm, not by exceptions, and on that basis, in the initial system, we are able to determine what (an ordinary person's) intentionality will dictate in a given interstitial case.

those that attest the transformed Judaism before us. The answer is negative, and that fact alerts us to yet another fundamental continuity between the two Judaisms.

As a matter of fact, the doctrine defining the appropriate attitude persisted pretty much unchanged from the beginning.[5] The repertoire of approved and disapproved attitude and intentionality remained constant through the half-millennium of the unfolding of the canon of Judaism from the Mishnah onward: humility, forbearance, accommodation, a spirit of conciliation. For one thing, Scripture itself is explicit that God shares and responds to the attitudes and intentionality of human beings. God cares what humanity feels – wanting love, for example – and so the conception that actions that express right attitudes of humility will evoke in Heaven a desired response will not have struck as novel the authors of the Pentateuch or the various prophetic writings, for example. The biblical record of God's feelings and God's will concerning the feelings of humanity leaves no room for doubt. What is fresh in the system before us is not the integration of the individual with the nation but the provision, for the individual, of a task and a role analogous to that of the nation.

With its interest in classifying large-scale and collective classes of things, the Mishnah's system treats matters of attitude and emotion in that same taxic context. For instance, while the Mishnah casually refers to emotions, for example, tears of joy, tears of sorrow, where feelings matter, it always is in a public and communal context. Where there is an occasion of rejoicing, one form of joy is not to be confused with some other, or one context of sorrow with another. Accordingly, marriages are not to be held on festivals (M. M.Q. 1:7). Likewise mourning is not to take place then (M. M.Q. 1:5, 3:7-9). Where emotions play a role, it is because of the affairs of the community at large, for example, rejoicing on a festival, mourning on a fast day (M. Suk. 5:1-4). Emotions are to be kept in hand, as in the case of the relatives of the executed felon (M. San. 6:6). If I had to specify the single underlying principle affecting all forms of emotion, for the Mishnah it is the profoundly philosophical attitude that attitudes and feelings must be kept under control, never fully expressed without reasoning about the appropriate context. Emotions must always lay down judgments.

---

[5] I have demonstrated that fact in my *Vanquished Nation, Broken Spirit. The Virtues of the Heart in Formative Judaism.* (New York, 1987: Cambridge University Press).

We see in most of those cases in which emotions play a systemic and indicative, not merely an episodic and random, role, that the basic principle is the same. We can, and must so frame our feelings as to accord with the appropriate rule. In only one case does emotion play a decisive role in settling an issue, and that has to do with whether or not a farmer was happy that water came upon his produce or grain. That case underlines the conclusion just now drawn. If people feel a given sentiment, it is a matter of judgment, therefore invokes the law's penalties. So in this system emotions are not treated as spontaneous, but as significant aspects of a person's judgment.

Whence then the doctrine, made so concrete and specific in the conception of *Zekhut* as made systemically generative in the successor-documents, that very specific attitudes, particular to persons, bear the weight of the systemic structure as a whole? It is in tractate Abot, which supplies those phrases cited at the outset to define the theology that sustains the conception of *zekhut*. Tractate-Abot, conventionally attached to the Mishnah and serving as the Mishnah's advocate, turns out to forms the bridge from the Mishnah to the Yerushalmi and its associated compilations of scriptural exegeses. That tractate presents the single most comprehensive account of religious affections. The reason is that, in that document above all, how we feel defines a critical aspect of virtue. The issue proves central, not peripheral. The very specific and concrete doctrine emerges fully exposed. A simple catalogue of permissible feelings comprises humility, generosity, self-abnegation, love, a spirit of conciliation of the other, and eagerness to please. A list of impermissible emotions is made up of envy, ambition, jealousy, arrogance, sticking to one's opinion, self-centeredness, a grudging spirit, vengefulness, and the like. Nothing in the wonderful stories about remarkable generosity does more than render concrete the abstract doctrine of the heart's virtue that tractate Abot sets forth.

People should aim at eliciting from others acceptance and good will and should avoid confrontation, rejection, and humiliation of the other. This they do through conciliation and giving up their own claims and rights. So both catalogues form a harmonious and uniform whole, aiming at the cultivation of the humble and malleable person, one who accepts everything and resents nothing. True, these virtues, in this tractate as in the system as a whole, derive from knowledge of what really counts, which is what God wants. But God favors those who please others. The virtues appreciated by human beings prove identical to the ones to which God responds as well. And what single virtue of the heart encompasses the rest? Restraint, the source of self-abnegation, humility, serves as the anecdote for ambition, vengefulness, and, above all, for arrogance. It is restraint of our own interest that enables us to deal generously with others, humility about ourselves that generates a liberal spirit towards others. And the correspondence of Heavenly and mortal attitudes is to be taken for granted – as is made explicit.

So the emotions prescribed in tractate Abot turn out to provide variations of a single feeling, which is the sentiment of the disciplined heart, whatever affective form it may take. And where does the heart learn its lessons, if not in relationship to God? So: "Make his wishes yours, so that he will make your wishes his" (Abot 2:4). Applied to relationships between human beings, this inner discipline of the emotional life will yield exactly those virtues of conciliation and self-abnegation, humility and generosity of spirit, that the framers of tractate Abot spell out in one example after another. Imputing to Heaven exactly those responses felt on earth, for example, "Anyone from whom people take pleasure, God takes pleasure" (Abot 3:10), makes the point at the most general level.

Then what has the successor-system contributed? Two things: [1] the conception that acts of omission or commission expressing an attitude of forbearance and self-abnegation generate *zekhut* in particular; [2] the principle that *zekhut* functions in those very specific ways that the system deems critical: as the power to attest to human transformation and regeneration, affording, in place of philosophical politics and philosophical economics, that power inhering in weakness, that wealth inhering in giving up what one has, that in the end promise the attainment of our goals. In a single sentence, the path from one system to the other is in three stages: [1] the philosophical Judaism, portrayed by the Mishnah, assigns to intentionality and attitude systemic centrality; [2] tractate Abot, in presenting in general terms the rationale of the Mishnah's system, defines precisely the affective attitude and intentionality that are required; [3] the religious Judaism of the Yerushalmi and associated writings joins together the systemic centrality of attitude and intentionality with the doctrine of virtue laid out in tractate Abot.

But in joining these received elements the new system emerges as distinct from the old.[6] For when we deem the attitude of affirmation

---

[6]This is not to suggest that the substance of the doctrine of virtue was richly revised in the successor-writings. That is not so. The transformation was systemic, not doctrinal. Emotions not taken up earlier in the pages of the Yerushalmi did not come under discussion. Principles introduced earlier enjoyed mere restatement and extensive exemplification. Some principles of proper feelings might even generate secondary developments of one kind or

and acceptance, rather than aggression, and the intentionality of self-abnegation and forbearance, to define the means for gaining *zekhut*, what we are saying is contrary and paradoxical: if you want to have, then give up, and if you want to impose your judgment, then make the judgment of the other into your own, and if you want to coerce Heaven, then evoke in Heaven attitudes of sympathy that will lead to the actions or events that you want, whether rain, whether long life, whether the salvation of Israel and its hegemony over the nations: to rule, be ruled by Heaven; to show Heaven rules, give up what you want to the other. *Zekhut* results: the lien upon Heaven, freely given by Heaven in response to one's free surrender to the will and wish of Heaven. And by means of *zekhut*, whether one's own, whether one's ancestors', the social order finds its shape and system, and the individual his or her place within its structure.

The correspondence of the individual to the nation, both capable of gaining *zekhut* in the same way, linked the deepest personal emotions to the cosmic fate and transcendent faith of that social group of which each individual formed a part. The individual Israelite's innermost feelings, the inner heart of Israel, the microcosm, correspond to the public and historic condition of the nation, of Israel, the macrocosm. In the innermost chambers of the individual's deepest feelings, the Israelite therefore lives out the public history and destiny of the people, Israel.

What precipitated deep thought upon fundamental questions of social existence was a simple fact. From the time that Christianity attained the status of a licit religion, the Jews of Palestine witnessed the formation of circumstances that had formerly been simply unimaginable: another Israel, in the same place and time, competed with them in their terms, quoting their Scriptures, explaining who they were in their own categories but in very different terms from the ones that they used. We need not explain the profundities of religious doctrine by reducing them to functions and necessities of public policy. But it is, a matter of simple fact, that the Jews in the fourth century had witnessed a drastic decline in their power to exercise legitimate violence (which is to say, violence you can make stick), as well as in their command of the real estate of Palestine that they knew as the Holy Land and its wealth. The system's

---

another. But nothing not present at the outset – in tractate Avot – drew sustained attention later on. The system proved essentially complete in the earliest statement of its main points. What then do the authors or compilers of the Yerushalmi contribute? Temper marks the ignorant person, restraint and serenity, the learned one. These are mere details.

Enchanted Judaism and The City of God

stress upon matters of intentionality and attitude, subject to the governance of even the most humble of individuals, even the most insignificant of nations, exactly corresponded to the political and social requirements of the Jews' condition in that time. The transformed Judaism made of necessity a theological virtue, and, by the way, the normative condition of the social order.

In the fourth century, from Constantine's great victory and legitimation of Christianity in the beginning, to the Theodosian code that subordinated Jewry and limited its rights at nearly the end, Jews confronted a remarkable shift in the character of the Roman empire. The state first legalized, then established Christianity as most favored religion, and – by the end of that century – finally undertook to extirpate paganism, and, by the way, to subordinate Judaism. Therein lies the urgency of the critical question addressed by the system as a whole – if not the self-evidence of the truth of its response to that question. Dealing with world-historical change in the character of the Roman Empire consequent on the legalization of Christianity by Constantine and the establishment of Christianity as the state-religion by his heirs and successors, the transformed Judaism made its statement in answer to the fundamental question confronting the social order: precisely what are we now to do?

That political question – the "do" part of the question – concerning the assessment of the legitimate use of violence in this Judaism called into doubt the legitimacy of any kind of violence at all, Jews' having none. But no less subject to reflection was that "doing" that referred to making a living, the economics of the acquisition and management of scarce resources, and, it goes without saying, the making of a life, the philosophy of rational explanation of all things in some one way. At stake, then, were the very shape and structure of the social order, reconsidered at what was, and was certainly perceived as, the critical turning.

This utter reordering of society framed a question that had to be faced and could not be readily answered.[7] It concerned the meaning

---

[7] And certainly had not been answered by the Mishnah's system, which treated history – composed of events in particular – as mere occasions for taxonomic inquiry: classifying this event in one way, according to one overriding rule, that event in some other, according to another rule; and neither rule bore any relationship to history. The regularization and ordering of disorderly events – counterpart to what we know as social science today – denied to history all status as the source of category-formation. I have spelled all this out in my Messiah in Context [= The Foundations of Judaism. Method, Teleology, Doctrine. (Philadelphia, 1983-5: Fortress Press. Second printing: Lanham, 1988: University Press of America. Studies in

and end of history, Israel's history, now that the prophetic promises were claimed by the Christian competition to have been kept in the past, leaving nothing in the future for which to hope. When, for a brief moment, in 361-3 the emperor Julian disestablished Christianity and restored paganism, proposing also to rebuild the Jews' Temple in Jerusalem, Christianity met the challenge and regained power. The Temple was not rebuilt, and Julian's brief reign brought in its wake a ferocious counter-revolution, with the Christian state now suppressing the institutions of paganism, and Christian men in the streets of the towns and villages taking an active role on their own as well. Julian's successors persecuted pagan philosophy. In 380 the emperor Theodosius (379-395) decreed the end of paganism:

> It is our desire that all the various nations which are subject to our clemency and moderation should continue in the profession of that religion which was delivered to the Romans by the divine Apostle Peter.

Paganism found itself subjected to penalties. The state church – a principal indicator of the Christian civilization that the West was to know – now came into being. In 381 Theodosius forbade sacrifices and closed most temples. In 391-392 a new set of penalties was imposed on paganism. And, while tolerated, Judaism, together with the Jews, suffered drastic change in their legal standing as well.

The upshot is simple. In the beginning of the fourth century Rome was pagan, in the end, Christian. In the beginning Jews in the Land of Israel administered their own affairs. In the end their institution of self-administration lost the recognition it had formerly enjoyed. In 300 the area of Palestine where Jews lived was mainly settled by Jews, hence, palpably and visibly, the Land of Israel, while in 400, the country was populated with Christian shrines.[8] In the beginning Judaism enjoyed entirely licit status, and the Jews, the protection of the state. In the end Judaism suffered abridgment of its former liberties, and the Jews of theirs. In the beginning, the Jews lived in the Land of Israel, and in some numbers. In the end they lived in Palestine.

As a matter of fact, each of the important changes in the documents first redacted at the end of the fourth century dealt with a powerful challenge presented by the triumph of Christianity in

---

Judaism series). I-III. II. Messiah in Context. Israel's History and Destiny in Formative Judaism].
[8]Constantine and his mother had built churches and shrines all over the country, but especially in Jerusalem, so the Land of Israel received yet another name, for another important group, now becoming the Holy Land.

Constantine's age.[9] The first change revealed in the unfolding of the sages' canon pertains to the use of Scripture. The change at hand specifically is in making books out the collection of exegeses of Scripture. That represents an innovation because the Mishnah, and the exegetical literature that served the Mishnah, did not take shape around the order of biblical passages, even when relevant, let alone the explanation of verses of Scripture. In the third, and especially, in the later fourth centuries, other writings, entering the canon, took shape around the explanation of verses of Scripture, not a set of topics. What this meant was that a second mode of organizing ideas, besides the topical mode paramount for the Mishnah, the Tosefta, the Yerushalmi (and the Bavli later on), now made its way.

The second concerned extensive consideration of the topic of the Messiah, formerly not accorded a principal place among the parts of the social system.[10] The philosophers of the Mishnah did not make use of the Messiah myth in the construction of a teleology for their system. They found it possible to present a statement of goals for their projected life of Israel which was entirely separate from appeals to history and eschatology. The appearance in the Talmuds of a messianic eschatology fully consonant with the larger characteristic of the rabbinic system – with its stress on the viewpoints and proof-texts of Scripture, its interest in what was happening to Israel, its focus upon the national-historical dimension of the life of the group – indicates that the encompassing rabbinic system stands essentially autonomous of the prior, mishnaic system.

Third, the Mishnah had presented an ahistorical and, in the nature of things, non-eschatological teleology, and did not make use of the messiah-theme to express its teleology. By contrast, the Talmud not only provides an eschatological and therefore a messiah-centered teleology for its system. Its authorship also formed a theory of history and found it appropriate to compose important narratives, episodic to be sure, concerning events that, in prior systemic writings, were treated as mere taxic indicators. Now what happened counted, not only that something happened, and the

---

[9]I have spelled these matters out in Judaism and Christianity in the Age of Constantine. Issues of the Initial Confrontation. (Chicago, 1987: University of Chicago Press); Midrash in Context [= The Foundations of Judaism. Method, Teleology, Doctrine. (Philadelphia, 1983-5: Fortress Press. Second printing: Atlanta, 1988: Scholars Press for Brown Judaic Studies) I-III. I. Midrash in Context. Exegesis in Formative Judaism]; .and, in summary, in Judaism in the Matrix of Christianity. (Philadelphia, 1986: Fortress Press. British edition, Edinburgh, 1988, T. & T. Collins).

[10]This is worked out in Messiah in Context, cited above.

details of events were to be narrated and preserved. So far as the definition of an event comprises a cultural indicator, the telling of stories about events tells us that, for the Talmud of the Land of Israel and related writings, the very formation of culture has been transformed.

No wonder, then, that the Mishnah's philosophical (therefore also social-scientific) and ahistorical Judaism, a Judaism of rules, gave way to the religious and historical (therefore also eschatological) Judaism of the Talmud of the Land of Israel, a Judaism of exceptions to the rules. These important shifts show that the later system set forth a Judaism intersecting with the Mishnah's but essentially asymmetrical with it. Given the political changes of the age, with their implications for the meaning and end of history as Israel would experience it, the foci of the connected but autonomous system now directed attention to the media for salvation in the here and now, for Israel and the individual alike, and in time to come for all Israel. A single word captured the whole: *zekhut* yielded a broad variety of answers to one urgent question. It was a question encompassing society and history, now and the coming age, Israel and the nations, the social order in the here and now and the great society comprised by nature and supernature. To the question posed by the simple statement of the religious system set forth in the late fourth and fifth century documents is this: the entire social order forms one reality, in the supernatural world and in nature, in time and in eternity.

The sages who wrote the Talmud of the Land of Israel, Genesis Rabbah, Leviticus Rabbah, and Pesiqta deRab Kahana, did not stand alone in their profound reflection on how earth and Heaven intersect, and how the here and the now forms a moment in history. As it happens, at the same time and, as a matter of fact, under similar circumstances of historical crisis, another system-builder was at work. When we appreciate the commonalities of the task facing each party and the dimensions that turn out to take the measure of the results of each, we realize how different people, speaking each to their own world, delivering each their own statement, turn out in the same time to answer the same question in what is, as a matter of fact, pretty much the same cosmic dimensions, and, it would turn out, with the same enduring results for the formation of Western civilization.[11]

---

[11]One need not exaggerate the influence of either St. Augustine or our sages of blessed memory to claim that the Christianity and the Judaism framed by each, respectively, defined norms and set the course for the two great religions of the West.

Augustine of Hippo's life, in North Africa and Italy, (354-430) coincided with the period in which, to the east, the sages of the Land of Israel produced their Talmud in amplification of the Mishnah as well as their Midrash-compilations in extension of Moses's books of Genesis and Leviticus. But he comes to mind, for comparison and contrast, not merely because of temporal coincidence. Rather, the reason is that, like the sages of Judaism, he confronted the same this-worldly circumstance, one in which the old order was coming to an end – and was acknowledged to be closing. And the changes were those of power and political. In 410 the Goths took Rome, refugees of Alaric's conquest fleeing to North Africa (as well, as a matter of fact, as to the Land of Israel/Palestine, as events even early in the story of Jerome in Jerusalem tell us[12]). At the very hour of his death, some decades later, Augustine's own city, Hippo lay besieged by the Vandals. So it was at what seemed the twilight of the ancient empire of Rome that Augustine composed his account of the theology of the social order known as the *City of God.* Within his remarkable *oeuvre,* it was that work that renders of special interest here the sages' contemporary and their counterpart as a system-builder.

Like the critical issue of political calamity facing sages in the aftermath of the triumph of Christianity and the failure of Julian's brief restoration of both paganism and (as to Jerusalem) Judaism, the question Augustine addressed presented a fundamental challenge to the foundations of the Christian order, coming as it did from Roman pagan aristocrats, taking refuge in North Africa.[13] What caused the

---

[12] I refer to J. N. D. Kelly, Jerome: His Life, Writings, and Controversies (N.Y., 1975: Harper & Row).

[13] In no way claiming to know the scholarship on Augustine, even in the English language, I chose to rely mostly upon a single work, consulting others mostly for my own illumination. It is the up-to-date and, I think, universally respected account by Peter Brown, Augustine of Hippo (Berkeley and Los Angeles, 1967: University of California Press). The pertinent passage is on p. 302. All otherwise unidentified page references to follow are to this work. My modest generalizations about the intersection of the two systems on some points important to each rests, for Augustine, entirely on Brown. I found very helpful the outline of the work presented by John Neville Figgis, The Political Aspects of S. Augustine's 'City of God' (London, 1921: Longmans Green and Co.), pp. 1-31, and the characterization of Augustine's thought by Herbert A. Deane, The Politician and Social Ideas of St. Augustine (New York & London, 1963: Columbia University Press). In Deane's lucid account, anyone in search of specific doctrinal parallels between sages' system and that of Augustine will find ample evidence that there is none of consequence. As will become clear, what I find heuristically suggestive are structural and functional parallels, not points of doctrinal coincidence of any material

186   *The Mind of Classical Judaism. II*

fall of Rome, if not the breaches in its walls made by Christianity? The first three books of *The City of God* responded, in 413, and twenty-two books in all came to a conclusion in 426: a gigantic work.[14] While *The City of God* (re)presents Christian faith "in the form of biblical history, from Genesis to Revelation,[15] just as sages present important components of their system in historical form of narrative, I see no important doctrinal points in common between the program of Israel's sages in the Land of Israel and that of the great Christian theologian and philosopher. Each party presented in an episodic way what can be represented as an orderly account of the social order,[16] each for the edification of its chosen audience; neither, I

---

importance. My sense is that the success of Brown's book overshadowed the important contribution of Gerald Bonner, St. Augustine of Hippo. Life and Controversies (London, 1963: SCM Press, Ltd.), a less dazzling, but more systematic and (it seems to me) useful presentation. A brief and clear account of the two cities is in Eugene Teselle, Augustine the Theologian (N.Y., 1970: Herder and Herder), pp. 268-278, who outlines the variety of approaches taken to the description and interpretation of the work: polemical, apologetic; philosophy or theology of history; analysis of political ideology; source of principles of political and moral theory; and of ecclesiastical policy; and the like. The achievement of F. Van der Meer, Augustine the Bishop. Religion and Society at the Dawn of the Middle Ages (New York, 1961: Harper & Row). Translated by Brian Battershaw and G. R. Lamp, is not to be missed: a fine example of the narrative-reading of religion by a historian of religion of one useful kind. Precisely what Augustine means by "the city of God" is worked out by John O'Meara, The Charter of Christendom: The Significance of the City of God (New York, 1961: The Macmillan Co.), who says (p. 43) that "the city of God exists already in heaven and, apart from certain pilgrim men who are on their way to it while they are on this earth, in heaven only." When I speak of sages' having extended the boundaries of the social system from earth to Heaven, I mean to suggest something roughly parallel, in that, when women and men on earth conform to the Torah, they find themselves in the image and after the likeness of Heaven. The sense of the concept "history," then, is "the story of two cities," so Hardy, pp. 267ff. (cf. Edward R. Hardy, Jr., "The City of God," in Roy W. Battenhouse, A Companion to the Study of St. Augustine (New York, 1955: Oxford University Press), pp. 257-286. I find the story of Israel among the nations as the equivalent, unifying and integrating conception of history in the doctrine(s) of history in the Yerushalmi and Leviticus Rabbah; this then means Israel forms the counterpart to the city of God, and I think that is the beginning of all systemic comparison in this context (and, I should suspect, in all others).
[14]p. 303.
[15]John H. S. Burleigh, The City of God. A Study of St. Augustine's Philosophy. Croall Lectures, 1944 (London, 1949: Nisbet & Co. Ltd.), p. 153.
[16]But the two parties have in common the simple fact that the representation of their respective systems is the accomplishment of others later on, indeed, in the case of sages, much later on indeed. Note the

think, would have understood a line of the composition of the other, in writing or in concept. And that unbridgable abyss makes all the more striking the simple fact that, from one side of the gap to the other, the distance was slight. For each party addressed questions entirely familiar, I think, to the other, and the gross and salient traits of the system of the one in some striking ways prove symmetrical to those of the other.[17]

The relationship of the opposing cities of God and the devil, embodied in the pilgrim Church and the empirical state, presents the chief systematic problem of *The City of God*.[18] Augustine covered,

---

judgment of Deane, Augustine "was not a system-builder...Virtually everything that Augustine wrote...was an occasional piece" (Herbert A. Deane, The Political and Social Ideas of St. Augustine (New York & London, 1963: Columbia University Press, p. viii). Sages' documents, it is quite obvious, do not utilize the categories for the description of the social order that I have imposed: ethos, ethics, ethnos; worldview, way of life, doctrine of the social entity. But systemic description in its nature imputes and of necessity imposes system, and that is so, whether the system is deemed social or theological in its fundamental character. I have no difficulty in defending the proposition that sages' system was in its very essence a system of society, that is, of the holy people, Israel, and the union of social and theological thought in Augustine is signaled by the very metaphors he selected for his work, in his appeal to "the city."

[17] When William Green recommended the choice of Augustine and I accepted it, the recommendation and recognition of its rightness bore a certain rationality too. Drawing a comparison with Augustine is by no means capricious, based merely on the temporal coincidence of our sages of blessed memory in the Yerushalmi and related writings and Augustine. What I think more compelling is the fact that sages inherited a Middle Platonic doctrine concerning the unity of all being and reworked it in historical-narrative terms, therefore finding in (among other concepts) the notion of zekhut a medium for the unification of the generations, past and present. Augustine, for his part, is everywhere described as a reworking the heritage of Platonism, drawing chiefly from Plotinus, so for instance Burleigh, p. 157. As a guess, therefore, I would venture that the principal shift in the large-scale modes of thought from the Mishnah through to the Yerushalmi along with Genesis Rabbah, Leviticus Rabbah, and Pesiqta deRab Kahana, was the movement away from Aristotelian modes of thought, such as characterized the Mishnah, to those of Middle Platonism. But not being a historian of philosophy in antiquity, I am able only to suggest that hypothesis as a subject for further inquiry. In any event one did not have to adopt the inheritance of Plato, in the formulation of Middle Platonism, Neo-Platonism, or Plotinus, to focus upon the social order as the centerpiece of philosophical, systematic thought and system-building. Aristotle (much less influential in this period, to be sure) provided an equally accessible model for anyone who might wish to rethink the foundations of the polis or of the social being of Israel, the holy people, in the Land of Israel, the holy land.

[18] So Teselle, p. 270.

in five books, "those who worshipped the gods for felicity on earth;" in five, "those who worshipped them for eternal felicity;" and twelve, the theme of the origin of "two cities, one of God, the other of the world, " "their unfolding course in the part," "their ultimate destinies."[19] True, sages reconsidered the prior disinterest in history, but they did not then produce a continuous account of everything that had every happened, and Augustine did. Nor do the two literary monuments, Augustine's and sages', bear anything in common as to form, style, sources, mode of argument, selection of audience, literary convention of any kind. Then why treat the system of sages and the systematic statement of Augustine as so connected as to warrant comparison? For the obvious reason that the authorship of Israel and the Christian author not only responded to the same circumstance but also framed the question deemed posed by that common circumstance in the same terms: a recasting, in historical terms, of the whole of the social order, a rethinking, in the image of Augustine, of God's city.

What then was the value of the polis, which throughout these pages I have rendered as "the social order," and exactly who lived in the city of the earth? It was "any group of people tainted by the Fall," any that failed to regard "the 'earthly' values they had created as transient and relative."[20] To this Augustine responds, "Away with all this arrogant bluffing: what, after all, are men but men!"[21] The rise of Rome is reduced, in Brown's words, "to a simple common denominator...the 'lust for domination.'" The Romans were moved by "an overweening love of praise: 'they were, therefore, "grasping for praise, open-handed with their money; honest in the pursuit of wealth, they wanted to hoard glory.'"[22] But the true glory resides not in Rome but in the city of God: "the virtues the Romans had ascribed to their heroes would be realized only in the citizens of this other city; and it is only within the walls of the Heavenly Jerusalem that Cicero's noble definition of the essence of the Roman Republic could be achieved."[23] The Judaic sages – we now realize – assuredly concurred on whence comes glory, whence shame: the one from humility, the other, pride.

The system of Augustine addresses the crisis of change with an account of history, and it is, therefore, in the same sense as is the

---

[19] pp. 303-304. Cf.. also Burleigh, pp. 166ff., on Augustine's attitude toward "the concrete political structures of history."
[20] p. 309.
[21] p. 309.
[22] p. 310.
[23] pp. 311-312.

Enchanted Judaism and The City of God

system of the Judaic sages, a deeply historical one: "The whole course of human history...could be thought of as laden with meanings which might be seized, partially by the believer, in full by the seer."[24] So Brown: "In his *City of God*, Augustine was one of the first to sense and give monumental expression to a new form of intellectual excitement." God communicates through both words and events. Specifically, history proves the presence of a division between an earthly and a heavenly city.[25] Why do I find this historical interest pertinent to my picture of a Judaism's social order? Because, in Brown's words, "there is room, in Augustine's view of the past, for the consideration of whole societies...."[26] But the building block of society is relationship, and the whole of human history emerges out of the relationship of Cain and Abel, natural man after the fall, citizen of this world, against a man who built no city, "by hoping for something else...he waited upon the name of the Lord."[27] Brown says:

> Augustine treats the tension between Cain and Abel as universal, because he can explain it in terms applicable to all men. All human society...is based on a desire to share some good. Of such goods, the most deeply felt by human beings is the need for 'peace:' that is, for a resolution of tensions, for an ordered control of unbalanced appetites in themselves, and of discordant wills in society...the

---

[24] p. 317.
[25] p. 319. See Burleigh, pp. 185ff., "A philosophy of history." He cites the following: "St. Augustine's De Civitate Dei...may be regarded as the first attempt to frame a complete philosophy of history...It was...a singularly unsuccessful attempt; for it contained neither philosophy nor history, but merely theology and fiction." Whether or not so of Augustine, that statement seems to me an apt description of the form of history as invented in the pages of the Talmud of the Land of Israel. My presentation of sages' thought on history is in my The Foundations of Judaism. Method, Teleology, Doctrine. Philadelphia, 1983-5: Fortress Press. II. Messiah in Context. Israel's History and Destiny in Formative Judaism. Second printing: Lanham, 1988: University Press of America. Studies in Judaism series. This matter has not played a principal role in my exposition of the successor-system, because it seems to me ancillary and not categorically-definitive. Burleigh describes the dominant philosophy of the age, characteristic of Augustine as well, as anti-historical. But Augustine's "Platonic Biblicism in effect brings them [history and philosophy] into the closest relation. Biblical History is Platonic idealism in time." That statement seems to me to run parallel to the characterization of the rabbinic uses of history in the form of persons and events as exemplary and cyclical, rather than unique and linear.
[26] p. 320.
[27] p. 320.

members of the [city of earth[, that is, fallen men, tend to regard their achievement of such peace in society as sufficient in itself...[28]

The city of Heaven is "the consecrated commonwealth of Israel," the city of earth, everybody else.[29] Brown's summary of Augustine's main point with slight alteration serves as epitome of sages' views:

> What was at stake, in the City of God and in Augustine's sermons, was the capacity of men to 'long' for something different, to examine the nature of their relationship with their immediate environment; above all, to establish their identity by refusing to be engulfed in the unthinking habits of their fellows.[30]

How alien can sages, concerned as they were with the possibilities of extraordinary conduct or attitude, have found Augustine's interest in establishing identity by reflection on what others deemed routine? The obvious answer justifies juxtaposing the two systems as to not only their ineluctable questions, but also their self-evidently valid answers.

Two further rhetorical questions seem justified: if Augustine spoke of "resident aliens" when referring to the citizens of God's city,[31] then how difficult can sages have found interpreting the identity of their social entity, their Israel, in the same way: here now, but only because of tomorrow: the pilgrim people, *en route* to somewhere else. And why should we find surprising, as disciples of Israel's sages, a city of God permeated, as was Augustine's, by arguments for hope:[32]

> "'Lord, I have loved the beauty of Thy house.' From his gifts, which are scattered to good and bad alike in this, our most grim life, let us, with His help, try to express sufficiently what we have yet to experience."[33]

Two systems emerged from the catastrophes of the fifth century, Augustine's[34] for the Christian, sages' for the Judaic West.

---

[28]p. 322.
[29]p. 322.
[30]p. 322.
[31]p. 323
[32]p. 328.
[33]p. 328.
[34]Note Burleigh, p. 218: "The Fifth Century...was a period of radical historical change." But just as Augustine expressed no sense of "the end of an era," so in the pages of the documents surveyed here I find no world-historical foreboding, only an optimistic and unshakable conviction that Israel governed by its own deeds and attitudes its own destiny every day. That seems to me the opposite of a sense that all things are changing beyond repair. I can find no more ample representation of the historical convictions of our sages of blessed memory than Burleigh's representation of Augustine's:

Constructed in the same age and in response to problems of the same character and quality, the systems bore nothing in common, except the fundamentally same messages about the correspondence of the individual's life to the social order, the centrality of relationship, the rule of God, and the response of God to what transcended all rules.

By both systems, each in its own way, God is joined to the social order because it is in relationships that society takes shape and comes to expression, and all relationships, whether between one person and another or between mortals and God, are wholly consubstantial.[35] That is why, for Augustine, the relationship between the individuals, Cain and Abel, can convey and represent the relationships characteristic of societies or cities, and that is why, for sages, the relationships between one person and another can affect God's relationship to the village needing rain or the householder needing to shore up his shaky dwelling-place.

True, we deal with the two utterly unrelated systems of the social order, fabricated by different people, talking about different things to different people, each meant to join the society of humanity (or a sector thereof) with the community of Heaven. But both formed quite systematic and well-crafted responses to one and the same deep (and in my judgment, thoroughly merited) perception of disorder, a world that has wobbled, a universe out of line. Rome fallen, home besieged, for Augustine, corresponding to the end of autonomy and the advent of another (to be sure, *soi-disant*) "Israel," for sages, called into question orders of society of very ancient foundation. And that produced a profound sense that the rules had been broken, generating that (framing matters in contemporary psychological terms)

"Rome might pass away. The protecting fostering power of her emperors might be withdrawn. But God endured. His purpose of gathering citizens into His Eternal City was not frustrated by transient circumstances. St. Augustine had no anxiety for the Empire or for civilization, even 'Christian' civilization, because he found a better security in God." It is interesting to note that Burleigh gave his lectures in 1944, responding it seems to me to the impending dissolution of the British Empire in his rereading of Augustine – and dismissing an interest in the fate of Empires as essentially beside the point for Augustine. So I think it was for our sages.

[35]Burleigh characterizes matters in this way: "He seems to have been satisfied to show...that the exposition and defense of the Christian faith necessitates a survey of all History, which is in its essence God's providential government of the human race" (p. 202).

alienation that was overcome by Augustine in his way, by sages in theirs.[36]

How, in the language of Judaism as our sages formulated it, may we express the answer to the question of the times? The shaking of the foundations of the social order shows how Israel is estranged from God. The old rules have been broken, therefore the remarkable and the exceptional succeeds. What is unnatural to the human condition of pride is humility and uncertainty, acceptance and conciliation. Those attitudes for the individual, policies for the nation, violate the rule. Then let God respond to transcending rules. And when – so the system maintains – God recognizes in Israel's heart, as much as in the nation's deliberation, the proper feelings, God will respond by ending that estrangement that marks the present age. So the single word encompassing the question addressed by the entire social system of the successor-Judaism must be *alienation*. The human and shared sense of crisis – whether Augustine reflecting on the fall of Rome, or sages confronting the end of the old order – finds its response in the doctrine of God's assessment, God's response. God enters the social order imagined by sages because God in the natural order proves insufficient, a Presence inadequate to the human situation. God must dwell in the city of humanity, and Israel in the city of God. So what in secular terms we see as a historical crisis or in psychological terms as one of alienation, in religious terms we have to identify as a caesura in the bounds of eternity. The psychological theology of the system joins the human condition to the fate of the nation and the world – and links the whole to the broken heart of God.

And yet that theological observation about the incarnate God of Judaism does not point us toward the systemic center, which within my definitions of what a system is must be social and explain the order of things here and now. For in the end, a religious theory of the social order describes earth, not Heaven.[37] It simply begs the question to claim that the system in the end attended to the condition of God's heart, rather than humanity's mundane existence.

---

[36]The basic motif of alienation, personal, cosmic, political, theological, as much as affective characterizes the two systems, because it defines the condition that provokes for each system the generative question, and because it is in the mode of reintegration that each system finds its persistent statement. True, alienation defines a purely contemporary category and forms a judgment made by us upon the circumstance or attitude of ancients. But the category does serve to specify, for our own understanding, what is at stake.

[37]To be sure, earth in the model of Heaven, or, as we might prefer, Heaven in the model of earth.

For a religious system is not a theological one, and questions about the way of life, world-view, and social entity, admittedly bearing theological implications or even making theological statements, in the end find their answers in the reconstruction of the here and now. So I have not identified the central tension and the generative problematic, nor have I specified the self-evident answer to that question that the system, in every sentence and all details means to settle. It is for identifying that generative problematic of the religious Judaism of the fifth century that the comparison between the Judaism of our sages of blessed memory and the Christianity of Augustine in his *City of God* proves particularly pertinent.

To state matters very simply, Augustine's personal circumstance and that of our sages correspond, so do Augustine's central question and the fundamental preoccupation of our sages. Augustine's *City of God* and the Talmud of the Land of Israel took shape in times that were changing, and both systemic statements accommodated questions of history. But we see the answer, therefore the question, when we realize that, as a matter of fact, both did so in the same way.

Specifically, Augustine, bringing to fruition the tradition of Christian historical thought commencing with Eusebius, provided for Christianity a theory of history that placed into the right perspective the events of the day. And our sages did the same, first of all affirming that events required recognition, second, then providing a theory of events that acknowledged their meaning, that is, their historicity, but that also subordinated history to considerations of eternity. The generative problematic of the successor-system concerned history: vast changes in the political circumstance of Israel, perceived mutations in the tissue of social relationship, clearly an interest in revising the plain meaning of ordinary words: value, power, learning. And the systemic answer for its part addressed questions of long-term continuity, framed in genealogical terms for the now-genealogically-defined Israel: the past lives in us, and the system explains in very precise and specific terms just how that takes place, which is through the medium of inherited entitlement or attained entitlement. The medium was indeed the same. The message carried by *zekhut* counseled performance of actions of renunciation, in the hope that Heaven would respond. Power was weakness, value was knowledge, and knowledge was power: all things formed within the Torah.

But if that was the message by way of answer to the historical question of change and crisis, then what how had the question of history come to be formulated? It was, of course, precisely what events should be deemed to constitute history, what changes matter, and what are we to do. The answer – our sages' and Augustine's alike – was that only certain happenings are eventful, bear consequence, require attention. And they are eventful because they form paradigms, Cain and Abel for Augustine, Israel's patriarchs and matriarchs for our sages.[38] Then what has happened to history as made by the barbarians at Rome and Hippo, the Byzantine Christians at Tiberias and Sepphoris? It has ceased to matter, because what happened at Rome, what happened at Tiberias, is no happening at all, but a mere happenstance. The upshot is not that history follows rules, so we can predict what will be, not at all.

Augustine did not claim to know what would happen tomorrow morning, and our sages interpreted events but did not claim to shape them, except through the Torah. The upshot is that what is going on really may be set aside in favor of what is really happening, and the story that is history has already been told in (for Augustine) the Bible and (for our sages) the Torah. But, then, that is no longer history at all, but merely, a past made into an eternal present. So, if I may specify what I conceive to be the systemic answer, it is, there are some things that matter, many that do not, and the few that matter echo from eternity to eternity, speaking in that voice, the voice of God, that is the voice of silence, still and small.

The systemic question, urgent and immediate and critical, not merely chronic, then, concerned vast historical change, comprising chains of events. The answer was that, in an exact sense, "event" has no meaning at all. Other than historical modes of organizing existence governed, and history in the ordinary sense did not form one of them. Without the social construction of history, there also is no need for the identification of events, that is, individual and unique happenings that bear consequence, since, within the system and structure of the successor-Judaism, history forms no taxon, being replaced by *zekhut*, a historical category that was – we now realize – in the deepest sense anti-historical. So, it must follow, no happening is unique, and, on its own, no event bears consequence.

Neither Augustine nor our sages produced narrative history; both, rather, wrote reflections *on* history, a very different matter. For neither did narrative history, ordinarily a sustained paraphrastic chronicle, serve as a medium for organizing and explaining perceived

---

[38]But while I think they are primary, as the formation of Genesis Rabbah at this time indicates, they are not alone; Israel at Sinai, David on the throne, and other historical moments serve as well. It is a mere impression, not a demonstrable fact, that the patriarchs and matriarchs provide the primary paradigm.

Enchanted Judaism and The City of God

experience. True, both referred to events in the past, but these were not strung together in a continuing account. They were cited because they were exemplary, not because they were unique. These events then were identified out of the unlimited agenda of the past as what mattered, and these occasions of consequence, as distinct from undifferentiated and unperceived happenings were meant to explain the things that mattered in the chaos of the everyday.

In responding as they did to what we conceive to be historical events of unparalleled weight, Augustine and our sages took positions that, from our perspective, prove remarkably contemporary. For we now understand that all histories are the creation of an eternal present, that is, those moments in which histories are defined and distinguished, in which events are identified and assigned consequence, and in which sequences of events, "this particular thing happened here *and therefore...*," are strung together, pearls on a string, to form ornaments of intellect. Fully recognizing that history is one of the grand fabrications of the human intellect, facts not discovered but invented, explanations that themselves form cultural indicators of how things are in the here and now, we may appreciate as far more than merely instrumental and necessary the systemic responses to the urgent questions addressed in common by our sages and by Augustine.

Shall we then represent the successor-Judaism as a historical religion,[39] in that it appeals for its world-view to not myth about gods in heaven but the history of Israel upon earth – interpreted in relationship to the acts of God in heaven to be sure? And shall we characterize that Judaism as a religion that appeals to history, that is, to events, defined in the ordinary way, important happenings, for its source of testing and establishing truth? I think not. That Judaism identifies an event through its own cognitive processes. Just as the canon that recapitulates the system, so events – things that happen given consequence – recapitulate the system. Just as the system speaks in detail through the canon, so, too, through its repertoire of events granted recognition the system delivers its message. But just as the canon is not the system, so the recognition of events does not classify the system as historical.

This brings me directly to the final question of systemic description: what exactly does the successor-Judaism mean by events? To answer that question succinctly is simple. In the canonical literature of the successor-Judaism, events find their place, within the science of learning of *Listenwissenschaft* that characterizes this

---

[39] I leave for Augustine-scholarship the counterpart-question on him.

literature, along with sorts of things that, for our part, we should not characterize as events at all. Events have no autonomous standing; events are not unique, each unto itself; events have no probative value on their own. Events form cases, along with a variety of other cases, making up lists of things that, in common, point to or prove one thing. Not only so, but among the taxonomic structure at hand, events do not make up their own list at all, for what is truly eventful generates *zekhut*. It is the act of *zekhut* that unites past and present, and it is the act that gains *zekhut* that makes history for tomorrow.

Events of other kinds, even those that seem to make an enormous, and awful, difference in Israel's condition, will appear on the same list as persons, places, things. And the contrary lists – very often in the form of stories – tell us events that in and of themselves change biography (the life and fate of an ass-driver) and make history. That means that events other than those that gain *zekhut* not only have no autonomous standing on their own, but also that events constitute no species even within a genus of a historical order. For persons, places, and things in our way of thinking do not belong on the same list as events; they are not of the same order. Within the logic of our own minds, we cannot classify the city, Paris, within the same genus as the event, the declaration of the rights of man, for instance, nor is Sinai or Jerusalem of the same order of things as the Torah or the Temple, respectively. But in the logic of the Judaism before us, Jerusalem stands for sanctity and for Temple; it is of precisely the same taxic order.

What then shall we make of a list that encompasses within the same taxic composition events and things? Answering that question shows us how our sages sort out what matters from what does not, and events, by themselves, do not form a taxon and on their own bear no means and therefore do not matter. For one such list made up of events, persons, and places, is as follows: [1] Israel at the sea; [2] the ministering angels; [3] the tent of meeting; [4] the eternal house [=the Temple]; [5] Sinai. That mixes an event (Israel redeemed at the sea), a category of sensate being (angels), a location (tent of meeting, Temple), and then Sinai, which can stand for a variety of things but in context stands for the Torah. In such a list an event may or may not stand for a value or a proposition, but it does not enjoy autonomous standing; the list is not defined by the eventfulness of events and their meaning, the compilation of matters of a single genus or even a single species (tent of meeting, eternal house, are the same species here). The notion of event as autonomous, even unique, is quite absent in this taxonomy. And once events lose their autonomy, that process of selection gets under way that transforms one event into history bearing meaning and sets aside as inconsequential in the exact sense all other events.

Since this point is systemically so fundamental, let me give the case of another such list, which moves from events to other matters altogether, finding the whole subject to the same metaphor, hence homogenized. First come the events that took place at these places or with these persons: Egypt, the sea, Marah, Massah and Meribah, Horeb, the wilderness, the spies in the Land, Shittim, for Achan/Joshua and the conquest of the Land. Now that mixture of places and names clearly intends to focus on particular things that happened, and hence, were the list to which I refer to conclude at this point, we could define an event for the successor-Judaism as a happening that bore consequence, taught a lesson or exemplified a truth, in the present case, an event matters because it the mixture of rebellion and obedience. But there would then be no doubt that "event" formed a genus unto itself, and that a proper list could not encompass both events, defined conventionally as we should, and also other matters altogether.

But the literary culture at hand, this textual community proceeds, in the same literary context, to the following items: [1] the Ten Commandments; [2] the show-fringes and phylacteries; [3] the *Shema* and the Prayer; [4] the tabernacle and the cloud of the Presence of God in the world to come. Why we invoke, as our candidates for the metaphor at hand, the Ten Commandments, show-fringes and phylacteries, recitation of the *Shema* and the Prayer, the tabernacle and the cloud of the Presence of God, and the mezuzah, seems to me clear from the very catalogue. These reach their climax in the analogy between the home and the tabernacle, the embrace of God and the Presence of God. So the whole is meant to list those things that draw the Israelite near God and make the Israelite cleave to God. And to this massive catalogue, events are not only exemplary – which historians can concede without difficulty – but also subordinated.

They belong on the same list as actions, things, persons, places, because they form an order of being that is not to be differentiated between events (including things that stand for events) and other cultural artifacts altogether. A happening is no different from an object, in which case "event" serves no better, and no worse, than a hero, a gesture or action, recitation of a given formula, or a particular locale, to establish a truth. It is contingent, subordinate, instrumental.[40] And why find that fact surprising, since all history comes to us in writing, and it is the culture that dictates how writing is to take place; that is why history can only paraphrase the affirmations of a system, and that is why events recapitulate in acute and concrete ways the system that classifies one thing that happens as event, but another thing is not only not an event but is not classified at all. In the present instance, an event is not at all eventful; it is merely a fact that forms part of the evidence for what is, and what is eventful is not an occasion at all, but a condition, an attitude, a perspective and a viewpoint. Then, it is clear, events are subordinated to the formation of attitudes, perspectives, viewpoints – the formative artifacts of not history in the conventional sense but culture in the framework of Sahlin's generalization, "history is culturally ordered, differently so in different societies, according to meaningful schemes of things."[41]

Events not only do not form a taxon, they also do not present a vast corpus of candidates for inclusion into some other taxon. Among the candidates, events that are selected by our documents are few indeed. They commonly encompass Israel at the Sea and at Sinai, the destruction of the first Temple, the destruction of the second Temple, events as defined by the actions of some holy men such as Abraham, Isaac, and Jacob (treated not for what they did but for who they were), Daniel, Mishael, Hananiah and Azariah, and the like. It follows that the restricted repertoire of candidates for taxonomic study encompasses remarkably few events, remarkably few for a literary culture that is commonly described as quintessentially historical!

Then what taxic indicator dictates which happenings will be deemed events and which not? What are listed throughout are not data of nature or history but of theology: the issue of history is one of relationship, just as with Augustine. Specifically, God's relationship with Israel, expressed in such facts as the three events, the first two in the past, the third in the future, namely, the three redemptions of Israel, the three patriarchs, and holy persons, actions, events, what-have-you – these are facts that are assembled and grouped. What we have is a kind of recombinant theology given narrative form through tales presented individually but not in a

---

[40]I can think of no more apt illustration of Geertz's interesting judgment: "an event is a unique actualization of a general phenomenon, a contingent realization of the cultural pattern." But my principal master in the present matter is Sahlin, cited in the next note.

[41]See his Islands of History (Chicago, 1985: The University of Chicago Press), p. ??.

sustained narrative. This recombinant theology through history is accomplished when the framer ("the theologian") selects from a restricted repertoire a few items for combination. What we have is a kind of subtle restatement, through an infinite range of possibilities, of the combinations and recombinations of a few essentially simple facts (data).

The net effect, then, is to exclude, rather than to include: the world is left outside. The key to systemic interpretation lies in the exegesis of that exegetical process that governs selection: what is included, what is excluded. In this context I find important Jonathan Z. Smith's statement:

> An almost limitless horizon of possibilities that are at hand...is arbitrarily reduced...to a set of basic elements....Then a most intense ingenuity is exercised to overcome the reduction...to introduce interest and variety. This ingenuity is usually accompanied by a complex set of rules.[42]

If we know the complex set of rules in play here, we also would understand the system that makes this document not merely an expression of piety but a statement of a theological structure: orderly, well-composed and proportioned, internally coherent and cogent throughout.

The canonical, therefore anything but random, standing of events forms a brief chapter in the exegesis of a canon. That observation draws us back to Smith, who observes:

> the radical and arbitary reduction represented by the notion of canon and the ingenuity represented by the rule-governed exegetical enterprise to apply the canon to every dimension of human life is that most characteristic, persistent, and obsessive religious activity....The task of application as well as the judgment of the relative adequacy of particular applications to a community's life situation remains the indigenous theologian's task; but the study of the process, particularly the study of comparative systematics and exegesis, ought to be a major preoccupation of the historian of religions.[43]

Smith speaks of religion as an "enterprise of exegetical totalization," and he further identifies with the word "canon" precisely what we have identified as the substrate and structure of the list. If I had to define an event in this canonical context, I should have to call it merely another theological thing: something to be manipulated,

---

[42] "Sacred Persistence: Towards a Redescription of Canon," in William Scott Green, ed., Approaches to Ancient Judaism 1978, 1:11-28. Quotation: p. 15.
[43] ibid. p. 18.

combined in one way or in another, along with other theological things.

In insisting that the successor-system remains connected to the initial one, I have until now left open the identification of the joining threads of thought. But now I scarcely need to elaborate. The systems are connected because the successor-system sustains the generative mode of thought of the initial one, which was list-making. But now the lists derive from data supplied by Scripture (as with the bulk of Augustine's historical events of paradigmatic consequence), rather than by nature. Now as before, list-making is accomplished within a restricted repertoire of items that can serve on lists; the list-making then presents interesting combinations of an essentially small number of candidates for the exercise. But then, when making lists, one can do pretty much anything with the items that are combined; the taxic indicators are unlimited, but the data studied, severely limited. So the systems connect because the successor-system in mode of thought and medium of expression has recapitulated the initial system.

The radical shift in category-formation, the utterly-fresh systemic composition and construction – these turn out to carry forward received modes of thought. So far as the two systems may both be called Judaisms, and so far as these Judaisms so join as to form one on-going Judaism, continuity is in not message but method. The history of religion is the exegesis of exegesis, and, for the case before us, the transformation of Judaism likewise tells two stories. The one portrays successive and essentially distinct, free-standing systems. The other narrates that enduring process that sustains and unites and nourishes – and, therefore, also defines.

South Florida Studies in the History of Judaism

240001	Lectures on Judaism in the Academy and in the Humanities	Neusner
240002	Lectures on Judaism in the History of Religion	Neusner
240003	Self-Fulfilling Prophecy: Exile and Return in the History of Judaism	Neusner
240004	The Canonical History of Ideas: The Place of the So-called Tannaite Midrashim, Mekhilta Attributed to R. Ishmael, Sifra, Sifré to Numbers, and Sifré to Deuteronomy	Neusner
240005	Ancient Judaism: Debates and Disputes, Second Series	Neusner
240006	The Hasmoneans and Their Supporters: From Mattathias to the Death of John Hyrcanus I	Sievers
240007	Approaches to Ancient Judaism: New Series, Volume One	Neusner
240008	Judaism in the Matrix of Christianity	Neusner
240009	Tradition as Selectivity: Scripture, Mishnah, Tosefta, and Midrash in the Talmud of Babylonia	Neusner
240010	The Tosefta: Translated from the Hebrew: Sixth Division Tohorot	Neusner
240011	In the Margins of the Midrash: Sifre Ha'azinu Texts, Commentaries and Reflections	Basser
240012	Language as Taxonomy: The Rules for Using Hebrew and Aramaic in the Babylonia Talmud	Neusner
240013	The Rules of Composition of the Talmud of Babylonia: The Cogency of the Bavli's Composite	Neusner
240014	Understanding the Rabbinic Mind: Essays on the Hermeneutic of Max Kadushin	Ochs
240015	Essays in Jewish Historiography	Rapoport-Albert
240016	The Golden Calf and the Origins of the Jewish Controversy	Bori/Ward
240017	Approaches to Ancient Judaism: New Series, Volume Two	Neusner
240018	The Bavli That Might Have Been: The Tosefta's Theory of Mishnah Commentary Compared With the Bavli's	Neusner
240019	The Formation of Judaism: In Retrospect and Prospect	Neusner
240020	Judaism in Society: The Evidence of the Yerushalmi, Toward the Natural History of a Religion	Neusner
240021	The Enchantments of Judaism: Rites of Transformation from Birth Through Death	Neusner
240022	Åbo Addresses	Neusner
240023	The City of God in Judaism and Other Comparative and Methodological Studies	Neusner
240024	The Bavli's One Voice: Types and Forms of Analytical Discourse and their Fixed Order of Appearance	Neusner
240025	The Dura-Europos Synagogue: A Re-evaluation (1932-1992)	Gutmann
240026	Precedent and Judicial Discretion: The Case of Joseph ibn Lev	Morell
240027	Max Weinreich Geschichte der jiddischen Sprachforschung	Frakes
240028	Israel: Its Life and Culture, Volume I	Pedersen
240029	Israel: Its Life and Culture, Volume II	Pedersen
240030	The Bavli's One Statement: The Metapropositional Program of Babylonian Talmud Tractate Zebahim Chapters One and Five	Neusner

240031	The Oral Torah: The Sacred Books of Judaism: An Introduction: Second Printing	Neusner
240032	The Twentieth Century Construction of "Judaism:" Essays on the Religion of Torah in the History of Religion	Neusner
240033	How the Talmud Shaped Rabbinic Discourse	Neusner
240034	The Discourse of the Bavli: Language, Literature, and Symbolism: Five Recent Findings	Neusner
240035	The Law Behind the Laws: The Bavli's Essential Discourse	Neusner
240036	Sources and Traditions: Types of Compositions in the Talmud of Babylonia	Neusner
240037	How to Study the Bavli: The Languages, Literatures, and Lessons of the Talmud of Babylonia	Neusner
240038	The Bavli's Primary Discourse: Mishnah Commentary: Its Rhetorical Paradigms and their Theological Implications	Neusner
240039	Midrash Aleph Beth	Sawyer
240040	Jewish Thought in the 20th Century: An Introduction in the Talmud of Babylonia Tractate Moed Qatan	Schweid
240041	Diaspora Jews and Judaism: Essays in Honor of, and in Dialogue with, A. Thomas Kraabel	Overman/MacLennan
240042	The Bavli: An Introduction	Neusner
240043	The Bavli's Massive Miscellanies: The Problem of Agglutinative Discourse in the Talmud of Babylonia	Neusner
240044	The Foundations of the Theology of Judaism: An Anthology Part II: Torah	Neusner
240045	Form-Analytical Comparison in Rabbinic Judaism: Structure and Form in *The Fathers* and *The Fathers According to Rabbi Nathan*	Neusner
240046	Essays on Hebrew	Weinberg
240047	The Tosefta: An Introduction	Neusner
240048	The Foundations of the Theology of Judaism: An Anthology Part III: Israel	Neusner
240049	The Study of Ancient Judaism, Volume I: Mishnah, Midrash, Siddur	Neusner
240050	The Study of Ancient Judaism, Volume II: The Palestinian and Babylonian Talmuds	Neusner
240051	Take Judaism, for Example: Studies toward the Comparison of Religions	Neusner
240052	From Eden to Golgotha: Essays in Biblical Theology	Moberly
240053	The Principal Parts of the Bavli's Discourse: A Preliminary Taxonomy: Mishnah Commentary, Sources, Traditions and Agglutinative Miscellanies	Neusner
240054	Barabbas and Esther and Other Studies in the Judaic Illumination of Earliest Christianity	Aus
240055	Targum Studies, Volume I: Textual and Contextual Studies in the Pentateuchal Targums	Flesher
240056	Approaches to Ancient Judaism: New Series, Volume Three, Historical and Literary Studies	Neusner
240057	The Motherhood of God and Other Studies	Gruber
240058	The Analytic Movement: Hayyim Soloveitchik and his Circle	Solomon

240059	Recovering the Role of Women: Power and Authority in Rabbinic Jewish Society	Haas
240060	The Relation between Herodotus' *History* and Primary History	Mandell/Freedman
240061	The First Seven Days: A Philosophical Commentary on the Creation of Genesis	Samuelson
240062	The Bavli's Intellectual Character: The Generative Problematic: In Bavli Baba Qamma Chapter One And Bavli Shabbat Chapter One	Neusner
240063	The Incarnation of God: The Character of Divinity in Formative Judaism: Second Printing	Neusner
240064	Moses Kimhi: Commentary on the Book of Job	Basser/Walfish
240066	Death and Birth of Judaism: Second Printing	Neusner
240067	Decoding the Talmud's Exegetical Program	Neusner
240068	Sources of the Transformation of Judaism	Neusner
240069	The Torah in the Talmud: A Taxonomy of the Uses of Scripture in the Talmud, Volume I	Neusner
240070	The Torah in the Talmud: A Taxonomy of the Uses of Scripture in the Talmud, Volume II	Neusner
240071	The Bavli's Unique Voice: A Systematic Comparison of the Talmud of Babylonia and the Talmud of the Land of Israel, Volume One	Neusner
240072	The Bavli's Unique Voice: A Systematic Comparison of the Talmud of Babylonia and the Talmud of the Land of Israel, Volume Two	Neusner
240073	The Bavli's Unique Voice: A Systematic Comparison of the Talmud of Babylonia and the Talmud of the Land of Israel, Volume Three	Neusner
240074	Bits of Honey: Essays for Samson H. Levey	Chyet/Ellenson
240075	The Mystical Study of Ruth: *Midrash HaNe'elam* of the Zohar to the Book of Ruth	Englander
240076	The Bavli's Unique Voice: A Systematic Comparison of the Talmud of Babylonia and the Talmud of the Land of Israel, Volume Four	Neusner
240077	The Bavli's Unique Voice: A Systematic Comparison of the Talmud of Babylonia and the Talmud of the Land of Israel, Volume Five	Neusner
240078	The Bavli's Unique Voice: A Systematic Comparison of the Talmud of Babylonia and the Talmud of the Land of Israel, Volume Six	Neusner
240079	The Bavli's Unique Voice: A Systematic Comparison of the Talmud of Babylonia and the Talmud of the Land of Israel, Volume Seven	Neusner
240080	Are There Really Tannaitic Parallels to the Gospels?	Neusner
240081	Approaches to Ancient Judaism: New Series, Volume Four, Religious and Theological Studies	Neusner
240082	Approaches to Ancient Judaism: New Series, Volume Five, Historical, Literary, and Religious Studies	Basser/Fishbane
240083	Ancient Judaism: Debates and Disputes, Third Series	Neusner

240084	Judaic Law from Jesus to the Mishnah	Neusner
240085	Writing with Scripture: Second Printing	Neusner/Green
240086	Foundations of Judaism: Second Printing	Neusner
240087	Judaism and Zoroastrianism at the Dusk of Late Antiquity	Neusner
240088	Judaism States Its Theology	Neusner
240089	The Judaism behind the Texts I.A	Neusner
240090	The Judaism behind the Texts I.B	Neusner
240091	Stranger at Home	Neusner
240092	Pseudo-Rabad: Commentary to Sifre Deuteronomy	Basser
240093	FromText to Historical Context in Rabbinic Judaism	Neusner
240094	Formative Judaism	Neusner
240095	Purity in Rabbinic Judaism	Neusner
240096	Was Jesus of Nazareth the Messiah?	McMichael
240097	The Judaism behind the Texts I.C	Neusner
240098	The Judaism behind the Texts II	Neusner
240099	The Judaism behind the Texts III	Neusner
240100	The Judaism behind the Texts IV	Neusner
240101	The Judaism behind the Texts V	Neusner
240102	The Judaism the Rabbis Take for Granted	Neusner
240103	From Text to Historical Context in Rabbinic Judaism V. II	Neusner
240104	From Text to Historical Context in Rabbinic Judaism V. III	Neusner
240105	Samuel, Saul, and Jesus: Three Early Palestinian Jewish Christian Gospel Haggadoth	Aus
240106	What is Midrash? And a Midrash Reader	Neusner
240107	Rabbinic Judaism: Disputes and Debates	Neusner
240108	Why There Never Was a "Talmud of Caesarea"	Neusner
240109	Judaism after the Death of "The Death of God"	Neusner
240110	Approaches to Ancient Judaism	Neusner
240111	Ecology of Religion	Neusner
240112	The Judaic Law of Baptism	Neusner
240113	The Documentary Foundation of Rabbinic Culture	Neusner
240114	Understanding Seeking Faith, Volume Four	Neusner
240115	Paul and Judaism: An Anthropological Approach	Laato
240116	Approaches to Ancient Judaism, New Series, Volume Eight	Neusner
240119	Theme and Context in Biblical Lists	Scolnic
240120	Where the Talmud Comes From	Neusner
240121	The Initial Phases of the Talmud, Volume Three: Social Ethics	Neusner
240122	Are the Talmuds Interchangeable? Christine Hayes's Blunder	Neusner
240123	The Initial Phases of the Talmud, Volume One: Exegesis of Scripture	Neusner
240124	The Initial Phases of the Talmud, Volume Two: Exemplary Virtue	Neusner
240125	The Initial Phases of the Talmud, Volume Four: Theology	Neusner
240126	From Agnon to Oz	Bargad
240127	Talmudic Dialectics, Volume I: Tractate Berakhot and the Divisions of Appointed Times and Women	Neusner
240128	Talmudic Dialectics, Volume II: The Divisions of Damages and Holy Things and Tractate Niddah	Neusner

240129	The Talmud: Introduction and Reader	Neusner
240130	*Gesher Vakesher:* Bridges and Bonds The Life of Leon Kronish	Green
240131	Beyond Catastrophe	Neusner
240132	Ancient Judaism, Fourth Series	Neusner
240133	Formative Judaism, New Series: Current Issues and Arguments Volume One	Neusner
240134	Sects and Scrolls	Davies
240135	Religion and Law	Neusner
240136	Approaches to Ancient Judaism, New Series, Volume Nine	Neusner
240137	Uppsala Addresses	Neusner
240138	Jews and Christians in the Life and Thought of Hugh of St. Victor	Moore
240140	Jews, Pagans, and Christians in the Golan Heights	Gregg/Urman
240141	Rosenzweig on Profane/Secular History	Vogel
240142	Approaches to Ancient Judaism, New Series, Volume Ten	Neusner
240143	Archaeology and the Galilee	Edwards/McCullough
240144	Rationality and Structure	Neusner
240145	Formative Judaism, New Series: Current Issues and Arguments Volume Two	Neusner
240146	Ancient Judaism, Religious and Theological Perspectives First Series	Neusner
240147	The Good Creator	Gelander
240148	The Mind of Classical Judaism, Volume IV, The Philosophy and Political Economy of Formative Judaism: The Mishnah's System of the Social Order	Neusner
240149	The Mind of Classical Judaism, Volume I, Modes of Thought:: Making Connections and Drawing Conclusions	Neusner
240150	The Mind of Classical Judaism, Volume II, From Philosophy to Religion	Neusner
241051	The Mind of Classical Judaism, Volume III, What is "Israel"? Social Thought in the Formative Age	Neusner
240152	The Components of Rabbinic Documents: From the Whole to the Parts, I. Sifre, Part One	Neusner
240153	The Theology of Rabbinic Judaism: A Prolegomenon	Neusner
240154	Approaches to Ancient Judaism, New Series, Volume Eleven	Neusner
240155	Pesiqta Rabbati: A Synoptic Edition of Pesiqta Rabbati Based upon all Extant Manuscripts and the Editio Princeps, V. I	Ulmer

South Florida Academic Commentary Series

243001	The Talmud of Babylonia, An Academic Commentary, Volume XI, Bavli Tractate Moed Qatan	Neusner
243002	The Talmud of Babylonia, An Academic Commentary, Volume XXXIV, Bavli Tractate Keritot	Neusner
243003	The Talmud of Babylonia, An Academic Commentary, Volume XVII, Bavli Tractate Sotah	Neusner
243004	The Talmud of Babylonia, An Academic Commentary, Volume XXIV, Bavli Tractate Makkot	Neusner

243009	The Talmud of Babylonia, An Academic Commentary, Volume XXVII, Bavli Tractate Shebuot	Neusner
243010	The Talmud of Babylonia, An Academic Commentary, Volume XXXIII, Bavli Tractate Temurah	Neusner
243011	The Talmud of Babylonia, An Academic Commentary, Volume XXXV, Bavli Tractates Meilah and Tamid	Neusner
243012	The Talmud of Babylonia, An Academic Commentary, Volume VIII, Bavli Tractate Rosh Hashanah	Neusner
243013	The Talmud of Babylonia, An Academic Commentary, Volume V, Bavli Tractate Yoma	Neusner
243014	The Talmud of Babylonia, An Academic Commentary, Volume XXXVI, Bavli Tractate Niddah	Neusner
243015	The Talmud of Babylonia, An Academic Commentary, Volume XX, Bavli Tractate Baba Qamma	Neusner
243016	The Talmud of Babylonia, An Academic Commentary, Volume XXXI, Bavli Tractate Bekhorot	Neusner
243017	The Talmud of Babylonia, An Academic Commentary, Volume XXX, Bavli Tractate Hullin	Neusner
243018	The Talmud of Babylonia, An Academic Commentary, Volume VII, Bavli Tractate Besah	Neusner
243019	The Talmud of Babylonia, An Academic Commentary, Volume X, Bavli Tractate Megillah	Neusner
243020	The Talmud of Babylonia, An Academic Commentary, Volume XXVIII, Bavli Tractate Zebahim A. Chapters I through VII	Neusner
243021	The Talmud of Babylonia, An Academic Commentary, Volume XXI, Bavli Tractate Baba Mesia, A. Chapters I through VI	Neusner
243022	The Talmud of Babylonia, An Academic Commentary, Volume XXII, Bavli Tractate Baba Batra, A. Chapters I through VI	Neusner
243023	The Talmud of Babylonia, An Academic Commentary, Volume XXIX, Bavli Tractate Menahot, A. Chapters I through VI	Neusner
243024	The Talmud of Babylonia, An Academic Commentary, Volume I, Bavli Tractate Berakhot	Neusner
243025	The Talmud of Babylonia, An Academic Commentary, Volume XXV, Bavli Tractate Abodah Zarah	Neusner
243026	The Talmud of Babylonia, An Academic Commentary, Volume XXIII, Bavli Tractate Sanhedrin, A. Chapters I through VII	Neusner
243027	The Talmud of Babylonia, A Complete Outline, Part IV, The Division of Holy Things; A: From Tractate Zabahim through Tractate Hullin	Neusner
243028	The Talmud of Babylonia, An Academic Commentary, Volume XIV, Bavli Tractate Ketubot, A. Chapters I through VI	Neusner
243029	The Talmud of Babylonia, An Academic Commentary, Volume IV, Bavli Tractate Pesahim, A. Chapters I through VII	Neusner

243030	The Talmud of Babylonia, An Academic Commentary, Volume III, Bavli Tractate Erubin, A. ChaptersI through V	Neusner
243031	The Talmud of Babylonia, A Complete Outline, Part III, The Division of Damages; A: From Tractate Baba Qamma through Tractate Baba Batra	Neusner
243032	The Talmud of Babylonia, An Academic Commentary, Volume II, Bavli Tractate Shabbat, Volume A, Chapters One through Twelve	Neusner
243033	The Talmud of Babylonia, An Academic Commentary, Volume II, Bavli Tractate Shabbat, Volume B, Chapters Thirteen through Twenty-four	Neusner
243034	The Talmud of Babylonia, An Academic Commentary, Volume XV, Bavli Tractate Nedarim	Neusner
243035	The Talmud of Babylonia, An Academic Commentary, Volume XVIII, Bavli Tractate Gittin	Neusner
243036	The Talmud of Babylonia, An Academic Commentary, Volume XIX, Bavli Tractate Qiddushin	Neusner
243037	The Talmud of Babylonia, A Complete Outline, Part IV, The Division of Holy Things; B: From Tractate Berakot through Tractate Niddah	Neusner
243038	The Talmud of Babylonia, A Complete Outline, Part III, The Division of Damages; B: From Tractate Sanhedrin through Tractate Shebuot	Neusner
243039	The Talmud of Babylonia, A Complete Outline, Part I, Tractate Berakhot and the Division of Appointed Times A: From Tractate Berakhot through Tractate Pesahim	Neusner
243040	The Talmud of Babylonia, A Complete Outline, Part I, Tractate Berakhot and the Division of Appointed Times B: From Tractate Yoma through Tractate Hagigah	Neusner
243041	The Talmud of Babylonia, A Complete Outline, Part II, The Division of Women; A: From Tractate Yebamot through Tractate Ketubot	Neusner
243042	The Talmud of Babylonia, A Complete Outline, Part II, The Division of Women; B: From Tractate Nedarim through Tractate Qiddushin	Neusner
243043	The Talmud of Babylonia, An Academic Commentary, Volume XIII, Bavli Tractate Yebamot, A. Chapters One through Eight	Neusner
243044	The Talmud of Babylonia, An Academic Commentary, XIII, Bavli Tractate Yebamot, B. Chapters Nine through Seventeen	Neusner
243045	The Talmud of the Land of Israel, A Complete Outline of the Second, Third and Fourth Divisions, Part II, The Division of Women, A. Yebamot to Nedarim	Neusner
243046	The Talmud of the Land of Israel, A Complete Outline of the Second, Third and Fourth Divisions, Part II, The Division of Women, B. Nazir to Sotah	Neusner
243047	The Talmud of the Land of Israel, A Complete Outline of the Second, Third and Fourth Divisions, Part I, The Division of Appointed Times, C. Pesahim and Sukkah	Neusner

243048	The Talmud of the Land of Israel, A Complete Outline of the Second, Third and Fourth Divisions, Part I, The Division of Appointed Times, A. Berakhot, Shabbat	Neusner
243049	The Talmud of the Land of Israel, A Complete Outline of the Second, Third and Fourth Divisions, Part I, The Division of Appointed Times, B. Erubin, Yoma and Besah	Neusner
243050	The Talmud of the Land of Israel, A Complete Outline of the Second, Third and Fourth Divisions, Part I, The Division of Appointed Times, D. Taanit, Megillah, Rosh Hashannah, Hagigah and Moed Qatan	Neusner
243051	The Talmud of the Land of Israel, A Complete Outline of the Second, Third and Fourth Divisions, Part III, The Division of Damages, A. Baba Qamma, Baba Mesia, Baba Batra, Horayot and Niddah	Neusner
243052	The Talmud of the Land of Israel, A Complete Outline of the Second, Third and Fourth Divisions, Part III, The Division of Damages, B. Sanhedrin, Makkot, Shebuot and Abldah Zarah	Neusner
243053	The Two Talmuds Compared, II. The Division of Women in the Talmud of the Land of Israel and the Talmud of Babylonia, Volume A, Tractates Yebamot and Ketubot	Neusner
243054	The Two Talmuds Compared, II. The Division of Women in the Talmud of the Land of Israel and the Talmud of Babylonia, Volume B, Tractates Nedarim, Nazir and Sotah	Neusner
243055	The Two Talmuds Compared, II. The Division of Women in the Talmud of the Land of Israel and the Talmud of Babylonia, Volume C, Tractates Qiddushin and Gittin	Neusner
243056	The Two Talmuds Compared, III. The Division of Damages in the Talmud of the Land of Israel and the Talmud of Babylonia, Volume A, Tractates Baba Qamma and Baba Mesia	Neusner
243057	The Two Talmuds Compared, III. The Division of Damages in the Talmud of the Land of Israel and the Talmud of Babylonia, Volume B, Tractates Baba Batra and Niddah	Neusner
243058	The Two Talmuds Compared, III. The Division of Damages in the Talmud of the Land of Israel and the Talmud of Babylonia, Volume C, Tractates Sanhedrin and Makkot	Neusner
243059	The Two Talmuds Compared, I. Tractate Berakhot and the Division of Appointed Times in the Talmud of the Land of Israel and the Talmud of Babylonia, Volume B, Tractate Shabbat	Neusner
243060	The Two Talmuds Compared, I. Tractate Berakhot and the Division of Appointed Times in the Talmud of the Land of Israel and the Talmud of Babylonia, Volume A, Tractate Berakhot	Neusner
243061	The Two Talmuds Compared, III. The Division of Damages in the Talmud of the Land of Israel and the Talmud of Babylonia, Volume D, Tractates Shebuot, Abodah Zarah and Horayot	Neusner
243062	The Two Talmuds Compared, I. Tractate Berakhot and the Division of Appointed Times in the Talmud of the Land of Israel and the Talmud of Babylonia, Volume C, Tractate Erubin	Neusner
243063	The Two Talmuds Compared, I. Tractate Berakhot and the Division of Appointed Times in the Talmud of the Land of Israel and the Talmud of Babylonia, Volume D, Tractates Yoma and Sukkah	Neusner

243064	The Two Talmuds Compared, I. Tractate Berakhot and the Division of Appointed Times in the Talmud of the Land of Israel and the Talmud of Babylonia, Volume E, Tractate Pesahim	Neusner
243065	The Two Talmuds Compared, I. Tractate Berakhot and the Division of Appointed Times in the Talmud of the Land of Israel and the Talmud of Babylonia, Volume F, Tractates Besah, Taanit and Megillah	Neusner
243066	The Two Talmuds Compared, I. Tractate Berakhot and the Division of Appointed Times in the Talmud of the Land of Israel and the Talmud of Babylonia, Volume G, Tractates Rosh Hashanah and Moed Qatan	Neusner
243067	The Talmud of Babylonia, An Academic Commentary, Volume XXII, Bavli Tractate Baba Batra, B. Chapters VII through XI	Neusner
243068	The Talmud of Babylonia, An Academic Commentary, Volume XXIII, Bavli Tractate Sanhedrin, B. Chapters VIII through XII	Neusner
243069	The Talmud of Babylonia, An Academic Commentary, Volume XIV, Bavli Tractate Ketubot, B. ChaptersVII through XIV	Neusner
243070	The Talmud of Babylonia, An Academic Commentary, Volume IV, Bavli Tractate Pesahim, B. Chapters VIII through XI	Neusner
243071	The Talmud of Babylonia, An Academic Commentary, Volume XXIX, Bavli Tractate Menahot, B. Chapters VII through XIV	Neusner
243072	The Talmud of Babylonia, An Academic Commentary, Volume XXVIII, Bavli Tractate Zebahim B. Chapters VIII through XV	Neusner
243073	The Talmud of Babylonia, An Academic Commentary, Volume XXI, Bavli Tractate Baba Mesia, B. Chapters VIII through XI	Neusner
243074	The Talmud of Babylonia, An Academic Commentary, Volume III, Bavli Tractate Erubin, A. ChaptersVI through XI	Neusner

South Florida-Rochester-Saint Louis Studies on Religion and the Social Order

245001	Faith and Context, Volume 1	Ong
245002	Faith and Context, Volume 2	Ong
245003	Judaism and Civil Religion	Breslauer
245004	The Sociology of Andrew M. Greeley	Greeley
245005	Faith and Context, Volume 3	Ong
245006	The Christ of Michelangelo	Dixon
245007	From Hermeneutics to Ethical Consensus Among Cultures	Bori
245008	Mordecai Kaplan's Thought in a Postmodern Age	Breslauer
245009	No Longer Aliens, No Longer Strangers	Eckardt
245010	Between Tradition and Culture	Ellenson

245011	Religion and the Social Order	Neusner
245012	Christianity and the Stranger	Nichols
245013	The Polish Challenge	Czosnyka
245014	Islam and the Question of Minorities	Sonn
245015	Religion and the Political Order	Neusner

South Florida International Studies in Formative Christianity and Judaism

242501	The Earliest Christian Mission to 'All Nations'	La Grand
242502	Judaic Approaches to the Gospels	Chilton
252403	The "Essence of Christianity"	Forni Rosa
242504	The Wicked Tenants and Gethsemane	Aus
242505	Messiah-Christos	Laato
242506	Romans 9–11: A Reader-Response Analysis	Lodge

BM
179
.N4775
1997
71535s
v.2

HIEBERT LIBRARY

3 6877 00151 5807